WHAT HAPPE   _ _.L.

What Happens When We Die?

ALISON MORGAN

KINGSWAY PUBLICATIONS
EASTBOURNE

Unless otherwise indicated, biblical quotations are from the
New International Version © 1973, 1978, 1984 by the
International Bible Society.

ISBN 0 85476 336 8

Produced by Bookprint Creative Services
P.O. Box 827, BN21 3YJ, England, for
KINGSWAY PUBLICATIONS LTD
Lottbridge Drove, Eastbourne, E Sussex BN23 6NT.
Printed in Great Britain.

CONTENTS

PREFACE

The initial impetus for this book has come out of personal experience, not of life after death, but of facing the death of three people to whom I was close. The first was Ruth Morgan, my Director of Studies in Cambridge, who died from cancer at the age of forty-one, leaving a husband and three young sons. The second was Davide Viazzo, a lively and highly intelligent five-year-old whom I had known since birth. The third was my own grandmother, who died at the age of ninety-five from old age. One person wrenched away from family and career in mid-flow; one full of promise and scarcely got going; and one ready to die.

The second impetus for the book came from the academic research I was engaged in at the time of Ruth's death, when I was working on popular beliefs concerning life after death in the Middle Ages and their relationship to Dante's *Comedy*. This was published in 1990 as *Dante and the Medieval Other World*. It meant looking at beliefs about the afterlife from Homer in the eighth century BC to Dante's death in 1321, and left me with a strong desire to bridge the gap between the fourteenth century and the twentieth. Is what was believed then what we believe now? Or is it because of the exaggerated teaching of the Middle Ages on heaven and hell that so many people feel today that the traditional Christian teaching is naïve and unacceptable?

7

And thirdly, ten years of marriage to an Anglican parish priest have taught me that when loved ones die, people do want answers to the questions we try so hard not to think about, and which I too had not thought about until death broke in on my life. At every funeral there is a coffin; in every coffin is a dead body; and every bereaved person thinks of that dead body and asks: 'Where are they now?' Most of us no longer have a ready answer.

This book therefore represents my attempts, twelve years after Ruth's death, to answer the questions I first asked myself then, and to which Ruth herself believed she knew the answers. The questions were these: Given that we must all die, what is the meaning of life? And can we know anything about what, if anything, happens after death? In order to answer those questions I have had to ask many more, and many years have passed in the search. I hope that in reading this book others will find that their search may be shorter.

My thanks are due to a number of people who have taken the time to read the manuscript of this book in whole or in part, and who have made many detailed comments and suggestions. In particular I am grateful to my husband Roger, to Bill Keymer, Helen Bence and Basil Scott. I am also indebted to those who have given me additional advice and support, most notably Roger Coleman, Jenny Ridge and Linda Angus; and to the congregation of St Columba's, Corby, among whom the book was first conceived.

INTRODUCTION

'As for man, his days are like grass, he flourishes like a flower of the field; the wind blows over it and it is gone, and its place remembers it no more.'

Psalm 103:15–16

'It's not that I'm afraid to die, I just don't want to be there when it happens.'

Woody Allen, Without Feathers, *1976*

As we are born, so must we die. Death is the sole certainty of life. It is the one thing which is truly universal; it happens to us all. It happened to David in the tenth century BC, and one day it will happen to Woody Allen. And however we die—old or young, a millionaire or homeless, alone or in the bosom of our family—this much is certain: sooner or later, we will die. One person out of one dies.

Given the one hundred per cent certainty of death, it is perhaps surprising that we do not talk about it more often. Indeed, we tend to avoid even thinking about it, consoling ourselves with the thought that we are unlikely to have to face it soon. We know we have an average life expectancy of about seventy-five years, and we take refuge in that, regarding it as the norm, almost indeed as a right. And so we pretend that death does not exist, that it will

9

not happen, and we live each day as if we were immortal. We know, for example, that smoking kills, yet so many people continue to smoke, thinking it will not kill *them*. We panic if a friend or relation is bereaved, not knowing what to say, desperately hoping they will get over it soon. We avoid mentioning death even to those who are terminally ill, feeling somehow that it must be kinder to let a person die without telling them what is happening, as if that will spare them the pain of thinking about it. They are of course thinking about it most of the time, but don't want to upset us by talking about it. And then we whisk the body away to a funeral parlour and cremate it behind velvet curtains—a sharp contrast with the practices of most societies, and with what we ourselves have done in the past. But in the past we had answers; previous generations believed the traditional Christian teaching on life after death, and drew consolation from it. Now we are not so sure; we live in a multi-faith society, and are faced with too many different religions to be sure of any of them. At the same time, science has advanced into areas which hitherto were matters of faith. And so now we tend to place our trust not in religion but in science. The result is that death—to which as yet science has no answer—has become a taboo subject, at best avoided, at worst shrouded in an agony of unexpressed fear.

In a way it is much harder for us to cope with the thought of death than it has been for previous generations. In 1348, bubonic plague wiped out a third of the population of Europe. There were no antiseptics, no antibiotics, no inoculations. Death was as likely to strike at the young as at the old. It could not be hidden away or ignored. It couldn't come as a tragedy or as a surprise. Whole communities were destroyed. In times of plague everyone knew that they could wake up next morning feeling ill, and that if they did then they would probably be dead within days. But even in the years between outbreaks of plague there was the same feeling that death was ever present. A long journey could mean death from malaria, or murder at the hands of highway robbers. Measles and diarrhoea were likely to be fatal, at least to children—as in many parts of the world they still are. Death was part of life.

Of course people still die; for each individual death will one day become the same reality it always has become. But the way our society as a whole experiences death has changed radically. Thanks to the expertise of the modern medical profession, the threat of unexpected death no longer hangs over us as it once did. Fatal plagues and epidemics are virtually non-existent in the Western world, and the seriously ill are cared for in well-equipped hospitals where the best treatment is available. In a way, however, this in itself prevents us from facing up to the fact of death. Five hundred years ago, the terminally ill were nursed at home, and died with their families and friends around them. Now they are admitted to anonymous hospitals where they are effectively cut off from the community. One thousand years ago, a death was marked by a long period of formal, public mourning. Now we hold a fifteen-minute service in a sanitised crematorium to the accompaniment of canned music, and try to get over it as quickly as possible. Two centuries ago books on the art of dying stood alongside the Bible in every home; now we have only articles in scientific journals on the most effective forms of pain relief. The result of all these changes, desirable though many of them are, is that death is, by and large, no longer a public matter. We die in private, and only the lives of those closest to us are touched.

Occasionally, however, death does burst into the public domain in a sudden and intrusive way. In recent years we have witnessed on our television screens horrendous wars in Kuwait and Bosnia; famines in Ethiopia and Somalia; cyclones, flooding and earthquakes in Bangladesh, America, Italy and Japan. Nearer to home, and therefore of even greater impact, have been a sinking cross-channel ferry, a burning football stadium, a fire in the London Underground, an aeroplane crashing on the M1, and another blown up in the air over Scotland. We look at mutilated children, sodden corpses, people with their hair on fire, dismembered limbs in the wreckage, and we respond first with compassion and then with anger. We feel that these things should not have happened, had no right to happen, and must be prevented from happening again. Death seems like an outrageous intrusion into the natural order of things.

This approach to death is most unsatisfactory, for two reasons. First, to deny death may work for a while, but sooner or later we will be brought face to face with either our own mortality or, more likely, with that of someone to whom we are close. Every day 260,000 people die, and tomorrow you could be one of them. Death cannot be avoided.

Secondly, if we cannot find an answer to death, we cannot find one to life either. In fact, we cannot even find an ultimately meaningful way of living it. How can we make decisions if we do not know what we are aiming for or what the purpose of life is? Nothing is potentially more frustrating. The author of a recent book on heaven wrote, 'If there is no God who created us for His eternal purposes, then human life is not only a meaningless accident but a cruel practical joke perpetrated by an impersonal cosmos that has somehow spawned beings who inexplicably long for meaning and purpose when there can be none.' If, on the other hand, there is a God who has created us for his eternal purposes, we need to understand what those purposes are—and what part death plays in them.

Sooner or later, therefore, we must face the thought of death, and ask the questions society does its best to protect us from, knowing that it no longer has an answer: What happens when we die? Is death the end, or is there something beyond it? If there is, how will we experience it? Is there any way of really knowing, or is it just a matter for conjecture?

I was not brought up in a religious family. Indeed, increasingly few people are brought up to believe the old certainties as previous generations have believed them. Our society embraces many faiths, and there seems little reason why any one of these should have a monopoly on truth over all the others. I have therefore had to take a hard look at several religions. Obviously one cannot examine in detail the hundreds of religions that there are in the world, so I have confined myself to the five which globally have the biggest following: Hinduism, Buddhism, Judaism, Islam and Christianity. What do they teach? What is their history? In what ways do they differ and what do they have in common? What are their beliefs about life after death? Do they fit with our own experience, and how convincing do they seem?

Then there is the question of science. It is to science, rather than to religion, that most people in the West today look for the answers to life's questions. Our lives are dominated by science, and we are reluctant to believe anything unless there is some scientific evidence to support it. Over the last few hundred years science and religion have fought one another, and in general science has won. But it was as I considered the scientific evidence for the existence of a life after death that I received the biggest surprises: it seems that modern scientific research is increasingly leading us towards the conclusion that there *is* a spirit world, that it exists independently of the material world, and that it interacts with it.

If we may approach the question of life after death from the point of view of religion or science, we may also approach it from the angle of history. There is a lot to be said for beginning at the beginning, so the first chapter of this book gives a brief survey of the history of belief in life after death. We find that almost all societies and cultures prior to our own have believed firmly that man survives death. Our Western twentieth-century democracy tends to regard itself as the most sophisticated society in the history of the human race, and therefore as knowing better than those which have preceded it. But can we really have the confidence to claim that in this matter *all* previous cultures have been wrong, including those which have been intellectually as highly developed as our own? Must they not have had sound reasons for believing in an afterlife?

These are the subjects of the first three chapters of this book, and they set the scene for the more detailed arguments of the remainder. If history, religion and science all point to the plausibility of a life after death, what if anything may we find out about that life? Those who have believed and do believe in it must find a foundation for their belief in their own experience; it must make sense of the things that happen. Many people in the world today believe in the doctrine of reincarnation. Why? In what way does it make sense of experience? Is there any evidence to support it? I have tried to answer some of these questions in Chapter 4 by looking at the evidence for and against reincarnation as taught by Hinduism, Buddhism and more recently proponents of the 'New Age'.

Many others believe in the teaching of men who have claimed to have received revelations and prophecies from God. What we need to ask ourselves here is whether these teachings are convincing, and whether we have any basis for trusting in the reliability of those who first expounded them. Chapter 5 therefore examines the personal histories and teachings of the prophets of Judaism, Islam and Mormonism.

Still others accept the Christian doctrine that Jesus was raised from the dead, and that therefore only he has the authority to speak about it—but is there any hard historical evidence to support this view? Did the resurrection really happen? This is the subject of Chapter 6, which examines the Christian and non-Christian evidence for the resurrection, and explains how I came to my own conclusion—one which I did not reach lightly.

The remaining chapters present the Christian teaching on the death of Jesus and on life after death as described by him and his closest followers, looking at the implications if we accept this remarkable teaching.

Notes

1. D. Hunt, *Whatever Happened to Heaven*? (Eugene, Oregon: 1988), p. 17.

I
THE BELIEFS OF PAST SOCIETIES

'It has become evident that there exists no human group, however primitive, which lacks all ideas of supernatural beings or entities.'

Geoffrey Parrinder[1]

Introduction

The question 'Is there life after death?' is not new. Indeed it is as old as humanity. And from the beginning of time it has been answered in the affirmative; every civilisation in human history has believed in some form of continued existence beyond the grave. Many people would feel that this is in itself a powerful argument for the reality of an afterlife. Others would suggest that surely we in the twentieth century have advanced far enough in our scientific understanding of the world we live in to be able to rise above such primitive superstition, and this is an argument to which we shall return in Chapter 3. But this initial chapter will be devoted to a survey of the historical continuity of human belief in an afterlife, and the difficulty in dismissing out of hand something which for 35,000 years has been almost universally regarded as self-evidently true.

There is however a second reason for studying the other-world beliefs of the past. It is that they influence the beliefs of the present. Although many of the details concerning the nature of the other world died with the societies that expounded them, a surprising number did not, surviving to enter the popular consciousness and re-emerge in later religious thinking. Some are even current today.

Prehistoric man

The first systematic study of the history of belief in life after death was undertaken 2,000 years ago by the Roman writer Cicero, who made it the subject of his *Tusculan Disputations*. He began with prehistoric man, and we shall follow his example.

The prehistoric era is defined as that which predates the invention of writing, which occurred in about 3000 BC. Because there are no written records our knowledge is necessarily limited; what we do know has been discovered through archaeology. We can however be reasonably certain that modern man, *homo sapiens*, first appeared around 30,000 years ago, and that both he and his predecessor, Neanderthal man, possessed not only a religious belief but also a belief in life after death.[2] The discovery of a number of Neanderthal graves suggests that the dead were buried according to careful ritual, sometimes with sacred objects. For early *homo sapiens* the evidence is stronger: grave goods, tools and precious possessions for the future use of the dead have been found at burial sites, and cave paintings and clay figurines point to a belief in some kind of sacred power. By Neolithic times, around 10000 BC, when the first settlements were formed, people had begun to build temples and other stone structures with religious significance.[3]

Belief in life after death seems therefore, as Cicero pointed out so long ago, to be as old as man himself.

Mesopotamia

The invention of writing occurred in around 3000 BC in Mesopotamia, a region often referred to as the 'cradle of civilisation'. The name 'Mesopotamia' means 'between the rivers', and designates the land lying between the Tigris and the Euphrates, now in Iraq and Syria. Between 3000 and 450 BC it was successively home to the Sumerian, Assyrian and Babylonian civilisations, and it was here that complex religious

ideas and practices first developed. Their influence is still to be
traced in the modern world religions today. Thanks to the
excavation of many settlements, in particular the early Sumerian
city of Uruk, we know a great deal about the beliefs of these
peoples.[4]

It is clear from the excavation of temples at Uruk that the
Sumerians worshipped a supreme god called Anu, and a mother
goddess called Inanna; other deities representing the powers of
nature were worshipped in other cities. It is also clear from a
number of early writings that the Sumerians believed in the
existence of a shadowy other world to which all men go after
death, and in which they eke out a somewhat miserable
existence. Their precise fate appears to have depended on
whether the correct funeral rites were followed, and on whether
their descendants continued to supply them with food and drink
in the tomb.

These beliefs were incorporated into a number of myths of
which we have later written copies dating from the Assyrian
period. They record the descent into the underworld of the
goddess Inanna (now called Ishtar) and the king Gilgamesh. The
underworld is described as a distant realm beyond desert and sea.
It is presided over by the goddess Ereshkigal, sister of Inanna,
and her husband Nergal. It has the appearance of a city with
seven gates, whose monster guardians progressively strip the
deceased of their clothing until they arrive naked at the palace
of Ereshkigal to be judged. Various demons do her bidding.
The Epic of Gilgamesh also describes a beautiful garden in
which heroes and great men recline, but from which the
majority of mankind is excluded.[5] This story is repeated in
different forms right through the classical period and up to
and including the Christian Middle Ages. The last major
example is the fictitious account of Dante's journey through
hell, purgatory and heaven given in his *Divine Comedy* at
the beginning of the fourteenth century. These descriptions
of the other world are an important source of information

concerning beliefs about life after death in at least five civilisations covering a period of up to 3,500 years.[6]

Because of the long journey necessary to reach the Mesopotamian underworld, the dead were often buried with appropriate equipment, particularly vessels for food and drink. For a few generations this appears to have been taken to extremes. The royal graves at Ur, dating from about 2600 BC, reveal that each (royal) person was buried with not only crockery and various tools, but also a complete entourage of soldiers, musicians and attendants, all of whom appeared to have died by voluntarily drinking a cup of poison which lay neatly by their sides! Even oxen and wagons were provided. Although it was not typical of the period as a whole, it does bear witness to the strength of the Sumerian belief in life after death.[7]

Ancient Egypt

The ancient Egyptian civilisation as we know it covered the period from about 3100 BC to about 30 BC, although there is evidence of religious activity stretching back as far as 4000 BC. It extended up and down the length of the Nile Valley, absorbing many local traditions and therefore encompassing a wide variety of beliefs. It was a polytheistic religion, with a large pantheon of gods among whom the creator god Atum, identified also with the sun god Re, was supreme. The gods were represented in either animal or human and animal form, and were worshipped in temples.

Tombs

The Egyptians went to lengths never attempted before and scarcely attempted since to ensure their post-mortem survival, and because of their careful creation of funerary monuments designed to last indefinitely, and the written texts deposited in them, we know a very great deal about their beliefs in this matter.[8]

The earliest Egyptian tombs were simple brick structures

known as *mastabas*. Then came the pyramids, the first of which was built in about 2700 BC, and which by their shape probably symbolised the ascent of the soul to heaven or to the sun. These in turn were superseded around 2000 BC by palace tombs carved into a cliff face; the tomb of Tutankhamen was of this type.

Texts

A number of texts have been found in the tombs, sometimes written on papyrus, sometimes inscribed on the coffin, and sometimes painted on the internal walls. There are three main groups of texts. The oldest are the so-called Pyramid texts, first found carved on the walls of the burial chamber of King Wenis in 2345 BC, but dating back earlier. They describe an afterlife in the stars, restricted to royalty and the aristocracy. Later come the Coffin texts, inscribed as the name suggests on coffins. They date from between about 2000 BC and 1800 BC and are effectively an expansion of the Pyramid texts. The afterlife was now seen as accessible to all who could afford to prepare themselves adequately for it. For the first time the dead person must face a post-mortem judgment, and the dead lived not in the heavens with the sun god Re, but in a pleasant land called the Field of Reeds with the god of the dead Osiris. The third group of texts are known collectively as the Book of the Dead, and date from about 1550 BC onwards. Each was written on a roll of papyrus and inserted in the tomb. All three groups of texts mostly consist of hymns, magical recitations and formulae for use by the deceased to ensure a smooth passage to the other world.

The preservation of the body

The funerary texts deal with the fate of the soul after death. But the ancient Egyptians are of course more famous for their preoccupation with the survival of the body. Egyptian funeral rites were extremely elaborate. First the corpse was ritually cleansed, and then it was subjected to a complex process of mummification. In its most elaborate form this involved the removal of the brain and intestines, their replacement by linen wads, spices, oils and natron (natural sodium), and their preservation in jars. The rest of the body was treated externally with the same substances and then bandaged. The heart, regarded as the seat of the soul, was not removed. After this process was complete, a special ceremony was conducted in which the life force was symbolically returned to the body, and it was placed in the tomb together with a vast array of objects necessary for its future life. Once buried, the dead person was sustained with daily offerings of food and drink.

The destiny of the soul

The Egyptian conception of the afterlife seems to have formed gradually. The idea of an underworld populated by the dead may well have developed from the practice of burial. By extension, the tomb came to be regarded as the house of the dead. This occurred not just in Egypt but throughout the ancient world, although it was only in Egypt that such elaborate post-mortem dwellings were built.

As time went by this idea was expanded, and the dead man was thought, if of aristocratic blood, to divide his time between his home in the tomb (by day) and the other world (by night); here he was carried in the chariot of the sun god Re. This other world was located in heaven among the stars. Eventually he was believed to alternate between the tomb and the realm of Osiris. Osiris, the fertility god, had according to legend been murdered by his brother, but lived on to become the ruler of the other world and a symbol of life after death. He presided over a rural paradise, conceived of as a heavenly version of Egypt, complete with Nile, and to which everyone was eligible for entry. Mostly the soul was believed to journey in a westerly direction to reach the other world.

The judgment of the dead

One of the key concepts in the teaching of many religions both ancient and modern has been that of the judgment of the individual at some point after death. This is a concept which appears for the first time in ancient Egypt. It is absent from the Pyramid texts, makes its first appearance in the Coffin texts, and occupies a central position in the Book of the Dead. The god Anubis, represented with the head of a jackal, leads the deceased by the hand to the scales, where he checks the balance. The heart of the deceased is then weighed against the feather of truth. A monster, Ammit, stands ready to devour those who weigh heavy in the scales, and the god Thoth stands by to write down the result. The acquitted soul is then introduced by the god Horus to Osiris, to whom he makes a ritual denial of a set list of sins. Other gods and goddesses are present as witnesses to the judgment. The scales remained an enduring symbol of the judgment of the soul right through to the Christian Middle Ages, when they were commonly painted on church walls with St Michael playing the part of Anubis.

Ancient Greece

The civilisation of ancient Greece was one of the greatest and most significant that human history has known, and it is the foundation on which our entire Western culture rests. Like the Egyptians, the Greeks developed a complex set of religious beliefs, which included a range of different teachings at different periods on the subject of life after death.[9]

The Greek archipelago has been inhabited from prehistoric times. The first people in the region about whom we have any real information, however, were the Minoans, whose civilisation lasted from about 3000 BC to 1450 BC. Their graves contain both votive figurines and articles of gold, suggesting that they believed in some form of life after death. They were succeeded by the Myceneans, who were dominant from 1450 BC to 1100 BC. The Myceneans buried their dead in underground vaults and provided them with weapons and other goods.

After the collapse of the Mycenean civilisation, Greece was

organised first into city states and then into a single state. Alphabetic writing was developed, giving us much more information than is available for the earlier periods. During this period three different cultural phases or movements may be distinguished, in all of which a belief in a life after death is strongly present. The first we might call the literary phase. The writing that has come down to us from this period is mostly in the form of poetry; the best-known figure is Homer. The second we might call the religious phase, in which a number of secret mystery religions developed, all of which were intimately concerned with the fate of the soul after death. And the third is what might be defined the philosophical phase, in which the key thinker was Plato, and in which the question of life after death was tackled not from a literary or religious point of view but from a philosophical one.

The literary tradition

It is not known precisely who Homer was or when he lived, but most scholars point to the ninth century BC as the most likely date for the composition of the two epic poems which are attributed to him. They are thought to be based on earlier material, and may go back to the twelfth century BC.

For our purposes it is the eleventh book of the *Odyssey* which is of the greatest importance. It contains an account of a visit to the other world made by Odysseus, who wishes to consult a certain prophet there. The other world is in this case an underworld, Hades—a shadowy realm in which the shades of the dead live a muted and passive existence. It is not dissimilar to the underworld of the Sumerians and, as we shall see in the next chapter, of the Jewish scriptures.

Odysseus begins his visit by offering a sacrifice of sheep. Blood was regarded as the seat of life, and so the shades to whom he will speak must drink of the blood of the sheep in order to regain their memories and talk with him. He is addressed first by his dead companion Elpenor, then by Tiresias, the prophet he has come to consult, and then by his mother. Twelve famous women of the past then come forward, followed by the heroes Agammemnon, Achilles and Aias. Later he speaks to Hercules.

Although this is the predominant picture of the other world given by Homer, two others are included in his narrative, possibly from separate traditions. First, Homer describes Tartarus, the prototype of hell. Here Odysseus sees the mythical king Minos, sitting in judgment over the dead, and three legendary figures undergoing punishment for their various offences. Tityus lies defenceless on the ground while vultures pick at his liver; Tantalus stands up to the chin in a pool of water beside laden fruit trees, but both water and fruit are out of his reach; and Sisyphus is required to roll a heavy rock up a steep hill, down which it repeatedly rolls again.

Secondly, Homer describes a happier realm, the Elysian Fields, 'the land where living is made easiest for mankind, where no snow falls, no strong winds blow and there is never any rain, but day after day the West Wind's tuneful breeze comes in from Ocean to refresh its folk' (*Odyssey* IV 561–68).

These concepts are echoed by the later poets Hesiod (eighth century BC) and Pindar (sixth century BC), who describe the Elysian Fields or, as they were also known, the Isles of the Blessed. These were variously located on the earth's surface, or in the sky, or underground. According to Hesiod, this is the happy place where man lived in a perfect Golden Age, and to which he may return after death. This concept is of course not dissimilar to the Judaeo-Christian tradition of an earthly paradise, the Garden of Eden. Pindar described the Isles of the Blessed as a realm ruled by the god Cronus, refreshed by sea breezes, fertile with trees and flowers, fields of crops and shady, sweet-smelling meadows. It is open to those who have lived three successive lives of purity and virtue. This is the first clear indication of inescapable moral criteria in the other world.

The religious tradition

The second major Greek tradition which concerns us is that of the mystery religions. The ancient Greeks were polytheistic in their religious beliefs, worshipping a pantheon of deities. This was, however, more a state or civic religion than a system of faith and worship for the individual, and by the fifth century BC a number of secret religious rites known as the mystery religions had developed. Principal among them were the Eleusinian Mysteries and the Orphic Mysteries. At their heart was a repudiation of the doctrine of a shadowy underworld; instead, they taught that there is a spiritual life which exists independently of the body and in which we may participate both before and after death.

We do not have a detailed knowledge of the mystery religions because they were by their very nature secret, revealing their truths only to the initiated. We do know that they were built around secret rites designed to bring the participant to a higher spiritual plane and to enable him to recapture something of the identification between the soul and the divine. In other words, these rituals were intended to provide a foretaste of life after death, and it was often proclaimed that initiation was necessary in order to secure a happy afterlife.

The Eleusinian Mysteries developed out of an agricultural festival centred on the earth goddess Demeter and celebrated at Eleusis. The Orphic Mysteries were formed around the legend of Orpheus, said to have been reborn after being killed by the Titans. Both were therefore concerned with the cycle of life and death. Orphism clearly taught the doctrine of reincarnation; the soul of an initiate would eventually, after many reincarnations, gain access to a heaven among the stars. It is thought that representations of the future life were enacted, and visions experienced. All the mystery religions are thought to have been influenced by Egyptian cults.

The mystery religions served to cement two concepts firmly

into the Greek consciousness: the idea of reincarnation or, more technically speaking, the transmigration of souls, which was not present in Homer but seems to have become accepted by the sixth century BC; and the idea of the moral dimension to the afterlife, present to some degree but not dominant in Homer. Both these are further developed in the philosophical tradition.

The philosophical tradition

The greatest Greek thinker, perhaps the most able thinker of all time, was Plato. He lived in the fourth and fifth centuries BC, and wrote a number of myths purporting to describe, in symbolic terms, the other world. He was influenced by the mystery religions, and in particular by Orphism.

The shortest of Plato's other-world myths is contained in his *Georgias*, where it is given to Socrates to describe the judgment of the soul after death. Socrates explains that the system described by Homer has been changed, and that men are now judged after death by Rhadamanthys, Aecus and Minos, and assigned to either Tartarus or the Isles of the Blessed; and that they will be judged on the basis of their physical appearance, in which their moral state is reflected. This doctrine is expanded in the *Phaedo*, which explains that the soul is immortal, that it will be reincarnated after death (not necessarily into a human) and that it is purified by the study of philosophy.

The other world is said to be divided into four different localities: a lake, in which those guilty of curable offences purge them for a fixed period of time; Tartarus, where the incurable live for ever; a pure dwelling, to which the righteous go; and somewhere even better, reserved for philosophers! So for the first time we have a sort of hell, a sort of purgatory and a sort of paradise—although it is to be remembered that in the vast majority of cases a stay there is followed by reincarnation.

Plato's most famous other-world myth is contained in the *Republic*, where he tells the story of Er, a soldier who was killed in battle but came back to life twelve days later to find himself lying on a funeral pyre. Er recounts his experiences. At death, his soul had left his body and journeyed to a place of judgment in the sky. Here he learned that each soul must pay ten times over for every crime committed in life, and conversely receives a tenfold reward for each good action. In exceptionally bad cases, the soul is led away to a separate place of torment. After an appropriate length of time it is allowed to choose between various selected reincarnations, made to drink of the river Lethe whose waters cause it to forget its experiences, and returns to earth. Er did not drink, and woke to find himself back in his body.

The fourth Platonic myth is contained in the *Phaedrus*, which pictures the soul ascending to heaven in a chariot. After a period of a thousand years, it is reincarnated; after ten such reincarnations, it may remain in heaven.

Other philosophical writers accepted the Platonic views. Aristotle, Plato's pupil, emphasised the idea of a single God who created the universe; Plotinus stated that the final destiny of the soul is union with that God, whom he also called the One. Several centuries after Plato, Plutarch took up again the theme of a journey up into the heavens in his two accounts of men who returned from the other world to tell of their experiences.[10]

However, although all three of the currents outlined above—literary, religious and philosophical—proclaimed a belief in life after death, there were times, as indeed there have been in our own society over the last couple of centuries, when spiritual matters were scorned, and a rationalist, purely scientific and non-religious approach prevailed. The greatest opponent of religious belief was perhaps Epicurus, who founded a school of philosophy in the third and fourth centuries BC which rejected the supernatural in all its forms. He taught instead that pleasure is the only thing which matters, and that it is to be found in the practice of virtue. His thought is summarised in the following ancient graffiti: 'Nothing to fear in God. Nothing to feel in

Death. Good can be attained. Evil can be endured.'[11]

But these beliefs were the exception rather than the rule. By and large the ancient Greeks believed that there is a life after death. In the earliest period this was thought to be a shadowy realm in which all men suffered the same fate. Later the heavens were the preferred location. Gradually the destiny of the individual became linked with his moral conduct on earth; and finally the idea of reincarnation was embraced.

Ancient Rome

Many of the beliefs of ancient Greece were absorbed by the Roman civilisation which followed it. The Romans seem originally to have believed that the dead would live on in their tombs, and many Roman tombs were designed as houses. The spirits of the dead were feared and honoured, and there was a strong belief in ghosts. But as Roman ideas developed, the three currents which we have identified in Greek belief also appeared.[12]

The underworld

The underworld is best described by the poet Virgil, who lived in the first century BC. The key passage is book six of the *Aeneid*, an epic poem whose hero, Aeneas, finds it necessary at a certain point in his adventures to consult the spirit of his dead father Anchises. At the entrance to the underworld he finds a river, a whirlpool and a marsh. The shores are crowded with people, who must spend a hundred years here before advancing further; everywhere there are threatening monsters of one kind or another. Beyond the entrance Aeneas finds the underworld proper, which is divided into three distinct areas. First comes a neutral place where he sees those who died as children, those condemned to death in innocence, certain suicides, those whose death was caused by love, and warriors. Their fate is decided by Minos. Aeneas then visits Tartarus, a pit enclosed in a castle surrounded by a river of fire; here those guilty of crimes such as treachery, hatred and avarice endure torment. Their judge is Rhadamanthus. Finally he enters Elysium, a pleasant wooded land peopled by both temporary and permanent residents who have completed their punishments in the other realms. Most return to earth and another life after a period of 1,000 years. The influence of both Homer and Plato is not hard to find. Similar accounts are given by the poets Lucan and Statius.[13]

Celestial immortality

In contrast to Homer, Plato had envisaged the other world as located in the heavens, and this belief also passed into Roman thought. Its main exponent was Cicero, who discussed it most fully in his *Tusculan Disputations*. He also wrote his own account of a journey to the other world and back, modelled on Plato's myth of Er. It describes the dream journey of the consul Scipio through the heavens to a point where he looks down on the earth and learns about the destiny of the dead. The term 'celestial immortality' has been coined to describe this pattern of classical belief.

The mystery religions

The mystery cults of Egypt and Greece were also influential on the thought of Rome. They too expounded a doctrine of a future life in the heavens or stars, and thus reinforced the teachings of the philosophers. The Greek cult of Pythagoreanism emerged in Rome during the first century BC as Neo-Pythagoreanism; its teachings had much in common with the other mystery religions discussed above, particularly Orphism—belief in the immortality of the soul, in reincarnation and in the possibility of attaining understanding of spiritual realities by participation in certain religious rituals.

A period of scepticism

Like the Greeks, the Romans generally believed in life after death, although they too had their sceptics. These were mostly philosophers and scientists. The Stoics taught that the soul would decompose like the body. The teachings of the Epicureans were taken up. The scientific approach began to emerge; Lucretius adopted the atomic theories of the Greek Democritus, and stated that a mechanistic universe leaves no room for a god or gods, or come to that for the existence of a non-material soul; and that there could therefore be no such thing as a life after death. Science, he might have said, has an explanation for everything. These are views with which we have become familiar ourselves. But they were not characteristic of Roman belief as a whole.

Greece and Rome: summary

By the end of the classical period two central beliefs had become widely accepted: belief in a divine being or God; and belief in the continuing life of the soul in the heavens after the death of the body. These beliefs persisted in the popular consciousness for centuries after the collapse of the Roman empire, and indeed survive today; the idea of a heaven 'up there' somewhere is one to which most people instinctively turn, unaware that its pedigree stretches back right through the classical period to ancient Egypt and beyond.

Conclusion

It is clear from this brief survey that from prehistoric times to the present, man has generally believed in some form of life after death, and that this belief has been anchored in a corresponding belief in a god or gods. We have also seen that scepticism is not new, and that at times attempts have been made to deny the existence of any form of purely spiritual life, either before death or after it. Nonetheless, these ideas have not found favour except among a small proportion of intellectuals. For the vast majority of the human race, throughout its history, it is the doctrine that man does possess an immortal soul, and that he does therefore survive death, which has commended itself to most people as making sense of life.

Of course we have not looked at all the civilisations of the past, confining ourselves rather to those which are the ancestors of our own. But a similar story is told in other parts of the world; in China, in India and in the many tribal or pre-literary societies which have been (and continue to be) strong in all five continents. There, as everywhere, man has believed in life after death.

Notes

1. G. Parrinder (ed.), *An Illustrated History of the World's Religions* (Feltham: 1983), p. 35.
2. For a summary of what we know about prehistoric man see the relevant sections in J. Bronowski, *The Ascent of Man* (London: 1973), and D. Attenborough, *Life on Earth* (enlarged edition, London: 1980); also R.P. Beaver et al (ed.), *The World's Religions* (Oxford: 1982).
3. See 'Prehistoric Religion', in *An Illustrated History of the World's Religions* ed. G. Parrinder (Feltham: 1983), ch. 1.
4. For the beliefs of ancient Mesopotamia see 'Mesopotamia', in *An Illustrated History of the World's Religions* (1983), ch. 8.
5. The *Epic of Gilgamesh* was written in about the seventh century BC, but is thought to date back to the twentieth BC or earlier. See L.E. Sullivan, *Death, Afterlife and the Soul* (New York: 1987), pp. 163–64.
6. An account of these texts is given by C. Zaleski, *Otherworld Journeys* (New York: 1987), and by A. Morgan, *Dante and the Medieval Other World* (Cambridge: 1990).
7. For the royal graves of Ur see G. Parrinder above, and I. Wilson and R. Bruce, *Life After Death?* (London: 1987), pp. 10–11.
8. Ancient Egyptian beliefs are outlined in 'Ancient Egypt', in *An Illustrated History of the World's Religions*, ed. G. Parrinder ch. 9. See also R.O. Faulkner (ed.), *The Ancient Egyptian Book of the Dead* (revised edition, London: 1985).

9. Ancient Greek beliefs are outlined in 'Ancient Greece', in *An Illustrated History of the World's Religions* ed. G. Parrinder (1983), ch. 10. See also L. Sullivan, *Death, Afterlife and the Soul* (1987) and R.P. Beaver, *The World's Religions* (1982).

10. The visions of Thespesius and Timarchus are contained in Plutarch's *Moralia*, ed. P.H. De Lacy, (London: 1959), pp. 269–99, 459–77.

11. *The Oxford Companion to Classical Literature* (Oxford: 1937), p. 162.

12. Roman beliefs on life after death are discussed in F. Cumont, *After Life in Roman Paganism* (New Haven: 1922). See also the relevant chapters in G. Parrinder, *An Illustrated History of the World's Religions*, and R.P. Beaver, *The World's Religions*.

13. Lucan, *Pharsalia* Book 6; Statius, *Thebaid* Book 4.

2

MODERN RELIGIOUS BELIEFS

'I do benefits for all religions—I'd hate to blow the hereafter on a technicality.'

Bob Hope

The history of the human race is a history of religious belief—belief in a god or gods, and belief in the existence of a life after death. But over the last 200 years, and particularly the last fifty, Western society has distanced itself from this religious inheritance and become secular to the point where most of us now reach adulthood with little religious education and no religious certainty.

However, we in the West are not typical of the world as a whole. Just as in history almost all peoples have held strong religious beliefs, so in the world today almost all societies adhere firmly to a clearly defined religious tradition. We, like the Epicureans in ancient Greece, are the exception rather than the rule. Furthermore, many people from other parts of the world have now made their home in Britain, bringing their religious beliefs with them, and so even within our own largely secular society we find a confusing array of different answers to those questions with which religion is concerned: Is there a God or gods, and is there a life after death?

It is not enough, therefore, to confine our enquiry to the religious tradition of which we are the heirs. This chapter will look at five major world religions, always bearing in mind the

questions with which we began: Is there a life after death, and if
so how do we obtain it? How do the major world religions
answer these questions, and are their answers convincing?

The world's religions

The current population of the world is estimated at about 5,000
million people. Of those, over 3,000 million follow one of five
major world religions.[1] Foremost among these is Christianity,
with a membership recently estimated at 1,382 million. It is
followed by Islam (819 million), Hinduism (653 million),
Buddhism (300 million) and Judaism (18 million). These are the
religions with which we shall be principally concerned in this
chapter. Other ancient religions are Chinese Confucianism (5.75
million) and Taoism (190 million, but to a large degree
influenced and assimilated by Buddhism), Japanese Shinto (3.2
million), and Zoroastrianism (which originated in Iran but is
today mostly confined to India, where its 150,000 followers are
known as Parsis). A further 200–300 million people continue to
follow one of the many primal religions of the so-called pre-
literary societies mentioned in the last chapter—tribal cultures
in, for example, Africa, Australia and South America. Millions
more follow religions of more recent origin but which are in effect
offshoots of the five major faiths: there are 16.5 million Sikhs
(source Hinduism and Islam), 4 million Jains (Hinduism) and 4.5
million Baha'is (Islam). Many others are members of modern sects
and religious movements which derive from one of the major
religions but are not generally regarded as a fully independent faith:
there are 6.75 million Jehovah's Witnesses (Christianity), half a
million Seventh Day Adventists (Christianity), 5 million Mormons
(Judaism and Christianity), 750,000 Unitarians (Christianity),
200,000 Moonies (Christianity and Taoism), and others.
Finally, many people live in countries which are officially atheist,
most especially those of the former Soviet Union, but where
Christianity and Islam in particular are becoming more popular.[2]

Hinduism

The oldest of the five major world religions is Hinduism; its development may be traced back as far as 5,000 years. It cannot be easily defined, for it has no founder, no prophets, no formal summary of belief, no single holy book, no unified code of practice and no organised structure. Throughout its history it has been largely confined to the Indian subcontinent—the words 'Hindu' and 'India' are both derived from 'Sindhu', the name for the river Indus—and perhaps this gives us its best definition; Hinduism is an umbrella term describing the many and diverse religious beliefs and practices of the peoples of India. In some ways it is not a religion at all, since its primary emphasis is not on belief but on conduct. One authority has stated that 'the theist and the atheist, the sceptic and the agnostic may all be Hindus if they accept the Hindu system of culture and life'. Another describes Hinduism as 'a great storehouse of all kinds of religious experiments'.[3]

The beginnings of modern Hinduism can be traced back to the middle of the second millennium BC when two distinct peoples came together. From about 2300 BC an advanced urban society known as the Indus Valley Civilisation had flourished in what is now Pakistan. The people of this society worshipped a mother goddess and a male consort, built temples and made use of icons and idols; localised cults honoured other female deities and revered trees, snakes and bulls. Sometime between 1200 and 1500 BC the Indus Valley was invaded by a fair-skinned people who called themselves Aryans. They spoke an early form of Sanskrit, and brought with them a polytheistic household religion of ritual, prayer, sacrifice and ancestor-worship. The merging of these two cultures provided the springboard for what was to become Hinduism.

The earliest Hindu scriptures (and indeed the oldest religious literature in the world still in use) are the *Vedas*, a series of hymns, prayers and ritual formulae composed by the Aryans in the period following their invasion, and dedicated to the gods of nature. But polytheism gradually gave way to monotheism, and around 800 BC a series of philosophical writings was composed to complement the *Vedas*. These writings are known as the *Upanishads*. They are principally concerned with the relationship between the *Brahman*, or divine being, and the *atman*, or individual soul. It was also in this period that the Aryan practice of sacrifice yielded to a system of ethics, and the Aryan rituals were replaced by a new emphasis on knowledge and devotion. These developments are revealed in the epic stories composed in the period leading up to 400 BC. The old gods came to be regarded as incarnations of the divine, and continued to be worshipped as more accessible personifications of a rather abstract single deity—not, as is often assumed, as independent deities within a polytheistic system. The *Ramayana* and *Mahabharata* epics also developed the doctrine of the *avatar*, the idea that God works his purposes by coming to earth periodically in human form. The best known avatar is perhaps Krishna, whose story is told in the *Bhagavad-Gita*, part of the *Mahabharata* epic. An avatar acts both as an intermediary between man and God and as a focus for the worship of God.

Hindu teaching has never been uniform, and in the early centuries AD the different philosophical schools taught everything from pantheism to agnosticism. The most influential was the *Vedanta*, which concentrated on the relationship between the individual soul and Brahman. But it was during our Middle Ages that the school of thought arose which perhaps most typifies Hinduism today. It is known as *bhakti*, or the path of devotion. In bhakti God is approached not directly but through devotion to the gods Vishnu and Shiva. Vishnu in turn may be worshipped in his incarnations or avatars, best known of whom is Krishna.

God, the human soul and the afterlife

Belief in some form of survival after death is present throughout the history and in all the major schools of Hinduism. God may be reached and immortality assured by following one of three paths: works, knowledge, or devotion. Broadly speaking the way of works has its roots in the *Vedas*, the way of knowledge in the *Upanishads*, and the way of devotion in the bhakti movement, although the way of works in particular was subject to later developments. All three paths are followed today.

The Vedas *and the path of works*

The *Vedas*, which are thought to date from some time in the second millennium BC, clearly set forth a doctrine of immortality—in fact, our very word 'immortality' is derived from the Sanskrit word '*amrta*' used in them. Literally, it means 'non-death'. The person who survives death is one who correctly and faithfully observes the prescribed practices and rituals of the Aryan faith. In particular, this involves worship of Brahman (by recitation of the *Vedas*), worship of the gods (by making offerings in the sacred fire kept alight in the home—fire symbolises immortality, which is why a corpse is disposed of by cremation), worship of the spirits of living things, worship of men, and finally worship of ancestors. This last duty is the most important. The ancestors must be offered rice, milk and water in order to ensure their continued blessing on the family. They dwell in the heavenly Land of the Fathers, where they retain their earthly identities and enjoy all the pleasures of life. Those not worthy of entry to heaven go instead to hell, an underground realm of darkness, silence and extremes of temperature, where a serpent or arch-demon is confined.[4]

This is the oldest formulation of the way of works. In later times, most particularly as expressed in the *Bhagavad Gita* (dating from the first millennium BC), the way of works has a different meaning. Belief in reincarnation is now firm, and salvation from rebirth is believed to come through the doing of deeds which produce no advantage to the doer. This doctrine of selfless work has influenced many generations of Hindus.

The Upanishads *and the path of knowledge*

The *Upanishads* give the earliest expression to three doctrines which together assert that death is not final, but might be followed by rebirth. The first is the doctrine that death occurs not once but many times, and is followed each time by rebirth. This is known as *samsara*. The second is the doctrine that the nature of that rebirth will depend on deeds done in the previous life. This is known as *karma*. And the third is the doctrine that there is a potential way of escape from these repeated cycles of death and rebirth. This is known as *moksha*. The path of knowledge seeks a proper understanding of these doctrines and the concepts which lie behind them and hopes through this understanding to find the way of escape or release.

The three teachings of samsara, karma and moksha are often thought of together in the West as the doctrine of reincarnation. Without a proper grasp of the Hindu concept of the individual, however, this doctrine is liable to be misrepresented.

The most influential philosophical school is that of the Vedanta. Vedanta distinguishes between the eternal soul (atman) and the embodied or empirical soul (*jiva*). I shall refer to the former as the soul and the latter as the self. Some might say 'spirit' and 'soul' respectively, but the important thing is that we clarify carefully the terms we are using. By the self here is meant the personality, that which experiences life, that which encompasses mind and emotion, action and reaction, that which constitutes an identity. It is subject to the law of samsara, and therefore bound for rebirth, not necessarily in human form. The nature of the next round will be determined by karma. Karma is the accumulated total of the actions of life, good and bad, like a sort of moral bank balance of deeds, arrested at the point of death. It will be either in credit (leading to a better state) or in debit (leading to a worse one). It is not however separate from the self but inextricably bound up with it; the self is the sum of its past actions.

It is important to grasp that the whole aim of life is not to achieve rebirth but to progress towards the ending of the cycle of death and rebirth. Salvation and immortality are not to be found in samsara. Indeed, the reverse is true; rebirth is an imprisonment, another wearisome round to be endured not enjoyed. The self may continue through one cycle after another, but it can never achieve immortality. Indeed it is transient and ultimately illusory.

The soul, or atman, on the other hand, is eternal but not personal. That is, it does not belong to the individual but represents that part of the divine reality, or Brahman, which is present in the individual. The goal of every Hindu, to attain release (moksha) from the endless cycle of death and rebirth, is achieved when the soul frees itself from the self and is reunited with Brahman. At that point the self is extinguished. So although moksha is salvation, it is not the salvation, the immortality, of the individual.

Furthermore, just as the salvation which may be achieved is not the salvation of an individual person, so the Brahman of the *Upanishads* is not the personal God we are used to in the West. Brahman does not have an identity; he is everything that is, the unique ultimate reality; he cannot be described except in terms of what he is not. He is the force through which the universe came into being. Everything is one, and the one is Brahman. That is the sense in which we have an immortal soul; it is not ours at all, but rather a manifestation of Brahman: 'As from a blazing fire there spring forth thousands of sparks like little fires, so . . . from God the Imperishable diverse life forms are produced and indeed go back again to Him' (*Mundakopanishad* II.1.1).

Within this system of rebirth and eventual restoration to Brahman the Vedic concepts of a heavenly realm and underground hell are retained, but in a revised form. Heaven and hell are now regarded as intermediate states, to be experienced as appropriate (depending upon one's karma) between death and rebirth. Seven levels of heaven stretch above the sky, and seven levels of hell reach below the ground. These are described in great detail in the epics. Hell is a place of great torment, where the wicked are devoured by dogs, worms and vultures; they are sawn in half, forced to stand on burning sand, boiled in oil, tossed onto sharp spears, beaten, or force-fed molten metals, urine and excreta. It is divided into twenty-eight regions, each of which has 144 chambers. Heaven, by contrast, is a land of beautiful palaces, perfumed maidens and incomparable banquets.[5]

Bhakti and the path of devotion

If salvation from rebirth may be sought through the practice of religious works or through the acquisition of knowledge and understanding, it may also be sought through love, and so the third path in Hinduism is the path of devotion, or bhakti.

In the early centuries AD a number of sects grew up in worship of the ancient gods Shiva, Shakti and Vishnu. These gods were not revered as independent deities but as manifestations of aspects of the supreme god Brahman. The devotee would move through successive stages of spiritual maturity as he performed certain rituals—in the case of the Shaiva sect, for example, bathing, laughing, dancing, singing, incantation, isolation through the abandonment of particular social conventions, and meditation. Generally, methods of achieving salvation included worship, meditation, yoga and penance.[6]

Bhakti finds its origin in the *Bhagavad-Gita*, which teaches that those who meditate on the Lord Krishna are united with him at death and thus freed from rebirth. The movement developed between the seventh and twelfth centuries in Southern India, and was marked by the composition of a large body of ecstatic religious poetry. It was only in the eleventh century that a theological basis was given to this essentially popular movement by Ramanuja, who reinterpreted the *Upanishads* to show that Brahman may be understood as a loving personal god with whom the devotee may be reunited at death through bhakti. Vishnu has been the most popular object of devotion, most particularly in the form of three of his avatars or incarnations—Krishna, Rama and the Buddha, all of whom are followed today. But many other deities are worshipped in this way, individual villages having their own particular god or goddess. The deity is worshipped in a temple, where he is represented by a statue in a central shrine, with rites of purification, hymns, prayers and offerings. He is also worshipped in the home, where a room may be set aside for the purpose.

The three paths today

Although the three paths of works, knowledge and devotion are all followed today, in practice they are not as clearly distinct from one another as the above outline implies. Most Hindus base their faith on elements derived from all three traditions.

Buddhism

Buddhism has much in common with Hinduism, and indeed it developed out of Hinduism. It is based on the teaching of one man, Siddhartha Gautama, who was born in India in the sixth century BC. Today it has over 300 million followers. Although now scarcely practised in the land of its origin, it is the main religion in Sri Lanka, Burma, Thailand, China, Korea, Tibet, Japan, Vietnam, Mongolia, Nepal and other smaller countries.

We have few reliable historical details concerning the life of Siddhartha Gautama, for neither his life nor his teaching was recorded in writing until several hundred years after his death. However, we do know that he was born into a ruling family in North India in about 563 BC. At the age of twenty-nine he was overwhelmed with a sense of the suffering inherent in the human condition, and the inadequacy of the conventional (Hindu) religious answers. Abandoning his rich lifestyle, he set out on a spiritual journey with the aim of finding whether there might not be some way of escape from the endless cycle of suffering, death and rebirth taught by contemporary Hinduism. He finally found his answer during a night of meditation some six years later. He became known as the Buddha, or Enlightened One, and from then until his death in about 483 BC he dedicated himself to the task of ensuring that the release he had found might become available to all who would seek it.[7]

What the Buddha taught

The Buddha once said: 'One thing I teach, suffering and the ending of suffering.'[8] He emphasised that suffering and death come to us all, but taught that there is a way of escape, a kind of spiritual release, which can be found by anyone who would seek it, without any outside assistance. The key to its discovery lies in the teaching which the Buddha formulated as the four noble truths and the eightfold path, and which was revealed to him during the night of his enlightenment. The four truths are these:

1. Suffering is bound up in every aspect of life. Disease, death, emotional pain, loss, the inability to make things go right, injustice, famine, frustration, loneliness, disillusionment, the very absence of what we yearn for; all these are forms of suffering.

2. The cause of suffering is desire. Desire is the craving for satisfaction and fulfilment; the attachment to things; the me-centredness of each one of us. It springs from the sense of 'I' and 'me' and 'mine'. It is this which binds us to a separate existence, prevents us from reuniting ourselves with the infinite, and which, at death, draws us into rebirth.

3. It is possible to escape from suffering and avoid rebirth by realising that 'I' do not exist; that there is in fact no such thing as an enduring 'I' or soul or atman, but only something which is constantly changing. Once we understand this, the root of desire and attachment is cut and with it suffering.

4. Desire may be conquered and suffering escaped by following the eightfold path. The culmination of the eightfold

path is enlightenment, or nirvana. No further rebirth will occur once this point is reached.

The path can be divided into three main stages. The first two steps are intellectual in nature, and involve right understanding (of the doctrines of Buddhism) and right attitude of mind (determination to aim for the right goals in the right way). The next three are ethical, and involve right speech, right action (the following of moral commandments: do not kill, steal, lust, lie or use drink/drugs), and right livelihood (an occupation consistent with the keeping of these commandments must be followed). The last three steps are spiritual, and concern right effort (the conquering of evil and the cultivation of universal love); right concentration (the ability to eliminate everything except a single point from the mind); and right meditation (the elimination of even that single point in favour of a direct awareness of 'the still centre of the turning world'). These steps will enable the individual to break free from the fetters which bind him to the wheel of life.

In its most essential form, Buddhism has been described as 'the finest moral philosophy extant', and as 'the most radical system of self-deliverance ever conceived', for it postulates no god and asks for no saviour. Buddhism is a do-it-yourself religion of the most sophisticated kind, perhaps most aptly summarised in the Buddha's own dying words: 'Work out your own salvation with diligence.'[9]

The soul

The Hinduism of the Buddha's time taught that salvation, or moksha, was to be found in the reuniting of the external self, or atman, with the ultimate reality, or Brahman. The Buddha's teaching contradicted this view, stating that there is no such thing as atman, and that therefore the possibility of uniting atman with Brahman does not arise. Everything is impermanent, everything is a wheel of becoming with no beginning and no end. In so far as there is an ultimate reality, it is a void. As for an individual soul, there can be nothing more in a man than a temporary association of five factors: body, emotion, perception, volition and consciousness. Human life is like the changing patterns and shapes of bubbles flowing together on the surface of a stream; and any concept we might have of selfhood, of individual identity, of an immortal soul, is no more than an illusion—and an illusion which it is vital to overcome if enlightenment is to be reached and rebirth escaped.

It follows that in continuing to teach the doctrine of rebirth, Buddhism does not teach that you or I will be reborn. All that can be reborn is the consciousness, which is little more than an integrating factor for the moving elements which make up a person. Everything else will be dissolved at death. The common Western understanding of reincarnation—that is, that we each possess an individual and immortal soul which has passed and will pass from one human body to another in a chronological succession of lives—has no basis in the teaching of the Buddha. As one authority reminds us, 'rebirth, not of a changeless soul, but of an ever-evolving, karma-created bundle of characteristics is accepted by the whole world east of Karachi'.[10] The Western concept that rebirth is desirable is also foreign to Buddhism, which like Hinduism regards it as a fate worth going to enormous lengths to avoid.

Nirvana

For the Buddhist, therefore, immortality or eternal life is to be found not in rebirth but in enlightenment, or nirvana. This is rather hard to describe. The Buddha himself expressed it thus:

> There is, Brethren, a condition where there is neither 'earth', nor 'water', nor 'fire', nor 'air', nor the sphere of infinite space, nor the sphere of infinite consciousness, nor the sphere of the void, nor the sphere of neither perception nor non-perception . . . that condition, Brethren, do I call neither a coming nor a going nor a standing still, nor a falling away nor a rising up; but it is without fixity, without mobility, without basis. It is the end of woe.[11]

A more recent description perhaps gives a clearer idea:

> *Nirvana* is an ethical state, a condition which eliminates any future rebirth, the extinction of all craving, the final release from suffering. It may be defined as deliverance from the trammels of the body, a supreme consciousness of peace and rest, a perfect, passionless happiness. It is a state of mind in which *karma* comes to an end. It is the cessation of becoming, for when a process is not continued it simply ceases. It is remainderlessness. It is the peace of the man for whom there will be no rebirth; separateness is ended, the flame of desire has gone out, the limitations of selfhood are extinguished.[12]

The word 'nirvana' literally means a 'going out', although it is a going out of the individual and not of life itself. Another authority comments that 'through the destruction of all that is individual in us, we enter into communion with the whole universe'.[13] The concept is not one that has gained popularity in the West, partly perhaps because it is so vague, and partly because it seems to be founded essentially on the idea of avoidance—the elimination of pain and suffering by cutting oneself off from it, and from oneself in the process.

Developments of the Buddha's teaching

Buddhism has continued to develop in the 2,500 years since the death of its founder, and it is now divided into four main schools. The original teaching is preserved by the Theravada school, and recorded in a body of scriptures dating (in written form) from the first century BC, and eleven times as long as the Bible. As time went on, however, the original teachings were expanded; other ancient oral traditions were gathered in, and elements from other religions were absorbed. The result was the Mahayana school, more flexible and dynamic than the Theravada, more popular in its appeal; based on the same central doctrines outlined above, but adding modifications of its own. In the sixth century AD the Zen school was founded in China; it is now followed mainly in Japan. And in the seventh century Buddhism reached Tibet, where the Tibetan school now holds sway. Both these schools are more closely related to the Mahayana than to the Theravada school.

The crucial modification made to the Theravada teaching by the Mahayana school concerns the means by which enlightenment may be obtained. The Buddha taught that salvation is achieved by self-effort alone; the Mahayana holds that help may be sought from a special person known as a *bodhisattva*. The bodhisattva is a person who achieves enlightenment but renounces it in order to bring it to others. This in itself is in harmony with the Theravada teaching. However, gradually the bodhisattva came to be seen as a kind of saviour, who by his love is able to confer salvation on others, thus enabling them to escape rebirth and achieve nirvana without following the long and arduous journey of self-improvement laid down by the Theravada teaching. Faith in the saving power of the bodhisattva becomes the only requirement. This doctrine is carried to the extreme by the Pure Land School of Japan (belonging to the Mahayana), which teaches that salvation is gained by simple trust in the bodhisattva Amida. For many ordinary people in India the chosen bodhisattva came to be worshipped as a local deity, and so the popular faith of rural areas was absorbed into the new religion.

The Mahayana claims by this development of the Buddha's teaching to have introduced love into an otherwise cold and logical philosophy, to have complemented the teaching of the head with the life of the heart, and above all to have made salvation accessible to everyone, not just to a spiritual elite. The Theravada regards the Mahayana as distorting the Buddha's original teaching to the point of transforming it into something quite different.

Heaven and hell in Buddhism

The Buddhist teaching on heaven and hell is similar to that of Hinduism; they are seen as intermediate and temporary states between one earthly existence and another. That which survives death (broadly speaking, consciousness plus karma) may pass into any one of the heavens or hells. There are eight subterranean hells, each with sixteen minor hells attached. Like the Hindu hells, these are extremely unpleasant in nature. The various heavens are arranged into three groups. The first six are sensual in character. The next thirteen to eighteen are material, but meditation is the occupation of their inhabitants. The last group are mental in nature, and are characterised by different levels of spiritual attainment. Nirvana transcends even the highest heaven.[14]

These concepts are modified by the Pure Land School, which teaches that there is a paradise in the west, a pleasant land of rivers, lakes, flowers, music and precious stones. Access to this paradise is granted by Amida to all who call on his name, and all who enter it will proceed to nirvana.[15]

Summary

Hindus take for granted that there is a continuing existence of the self after death. This may take the form of almost immediate rebirth, or of time in heaven or hell. Some Hindus hope that they will obtain salvation and become one with God. Buddhists also believe in rebirth, but hold that there is no such thing as an individual soul, and that salvation is to be found only in the realisation of this truth and the consequent elimination of self. For both the Hindu and the Buddhist rebirth is an unfortunate law of life, and not something to be sought.

There are other differences between Hinduism and Buddhism. The Hindu lives in a world of many gods, one or more of whom he may worship as a way of progressing spiritually towards his goal of release from rebirth. The Buddhist is an agnostic, who holds no firm belief in a God or gods, but only in men who have achieved spiritual maturity and may act as guides for other men. In a sense, Buddhism is not a religion at all, but rather a moral philosophy.

We will return to both these religions in Chapter 4, when we come to look at the concept of reincarnation in more detail.

Judaism

Like Hinduism, Judaism is primarily the faith of a people, in this case the Jewish people. And like Buddhism, Judaism can trace its origins back to a specific point in history, in this case the contract, or covenant, made between God and Abraham in the eighteenth century BC or thereabouts.[16] But in every other way Judaism is radically different from these other two ancient religions. In particular, it is founded on the concept of a single, personal deity who has a special relationship with the Jewish people and who has revealed his will in a written law given to that people. The history of the relationship between God and the Jews is recorded in what we know as the Old Testament.[17]

The development of Judaism

The Jewish people trace their ancestry back to Abraham, whose story is recorded in the Book of Genesis. Abraham came from Ur, in Mesopotamia, but was told by God to go with his wife to the land of Canaan—modern Israel. There he was given a double promise of land and family:

> Behold, my covenant is with you, and you shall be the father of a multitude of nations. . . . And I will establish my covenant between me and you and your descendants after you throughout their generations for an everlasting covenant, to be God to you and to your descendants after you. And I will give to you, and to your descendants after you, the land of your sojournings, all the land of Canaan, for an everlasting possession; and I will be their God (Genesis 17:4–8).

The Jewish people are themselves the fulfilment of the first element in this covenant—the promise that Abraham would have many descendants. The second element, the promise of land, has sustained them throughout their history.

Abraham had a son, Isaac. He in turn had a son, Jacob, renamed Israel or 'he who strives with God'. Jacob had twelve sons, one of whom was Joseph, who in the familiar story was sold into slavery in Egypt, became one of Pharaoh's trusted advisers and was followed by his family who settled there. God's promise had been that the Jewish nation, Abraham's family, would inhabit Canaan and not Egypt. Over the years they became enslaved there, and at the beginning of the thirteenth century BC they were led back out of Egypt by Moses, in what became known as the Exodus. Eventually they were able to reach and capture Canaan under the leadership of Moses' successor Joshua. This was seen as the first fulfilment of God's covenant with his people. It was marked by the giving of a body of law. The Israelites were to demonstrate their continued faith, and their acceptance of the covenant, through the keeping of this law. It began with the Ten Commandments:

1. I am the Lord your God; you shall have no other gods before me.
2. You shall not make a graven image, or any likeness of anything; you shall not bow down and serve them.
3. You shall not take the name of the Lord your God in vain.
4. Remember the sabbath day.
5. Honour your father and mother.
6. You shall not kill.
7. You shall not commit adultery.
8. You shall not steal.
9. You shall not bear false witness against your neighbour.
10. You shall not covet.

(Exodus 20)

In this way the original covenant was strengthened; the Israelites now regarded themselves as a chosen people or holy nation, watched over by God and bound for their part to live according to his will.

In Canaan, after a period of consolidation under various leaders, David was appointed king in about 1000 BC. He was succeeded by his son Solomon, who built a magnificent national temple in Jerusalem. But the faith of the people grew weak, and the law was not kept; the covenant was therefore broken, and the land lost; in the sixth century BC the two kingdoms of Judea and Israel, into which Canaan had been divided on the death of Solomon, were captured by the Babylonians. The temple was destroyed, and the Israelites carried into exile. With the exile, however, came the opportunity for reflection and reform, and it was during this period that the law was revised and written down. God responded to their renewed faith with a second fulfilment of his promise to Abraham; after sixty years the Babylonians were defeated by the Persians, and the Israelites allowed to return home. Jerusalem was rebuilt under the governorship of Zerubbabel.

In the fourth century BC the Persians were defeated by the Greeks, and in the new Hellenistic culture the Jewish faith flourished and developed. In particular, this period saw the emergence of the idea of a future messiah or saviour: a man who, like Moses, Joshua, David and Zerubbabel, would be ordained by God to bring the people into fulfilment of the double promise—but this time permanently.

The first century AD however brought another setback. The Greek empire was succeeded by the Roman empire. Jerusalem was sacked, the temple destroyed once more, and the Israelites dispossessed.

The same pattern has continued up to the present day. On a political level, expansion and prosperity have alternated with persecution and hardship, most notably of course during the Holocaust. On a spiritual level, periods of obedient faith on the part of the people have alternated with periods of disobedience and decline, and God has responded with blessing or withdrawal of blessing. For many Jews, God again fulfilled his covenant in the founding of the state of Israel in 1948; and yet, as we know,

Israel's difficulties are far from over.

Within modern Judaism a number of different perspectives exist. Some, the Orthodox, continue to await a political messiah who will give permanent fulfilment to the promise of land, and therefore continue to express their faith in the traditional observance of the law. Others, while preserving a clear Jewish identity, show less certainty regarding the future, preferring instead to emphasise the present, and the need to adapt traditional practices to fit the demands of modern society.

The scriptures

The core of the Hebrew scriptures is the Mosaic law, recorded in the Pentateuch or first five books of the Bible. This law was repeated and developed in later writings. It is known as the *Torah*, or 'divine instruction'. The *Torah* is complemented by the *Talmud*, which has two main elements. One is the *Mishnah*, a body of oral law composed as a commentary to the *Torah* and first committed to writing in about AD 200. The other is the *Gemara*, a commentary on the *Mishnah* completed by about AD 500. In addition there are later commentaries and codes which interpret and systematise the earlier teaching. Alongside the Law, the Jewish scriptures contain two other kinds of literature: the Prophets and the Writings. These three together are known as Tanak, and are essentially what Christians know as the Old Testament.

Major doctrines

Judaism has no formal statement of doctrine. The first attempt to summarise its main beliefs was made in the twelfth century by the philosopher Maimonides, who drew up a list of thirteen articles of faith. These are still to be found printed in the Authorized Jewish Prayer Book. Six of them are concerned with God, who is believed to be the one eternal creator and provider, incorporeal and omniscient, to whom alone worship is due. Four are concerned with the law, which is unchangeable and was first given by God to Moses and subsequently confirmed by later prophets. One is concerned with the Messiah, a future reformer who will redeem the Jewish nation and establish peace and prosperity on earth. And two are concerned with the afterlife, affirming the resurrection of the dead and the doctrine of retribution in the hereafter. These doctrines are mostly upheld today, although most Jews place little emphasis on the afterlife, and indeed some, notably the Reconstructionists, deny its existence altogether. The emphasis of Judaism as it is lived lies in obedience to the law—often summarised in the words of the Book of Leviticus as 'love your neighbour as yourself' (Leviticus 19:18).

Life after death

Belief in the existence of an afterlife has never been as prominent in Judaism as in the religions of the Far East or, as we shall see, in Christianity. This is essentially because the basis of Judaism is the covenant between God and the Jewish people; Jews have traditionally looked forward first and foremost to a future on this earth, and have striven to keep the law, their part of the covenant relationship. At the same time, it seems unlikely that a God who would take such trouble to look after his people on this earth would abandon them at death, and it is clear from the scriptures that from the earliest times the Hebrew people have believed in the existence of an afterlife. Furthermore, it is clear that their belief has not been static but shows a gradual development which continues to this day.[18]

According to Hebrew teaching, and in sharp contrast with the tenets of Hinduism and Buddhism, the soul and body are indivisibly one. Such a doctrine obviously affects what is believed about the afterlife, and for many centuries life after death was conceived as a shadowy existence of both body and soul in a place known as Sheol. The scriptures describe Sheol as located deep beneath the earth's surface; it is a place of darkness, mist and gloom, to which all people go irrespective of their spiritual or worldly status. It is commonly referred to as a pit in which men are swallowed up; it is a land of no return.[19]

From the sixth century BC this doctrine began to be modified, and suggestions appear, particularly in the Psalms, that there may be something more to hope for than an eternally shadowy existence in Sheol. As the Jewish understanding of the covenant developed, the concept arose of heaven as a relationship between the righteous and God, and thence the idea of a positive, individual life after death—the idea of resurrection.[20] By the second century BC Jewish writing was affirming that all will be resurrected after death, that all will face judgment, but that immortality will be gained only by some. Sheol became a place for the wicked, while the righteous would go to 'paradise'—literally meaning 'garden', and referring back to the Garden of Eden.[21] Other texts from the second century BC to the second century AD elaborate still further, describing in great detail not a garden but up to ten consecutive heavens in which the righteous will dwell, and a subterranean hell of excruciating physical torment.[22]

By the first century AD various positions had been adopted concerning life after death. The Sadducees denied survival in any form. The Pharisees taught that the individual has an immortal soul, and that the good will be resurrected while the bad will undergo suffering. The Essenes believed that the good will find rest in a pleasant land beyond the sea, whereas the bad will be confined to an underground realm of suffering. And the Zealots taught that eternal life is to be found only in the release of the soul from the body at death.[23] The influence of Greek thought on the formation of some of these beliefs is apparent.

Of these four schools, it was the Pharisees who came to occupy the dominant position over the first few centuries AD, and belief in the resurrection of the body and the judgment of the dead became established. However, during the last two centuries various challenges have been mounted to this position. Of the modern schools, Reform Judaism no longer believes in the resurrection of the body, Conservative Judaism believes in both the resurrection of the body and the immortality of the soul, and the Reconstructionists, like the Sadducees before them, deny altogether the existence of any form of life after death. It is nonetheless true to say that throughout the last 2,000 years the majority of Jews have believed, and still do believe, in some form of life after death—and pray daily 'Blessed art thou, O Lord, who makest alive the dead.' In particular, the Jew expects to be judged according to the law, and to be admitted to heaven; he also expects those who have not kept the law to receive some form of appropriate punishment.

And so Judaism, although it places the emphasis of its teaching firmly on this life rather than on the next, offers a third view of salvation. Hinduism teaches that salvation may be achieved only by dedicated following of the paths of work, knowledge or devotion, and that it may take many lives to do so. Buddhism teaches that suffering is universal, that it is caused by desire, and that salvation is gained only by the abandoning of these desires and the transcending of the self; it offers a complex and rigorous method for achieving this. Judaism teaches that a Jew stands in a covenant relationship with God which, although to be fulfilled primarily on this earth, may be expected to lead to salvation after death also. It may be sought through faith in God, expressed essentially in the keeping of the law.

Christianity

Christianity is a much younger religion than any of those discussed so far, although it traces its ancestry back through Judaism and so properly speaking likewise begins with the Book of Genesis 4,000 years ago. Its impact has been enormous— signalled by the worldwide adoption of a calendar based on the date of Christ's birth—and it now has more followers and a wider distribution than any other religion. Indeed, something approaching one third of the entire world population currently professes the Christian faith.[24]

Whereas other religions are based on the religious experience of a people, like Hinduism, or the teaching of a particular man, like Buddhism, or the messages of a prophet, like Islam, the Christian faith is based on a number of key historical events. In this it is most similar to Judaism. The crucial events for Christians were the birth, crucifixion and resurrection of Jesus Christ in Palestine (Israel) 2,000 years ago. The importance of these events lies in the identity of Jesus, who claimed to be the Son of God incarnated as a man, and the only vehicle through which men might be saved from what comes through death. Christians believe that he validated this claim not only through his teaching and the miracles he worked while alive, but most particularly by the fact that he reappeared, alive, two days after being buried. The vast majority of Christians worldwide believe, and have always believed, the resurrection of Jesus to be literally true—that is, that Jesus was actually bodily restored to life after his death. A minority of Christians in recent times have however suggested that the traditional teaching of the incarnation and resurrection refers not to historical events which actually took place, but rather to universal truths cast in this particular 'mythical' form. These Christians are known as liberals. The evidence for the resurrection of Jesus will be discussed in Chapter 6.

Christianity and Judaism

Christianity grew out of Judaism, and the two faiths have much in common. Christians worship the same God as Jews. They look back on the same history and share the same scriptures, which they know as the Old Testament and to which they have added the New Testament. They regard the Jews as the people chosen by God for a special purpose. And most importantly, Christians share with Jews the belief in a Messiah, a man appointed to come in order to rule over all nations. This, however, is also where Jews and Christians part company:

Christians regard Jesus as the promised Messiah; Jews believe that the Messiah is yet to come.

The Hebrew word 'Messiah' means 'Anointed one', as does the Greek word 'Christ', which is a translation of it. In Jewish thought it came to designate a future descendant of King David, who is expected to lead Israel to victory over a hostile world power and establish a kingdom of peace and prosperity.[25] Jesus of Nazareth, a Jew who spent his life among Jews, and a descendant of David whom his followers believed to be the promised Messiah, was not recognised by many Jews as such because he failed to achieve the political victory which was expected, and indeed died the death of a common criminal.

For many first-century Jews, however, Jesus had demonstrated that he was the Messiah by rising from the dead and establishing a revolutionary new kingdom which was not political but spiritual in nature. They believed that this kingdom began immediately in the life of the individual but that it would be universally established after an appointed Day at the end of time. They pointed to the many Old Testament prophecies which appeared to have found fulfilment in the particular circumstances of his life and death.[26]

The Christian church

The new faith grew rapidly as the news of the resurrection spread, at first through the Jewish synagogues. By the end of the first century there were communities, or churches, of Christians all round the Mediterranean; by the end of the second there were Christians in Egypt, North Africa and Gaul. In 380 Christianity became the official religion of the Roman Empire, and thence spread to Mesopotamia, Ethiopia, Persia, Armenia and the Gothic lands of middle Europe. In the fifth century it reached Britain, and from there was carried to Holland, Denmark and Germany. In 800 Charlemagne established it throughout his Holy Roman Empire. By the sixteenth century there were churches in the Far East, North and South America and the

Philippines; by the eighteenth in India and Jamaica. The last couple of centuries have seen the Christian faith adopted in countries all over the world, and at present it is growing most rapidly in Africa, South Korea, and parts of Latin America. There appears to be a revival of adherence also in Eastern Europe and the former Soviet Union.

Today there are many different churches and denominations, all of which adhere to the same basic doctrine, although they differ over many details of belief and especially practice. The major churches are the Roman Catholic Church, the Eastern Orthodox churches, the Protestant churches and the Pentecostal churches. They have different emphases, but are all founded on belief in Jesus.

Major doctrines

The term 'Christian' dates from within a year of the death and resurrection of Jesus, and was coined by the people of Antioch to describe his followers as they taught there (Acts 11:26). The name has stuck, for it goes to the heart of the new faith; it is founded on Christ. The major beliefs of the Christian faith are stated in the Creed (from the Latin word for belief). The one in use today was formulated in the fourth or fifth century, but probably dates back in essence to the early church in Jerusalem. In its shortest form it goes like this:

I believe in God, the Father almighty, creator of heaven and earth.

I believe in Jesus Christ, his only Son, our Lord. He was conceived by the power of the Holy Spirit, and born of the Virgin Mary. He suffered under Pontius Pilate, was crucified, died and was buried. He descended to the dead. On the third day he rose again. He ascended into heaven, and is seated at the right hand of the Father. He will come again to judge the living and the dead.

I believe in the Holy Spirit, the holy catholic [universal] church, the communion of saints, the forgiveness of sins, the resurrection of the body, and the life everlasting.

The essence of the Christian faith is therefore this: Christians believe in God the Father who created the world; in Jesus his Son who came to earth as a man, who was crucified and rose from the dead, and will one day judge all mankind; and in the Holy Spirit, who sustains and speaks to man. We will return to the doctrine of the Holy Spirit, for it is the essence of the Christian belief and experience.

Life after death

The question of life after death is central to the teaching of Jesus. Jesus taught that although everyone must die, the spirit will not die with the body, and that one day, on the Day of Judgment, every person who has ever lived will have to give an account of himself or herself. He or she will then either be allowed to live on in heaven, or be condemned to hell. The Christian teaching on heaven and hell will be examined in greater detail in the last chapter.

Jesus also taught that nobody is left just to hope for this 'eternal life'; there would be two guarantees. The first guarantee would be his own resurrection; he would not only talk about life after death, but actually demonstrate it. This of course would be most convincing for those who actually saw it with their own eyes, which many did. The second guarantee would be what Jesus described as the coming of the Holy Spirit. He promised that those who followed him would have the presence of God with them, to such a degree and in such a way that they could not doubt it. This experience of God's presence in a person would bear witness to the promise that he or she would survive physical death and receive eternal life—that the person has already crossed over from death to life, to put it in biblical terminology. The Holy Spirit makes it possible to know God through prayer, and testifies to a spiritual life which will not end with the grave.

The main intellectual question posed by Christianity is therefore this: Did Jesus really rise from the dead? If the resurrection occurred, it is a most powerful demonstration that

Christianity is true, and this would cast a shadow on the claims of other religions. If on the other hand the resurrection did not occur, then the whole of the Christian faith stands on a very shaky foundation. Then there is a secondary question, more practical in nature: How do I as an individual claim a share in this eternal life, or—for it amounts to the same thing—how do I obtain an experience of God's presence with me now?

Jesus was quite clear on this, although what he said has often been forgotten. He taught that eternal life is not obtained by meditation and understanding, nor by good works, nor by devotion to gods who may intercede for us; it is not obtained by programmes of self-enlightenment, however commendable these may be, nor yet by striving for obedience to the law, honourable and God-given though the law may be. It is obtainable only through him, the Son of God; through a willingness to believe in him, trust him, and live according to his will.

Islam

Islam is the third, in chronological terms, of the major monotheistic religions. It was founded in the seventh century AD by Muhammad and, like Christianity, has its origin in Judaism. Today it is practised by over 800 million people, mostly in the Middle East and North Africa.[27]

The history of Islam

The founder of Islam was Muhammed ibn Abdullah, who was born in AD 570 in Mecca, in present-day Saudi Arabia, where he grew up to earn his living as a caravan trader. At that time Mecca had become the major commercial centre in what was essentially a tribal, polytheistic culture. Muhammad, as a result of receiving a number of detailed divine relevations, sought to bring the people of Arabia back to the monotheistic faith of their father Abraham, from whom the Arabs trace their descent through his son Ishmael (the Jews also trace their descent from Abraham, but through Isaac). These revelations to Muhammad continued for a period of twenty-two years, and after Muhammad's death were collected and recorded in what became the holy book of Islam, the *Quran*.

Muhammad regarded himself not as the founder of a new religion but as a reformer, a messenger and prophet in the line of Abraham, Moses and Jesus. And so the Muslim regards both the Old Testament and the New with respect. However, he believes the *Quran* to be the only uncorrupted version of the word of God, or Allah as he had been known in the region; the Jewish and Christian scriptures are seen as a mixture of divine revelation and human error. The *Quran* is written in Arabic, and consists of 114 chapters arranged according to length rather than subject matter, which makes it rather difficult of access for the Western reader.

Muhammad gradually built up a community of believers, first in Medina, a city to the north of Mecca, and then in Mecca itself. This was achieved initially by the courageous preaching of his message, and subsequently by the use of military force. By the time he died in 632, the whole of Arabia was under Islam. Within another twelve years the Muslims had occupied Egypt, Syria and Iraq; within a century they had gained control of the entire breadth of North Africa, and spread to the north as far as Constantinople (now Istanbul) and to the east as far as Persia (Iran), and modern Afghanistan and Pakistan. By the Middle Ages Islam was expanding into Spain, and then to India, from where it spread to Malaysia, Indonesia and the Philippines. During the eighteenth and nineteenth centuries the Islamic lands were first developed and then colonised by Western powers, but this century has seen a strong Muslim resurgence in many countries, and Islam has again become a powerful modern force, both culturally and politically.[28]

The divisions of modern Islam

When Muhammad died he did not leave a designated successor, and this has caused many divisions within Islam. Initially there were those who held that Muhammad should be succeeded by elected leaders, and this was indeed what happened at first. However, there were also those who believed that his position as leader of the Muslim community should be hereditary, passing to his son-in-law Ali and then to his grandsons. The first group were, and remain, in a majority; today they are known as Sunni Muslims, and they look for their authority to the example of Muhammad and the first four elected caliphs ('sunna' means 'custom') and to the community law which has been carefully developed over the centuries. They continued to be' led by an elected caliph until 1924, when the office was declared redundant.

The second group, who today constitute only about ten per cent of the total Muslim population, are known as Shiah or Shi'ite Muslims. The Shiahs have split into further sub-groups at various stages when the line of succession has been in doubt. They look for authority to the hereditary leader or *imam*, who is believed to be infallible in his interpretation of the *Quran* and in his leadership of the community. The heartland of the Shiahs today is Iran.[29]

The doctrine of Islam

The major emphasis of Islam is not doctrine or belief, as in Christianity; rather it is the observance of the law, as in Judaism. The doctrinal teaching of Islam can in fact be summarised in one key statement: 'There is no god but God, and Muhammad is the messenger of God.' This is the basis of Muslim belief and practice.

God is Allah, the name of the High God of the tribal faiths to whom Muhammad first preached his message of reform. He is the creator, sustainer and ultimately judge of the universe. He cannot be known, only obeyed; he is awesomely powerful but also merciful. He has no associates—the Christian doctrine of the Trinity is repudiated, and Jesus regarded as human, not divine. Muhammad believed that Jesus was not crucified and not resurrected.[30] Allah is recognisably the same God as the God of the Jews and the Christians, but different aspects of his nature are stressed. As a broad generalisation, Muslims emphasise God's power, Jews his justice, and Christians his love.

The second part of the Muslim creed states that Muhammad is the messenger of God. A messenger is more than a prophet. Both are regarded as divinely inspired recipients of God's word, but the role of a messenger is more significant than that of a prophet. A messenger receives the perfect word of God, complete and incorruptible; his message is for an entire community. Muhammad was such a messenger. (The title messenger is also given to the main figures from the Bible who are mentioned in the *Quran*, from Adam to Jesus.) But although Muhammad's message came from God, he himself was a man. Unlike Jesus, he did not claim and has never been accorded any divine status.

The practice of Islam

At the heart of the Muslim way of life are the so-called Five Pillars of Islam, five practices regarded as obligatory by all Muslims. These are as follows.

First, and most important, is the profession of faith. A Muslim is one who can acknowledge the simple creed quoted above: 'There is no god but God (Allah), and Muhammad is the messenger of God.'

Secondly, a Muslim is called to prayer. He is required to perform this duty at five set times each day, prostrating himself, reciting fixed prayers (which include passages from the *Quran*) and declaring his faith using the formula quoted above.

Thirdly, a Muslim must pay a special tax, the *zakat*, which is used for the support of the poor and to assist in the spread of Islam.

Fourthly, a Muslim is required to fast each year for the duration of the month of Ramadan, when he may not eat between the hours of sunrise and sunset.

Fifthly, every Muslim is expected, circumstances permitting, to undertake a pilgrimage to Mecca at least once in his lifetime. Here he will join a procession which encircles the Kaaba, a building which houses a sacred black stone or meteorite believed to have been given to Abraham by Gabriel. He will also perform a number of special ceremonies and sacrifices.

In addition to the Five Pillars of Islam there is a further practice sometimes unofficially regarded as a sixth pillar. This is the *jihad*, or 'struggle'. In general terms this refers to the obligation of all Muslims to live according to God's will and to promote Islam. By extension it also refers to the holy war which is sometimes necessary for the defence of the faith. Jihad does not include either aggressive warfare or warfare against fellow Muslims, although it has been cited as a justification for both in recent years.

The Five Pillars cover the duty of the individual Muslim to God. In addition, of course, he has obligations to his fellow men, and these obligations are regulated by the sacred law or *Shari'a*. The Shari'a is far more than a legal system, however, since it covers not only those things which are prohibited by God, but also those which are commanded, desirable, optional and undesirable. It therefore acts as a guide to every aspect of life. The Shari'a is regarded as divinely revealed through four sources: the *Quran*, the practice of Muhammad, the consensus of scholars, and deductions based on these first three sources. During the nineteenth century much of the Shari'a was in effect superseded by Western legal codes, but it remains in force as far as family law is concerned, and is becoming more influential in other areas.

It is perhaps the Shari'a which gives Islam its distinctiveness, and has made integration with peoples of other faiths so difficult. Islamic law provides detailed regulations for the whole of life, including for example politics and education, which we might think of as non-religious areas. The very word 'Islam' means 'surrender to God's law', and a 'muslim' is 'one who submits'. As the essence of Islam is the law, it is difficult to be a Muslim unless the whole of the society in which you live is organised according to that law. This is not the case to nearly the same extent for any of the other major religions—although of course Judaism and Christianity in particular contain much teaching which applies not just to the individual but to society as a whole.

Life after death

The hereafter occupies a central position in Islamic thought, and many pages of the *Quran* are devoted to it. The Muslim believes that salvation depends both on the mercy of God and on the repentance, faith and correct conduct of man. He expects to be judged after death according to the way in which he has lived his life, and to be either admitted to paradise or consigned to hell. Hell may be either a temporary or a permanent abode.[31]

The Last Judgment. The Muslim believes firmly in the future coming of a Day of Judgment. This day cannot be foretold, but will be heralded by a trumpet blast and the destruction of the world. The skies will part, and angels bear down the throne of God. A general resurrection will occur, in which the soul of every person who has ever lived will be reunited with the body from which it was parted at death. Each individual will be brought before the throne to be judged according to the record of his deeds. The good Muslim hopes that his good deeds will outweigh his bad deeds when his actions are weighed in the balance. After the judgment he will be required to pass over the bridge of al-Araf, from which the infidel will fall into the pit of hell, but over which the true Muslim will pass to paradise.[32]

Hell. Hell is for the infidel or unbeliever, and for those Muslims who by their failure to observe the law have behaved as unbelievers. It is described in highly material terms as a place of fire and torment. It is in the shape of an inverted funnel divided into seven horizontal layers. The torments increase with depth, and are presided over by guardians. Demons abound. The various levels are named after hypocrites, idolators, Sabaeans (Yemenis), Muslims, Christians, Magi (Zoroastrians) and Jews, and separated by guarded gates. Other deeds specified in the Quran as deserving of torment in hell are lying, corruption, unbelief, blasphemy, denial of the Last Judgment and hell fire, and failure to give alms. The torments themselves include scorching, the wearing of burning clothes, chains and collars, immersion in boiling water and manhandling with iron hooks.[33]

Paradise. Corresponding to the seven levels of hell are seven layers of heaven, through which the righteous person will journey in the company of Gabriel to reach the garden of paradise. This is a realm of perfect bliss, watered by fountains, protected from the heat of the sun and the chill of winter, and pervaded by an atmosphere of peace. Here the blessed may relax on cushions, couches and carpets, drink and eat from vessels of silver and enjoy the company of beautiful women and youths.[34]

These details are all taken from the *Quran*, which is the major source of the Islamic teaching concerning the afterlife. The traditional teaching, while never discarded, has however been variously interpreted by some of the many groups within Islam. This has particularly concerned the exact definition of an unbeliever—always bearing in mind that belief is measured principally by action. Some modern Muslims have also sought to place greater spiritual, as opposed to literal, emphasis on the descriptions of the afterlife. However, these differences are not of major significance, and it remains the case that Muslims today, in the words of one authority, 'take the attitude that if they recite the Muslim creed from their hearts, and if they make some attempt to fulfil their obligations in fast and prayer, they may have to taste the fire of judgment for a time but will eventually be "saved" and admitted to Paradise by the timely intercession of their Prophet'.[35]

Conclusion

These, therefore, are the major religious movements in the world today. They all have a long history. They provide various answers to the questions with which we began this chapter: Is there a life after death, and how may we obtain it? But their answers are not only different from one another, they are often irreconcilable. It cannot be the case, for example, that there is no survival of the individual after death except within Braham, of whom the individual is truly a part, and also that the individual is uniquely created by God and can, through a relationship of faith in his Son Jesus Christ, pass after death to a new life, in a new world, in which that individuality is preserved.

But there is some common ground between all these religions. They are all unanimous that there is more to life than just the material; that we have not just a bodily but also a spiritual existence; and that this spiritual existence is independent of the body and will outlive it. These convictions have sustained so many, for so long, that they cannot be easily dismissed. But— and this will be the subject of the next four chapters—is there any hard evidence to support them?

Notes

1. Clear summaries of the beliefs and practices of the major world religions are given in *The World's Religions* ed. N. Anderson (Leicester: 1975), and *The World's Religions, A Lion Handbook* eds. K.P. Beaver et al, (Oxford: 1982).
2. Recent statistics for the world religions are given in *Hutchinson Gallup Info 92* (London: 1991), pp. 161–70.

3. An excellent general introduction to Hinduism is K.M. Sen's *Hinduism* (London: 1961). See p. 38 (Radhakrishnan) and
   p. 37.
4. These beliefs are described in the *Rigveda*, a collection of funeral hymns. For further details see *Death, Afterlife and the Soul* ed. L.E. Sullivan (New York: 1987), pp. 154–55, 130, 261. The practice of ancestor-worship is described in *An Illustrated History of the World's Religions* ed. G. Parrinder (Feltham: 1983), pp. 194–98.
5. Heaven and hell are described in the *Ramayana* 7, the *Mahabharata* 12, and the *Agni Purana* 340, 342. See L. Sullivan, *Death, Afterlife and the Soul*, pp. 155, 171.
6. The development of *bhakti* is outlined in *An Illustrated History of the World's Religions*, ed. G. Parrinder pp. 216–233.
7. The best general introduction to Buddhism is that by C. Humphreys, *Buddhism: An Introduction and Guide* (London: 1951).
8. C. Humphreys, *Buddhism*, p. 81.
9. C. Humphreys, *Buddhism*, p. 19.
10. C. Humphreys, *Buddhism*, p. 21.
11. *Udana* ch. 8, quoted in C. Humphreys, *Buddhism*, p. 127.
12. D. Bentley-Taylor and C.B. Offner, "Buddhism", p. 176.
13. Radhakrishnan, quoted in C. Humphreys, *Buddhism*, p. 128.
14. For further detail see L. Sullivan, *Death, Afterlife and the Soul*, pp. 156–57. The heavens and hells are described in the *Theravada Pali Canon*, but not systematically. For hell see in particular the *Pali Abhi dhamma Pitaka*.
15. The Pure Land Western Paradise is described in the *Saddharmapundarika* and the *Sukhavativyuka*. See L. Sullivan, *Death, Afterlife and the Soul*, p. 158.
16. The exact date is unknown; see B.W. Anderson, *The Living World of the Old Testament* (3rd edition, Harlow: 1978), p. 29.

17. The history of the Jewish people is outlined in *An Illustrated History of the World's Religions*, ed. G. Parrinder (Feltham: 1983), and in *The World's Religions: A Lion Handbook* (Oxford: 1982), pp. 272–300. Current belief and practice is outlined by H.D. Leuner, 'Judaism', in *The World's Religions*, ed. N. Anderson (Leicester: 1975), pp. 63–64.

18. The history of Hebrew belief in an other world is traced by L. Sullivan, *Death, Afterlife and the Soul*, p. 268. For a detailed study of Jewish belief in an afterlife see R.H. Charles, 'Eschatology', in *Encyclopaedia Biblica* (vol 2, London: 1901), cols 1335–92. A readable account is given by R. Cavendish, *Visions of Heaven and Hell* (London: 1977).

19. Sheol is described in, for example, Job 3:11, 10:21–22, 26:6–10; Isaiah 14 and 38; Psalm 87:5–7.

20. See, for example, Psalm 49:16; Proverbs 15:24.

21. For statements about resurrection see 2 Maccabees 7:14; Isaiah 25:8, 26:19; Daniel 12:2–3; Ezekiel 26. For the distinction between Sheol and paradise see L. Sullivan, *Death, Afterlife and the Soul*, p. 219.

22. The most important of these texts are the Book of Enoch, Apocalypse of Esdras, Apocalypse of Baruch, and Testament of Abraham.

23. Our main source for the beliefs of the period is the Jewish historian Josephus, *The Jewish War* II. 154–58, VII 343–44.

24. A good summary of Christian belief and practice is given in *The World's Religions: A Lion Handbook*. The historical development of Christianity is discussed in *An Illustrated History of the World's Religions*, ch. 20.

25. The development of the concept of a Messiah is outlined in 'Messiah', *The Interpreter's Dictionary of the Bible*, ed. G.A. Buttrick (Nashville: 1962), vol. 3.

26. Old Testament references to the Messiah include Genesis 49:10–12; Isaiah 7:10–17, 9:1–7, 11:1–9; Micah 5:2–5; Jeremiah 23:5–6; Ezekiel 34:23–24, 37:22–25; Haggai

2:21–22; Zechariah 6:9–14, 9:9–10.

27. Good general introductions to Islam are J. Esposito, *Islam: The Straight Path* (Oxford: 1988), and the section in *The World's Religions: A Lion Handbook*, ed. R. Beaver, Oxford 1982.

28. For the history of Islam see *An Illustrated History of the World's Religions*, ed. G. Parrinder (Feltham: 1971).

29. For the divisions of modern Islam see N. Anderson, *Christianity and World Religions* (Leicester: 1984), pp. 64–65.

30. *Quran* 4.156.

31. The Muslim concept of life after death is discussed by N. Anderson, *The World's Religions* (Leicester: 1975), pp. 117–18; J. Esposito, *Islam*, pp. 34–35; L. Sullivan, *Death, Afterlife and the Soul*, pp. 105, 154, 168, 275–77.

32. References in the *Quran*: *Suras* 11, 18, 36, 50, 51, 55, 56, 69, 70, 81, 84, 99.

33. *Quran* 7, 15, 40, 74, 79, 83, 88, 89. See also L. Sullivan, *Death, Afterlife and the Soul*, pp. 169–70.

34. *Quran* 2, 7, 15, 52, 76, 88.

35. N. Anderson, *Christianity and World Religions* (Leicester: 1984), p. 105.

3
EVIDENCE FROM SCIENCE
AND THE PARANORMAL

Western religion and modern science

Although religion is a powerful influence in the East and in the Third World, most people in the West don't look to religion for the answers to their questions; they look to modern science. And many of the ideas of the religions we have discussed have been disproved by science. We know that there is no heaven in the stars or in the East. We know that beneath the earth's surface there is no underground hell. We know that mummification can't preserve our bodies for the next life. Other religious beliefs cannot be disproved but seem to have no scientific evidence to support them—the Hindu belief that a person may be reincarnated as a god, human being or even animal, or the Buddhist's belief in celestial beings called *bodhisattvas*. So people are coming increasingly to believe that we do not survive death at all. And unless modern science, which in a way has become our religion, suggests that there is a life after death, we will remain disbelievers and doubters—or at the very best, merely hopeful.

Examining the evidence

Most people assume that science advances by a simple process of gradual discovery. We tend to think of current scientific knowledge as a partly completed jigsaw, and to expect that new pieces will continue to be added as research projects unearth new facts, until one day the jigsaw will be finished and we will have a 'proper', 'scientific' explanation for everything. And this is indeed how the scientists of the past saw their task. But it is not the view of modern scientists. Modern science proceeds not by discovering facts but by examining evidence and then forming theories to explain that evidence. Henry Margenau, a physicist, defines science like this:

> Science is more than a mere collection of facts, a catalogue of observations. . . . . Science is a style of inquiry; it is a peculiar way of organizing human experience which integrates and thereby confers lucidity, clarity, and cohesion upon our immediate sense impressions and upon our observations. Every kind of human experience, or fact, is at first vague, meaningless, incoherent. Because of this, the scientist finds it necessary to set up or construct, vis-à-vis every given set of unorganized experiences, a model, originally invented by the human mind, which stands somehow in correspondence with the facts themselves.[1]

In other words, scientists observe the facts, and then they try and find the simplest hypothesis which will explain those facts. And so science should be compared not to a jigsaw but, Margenau suggests, to a crystal—unorganised, irregular in shape, always growing in one direction or another, and never reaching the point where a neat explanation can be provided for everything.

Over the last 150 years this approach has provided us with a far greater understanding of the universe in which we live than had even been dreamed of by our ancestors. Darwin studied the world's wildlife and invented the theory of evolution. Rutherford and Bohr explained the structure of the atom. Einstein came up with the theory of relativity. Wilkins, Crick and Watson identified the DNA molecule and explained the function of chromosomes in genetic transmission. We now understand comets and black holes, and have a theory to describe the creation of the universe. We have landed on the moon. Freud, Jung and their successors have provided us with many insights into the way our own minds work. Our understanding of both ourselves and our environment is greater than ever before. But still the crystal is growing, and now new hypotheses are being formed to take account of a new kind of evidence.

What is this evidence?

In the main, scientists have so far been concerned with explaining how the world we see and touch is put together, and with discovering the laws that govern it. They have tended to shy away from the examination of non-material phenomena, and even to deny that such phenomena exist. But increasingly it is becoming clear that the universe will never be explained in purely material or mechanical terms. Indeed, strong evidence is emerging to suggest that many forces and phenomena which have hitherto been dismissed as the figment of people's imaginations really do exist, and a new discipline has been founded in recent years to examine them. This discipline is known as parapsychology, or the study of the paranormal. It takes as its subject phenomena such as ESP, telepathy, psychokinesis and ghosts, and activities as varied as spiritualism, divination and astral travelling.

One authority on the paranormal has summarised the position like this:

> In science a new cycle has begun, a revolt against the old rigid reductionism, a recognition that 'materialism' leaves half the universe unexplained. Biologists, psychologists and even physicists are cautiously trying to feel their way into new worlds. They are acknowledging at last that they are dealing with a living universe, a universe full of strange forces. The magic of the past was an intuitive attempt to understand and control these forces: the science of the future will be a fully conscious attempt.[2]

This new research is of the greatest importance to our enquiry, for it concerns itself with many of the phenomena which have traditionally been taken to indicate that life is more than just material or bodily existence, and that therefore we may survive material death. Indeed, parapsychologists are beginning to examine experiences which have hitherto been regarded as matters for religion—or superstition. The scientific method is to look for the simplest hypothesis which explains the observable facts, and many parapsychologists are beginning to suspect that it is this: that there is a spirit world of which we are ordinarily unaware, but in which we can at times participate. Could the existence of this spirit world have been what persuaded so many societies that a part of us lives on after death? Certainly many authorities think so. Consider statements such as this, by Allan Barham:

> Compulsive sceptics are fewer than they used to be, for those academic disciplines which include within their scope the consideration of the nature and function of the human mind are not so dogmatic as they once were in declaring that the whole man dies with the death of the body. The mechanistic view of the universe has largely gone, and psychologists and philosophers of considerable stature. . . are willing to admit the possibility of mental activity existing independently of the body, and consequently the possibility of a post-mortem existence.[3]

And later:

> I can conceive of no greater service to man than to provide him with a credible picture of a life beyond death; a life which reunites him with those whom he has loved and have died, which makes sense of his striving and suffering on earth, which points to love as the principle of the universe, and which shows a progression towards ultimate union with that love which is God. . . . This is what Psychical Research can do. Not only does it provide evidence that death is not the end; it goes on to demonstrate, if the evidence can be

accepted, that the life that follows death can be infinitely worth while, and satisfying beyond all our hopes and desires.[4]

The aim of this chapter is to summarise some of the research that has led to conclusions such as these.

The near-death experience

What is a near-death experience?

One of the phenomena most often brought forward as evidence that we survive death is the so-called 'near-death experience' (NDE). A person who is critically ill, or who is the victim of a near-fatal accident, may experience the sensation of leaving his body as if in death. Typically he will then acquire a 'spiritual' body; he will meet dead friends or relatives, and encounter a 'being of light'. He approaches a sort of barrier, as if between this world and the next, but learns that his time has not yet come. He is next aware of being back in his body.

These experiences are sufficiently common to have excited a certain amount of attention in the medical world. An article in the *Lancet* of 24 June 1978 reported as follows:

Collected accounts volunteered by survivors ... bear striking similarities. Amongst the experiences many have described are an initial period of distress followed by profound calm and joy; out-of-the-body experiences with the sense of watching resuscitation events from a distance; the sensation of moving rapidly down a tunnel or along a road, accompanied by a loud buzzing or ringing noise or hearing beautiful music; recognising friends and relatives who have died previously; a rapid review of pleasant incidents from throughout the life as a panoramic playback (in perhaps twelve per cent of cases); a sense of approaching a border or frontier and being sent back; and being annoyed or disappointed at having to return from such a pleasant experience—'I tried not to come back', in one patient's words. Some describe frank transcendent experiences and many state that they will never fear death again. Similar stories have been reported from the victims of accidents, falls, drowning, anaphylaxis, and cardiac or respiratory arrest.

How common is it?

The near-death experience is neither rare nor new. The oldest written account of the phenomenon in the Western tradition dates from 375 BC, when Plato described the experience of Er the Pamphilian as a basis for an account of the other world. Er was a soldier who was apparently killed in battle but revived after twelve days to relate how he had seen the place where the souls of the dead assemble for judgment, some being sent for reward, some for punishment. Another classical account is given by Plutarch in his *Moralia*, where it is recounted how a man named Thespesius fell unconscious for three days following a concussion. During this period he travelled to another region where he met a deceased relative who acted as his guide through various regions of the other world. He returned to life and, in common with many modern subjects, reformed his habits.

In the sixth century AD Pope Gregory the Great recorded a number of near-death experiences in his *Dialogues*, a highly popular work full of up-to-date stories and anecdotes; and from then on many NDEs were written down, mostly by the clergy, and used to teach people about the nature of the other world and the importance of right living. The best known and most sophisticated work in this tradition was Dante's *Divine Comedy*, written at the beginning of the fourteenth century.[5]

Many common 'ingredients' of the NDE remain unchanged from the earliest times throughout the Middle Ages and to the present day: a life review, the meeting of people known on earth, a vision of overwhelming light, a glimpse of another realm—sometimes peaceful, sometimes terrifying—sudden return to the body, and a new outlook on life. What changes is not so much the core experience, but rather the way in which it is expressed. Classical writers tend to use ethical language and terminology to relate the NDE; medieval authors use religious language and terminology; and modern accounts use scientific language and terminology. In other words, the NDE is reported in a way which makes it acceptable to the philosophy of the day; the experience itself remains essentially the same.

The near-death experience appears to occur not just in the West but also in many other cultures and societies in both the past and the present. Professor Frederick Holck reports examples of NDEs in the Tibetan Book of the Dead, in sacred Buddhist and Zoroastrian writings, and in the modern communities of the American Indians, the Dayaks of Borneo, the Maoris and others.[6]

Who has a near-death experience?

It seems that anyone can have an NDE. Various studies have shown that its occurrence is independent of any clearly identifiable factor in those who experience it. Age, sex, religious belief, social class, education, occupation, medical circumstances, psychiatric history, even interest in psychic matters have all been found to be irrelevant. In her 1987 survey Carol Zaleski concluded that

> suicide victims seeking annihilation, fundamentalists who expect to see God on the operating table, atheists, agnostics and *carpe diem* advocates find equal representation in the ranks of near-death experiencers. And their answers to survey questions show that, for all the religious implications of near-death experience, a person's beliefs about God, life after death, and heaven and hell do not determine the content of his vision.[7]

People do not experience what they expect to experience; the NDE is not determined by the religious beliefs of the individual. And it is very common. Different researchers come up with different statistics, but one of the most recent studies claims that up to sixty-eight per cent of those who survive acute life-threatening situations have some kind of near-death experience.[8]

Some examples

Most modern near-death experiences are positive in nature. Cardiologist Maurice Rawlings quotes a typical account given by one of his patients:

'I could see the other car swerving before he jumped the median. Out of the corner of my eye I could see that he was coming right at me. There was no way I could get out of his way. I said, "This is it." Although I was never sure I believed in God, I remember saying, "God help me!" Then the last thing I remembered was hearing this terrible crash with glass splintering like an explosion. The steering wheel must have gone into my chest, it hurt so much. In a split second the explosion was gone and then the pain was gone; I knew I must be dead! I remember other cars stopping and people peering into the car through the broken windows; it all seemed so strange.

It was then that I knew I had been looking down on the scene of the accident, completely free of pain and without a worry in the world. I felt completely at ease, just floating up there. I heard one of them say, "Call an ambulance." They were dragging my body out of what was left of the car. The driver of the other car already seemed to be dead.

After they had stretched me out on the ground, one of them started blowing through my mouth and another one pushing on my chest; it was hard for me to believe that that body was actually mine!

Traffic seemed to be piled up for a half mile behind the accident, and I could hear an ambulance trying to get through.

By this time I heard a strange noise and then found myself tumbling head over heels through some big tube or tunnel. It was awfully dark in there, but I was glad to see a light at the far end which seemed to get bigger and bigger. I got out into a beautiful valley lit by something as bright as the sun, but I couldn't tell where it was coming from.

And there I saw both of my parents (who had died before) coming to greet me down a pathway between these large groups of trees and flowers. They seemed awfully glad to see me and said they had been looking for me. Each put an arm around my waist, and we walked down the path deeper into the valley where we came to a stream. It was too wide to cross without wading. As I was getting ready to cross this stream, I felt something like a baseball bat suddenly hit me in the chest and everything went black.

I awakened to find myself back in my body at the scene of the accident. Everything was hurting. They were applying an electric shock from a "defibrillator" gadget. Afterwards, I felt sad about leaving my parents and that place in the valley. It was so beautiful. I can't describe it.

Instead, I was back here, all bloody and cut up and on my way to the hospital.

Now, this wasn't a dream. I've had many dreams, but this was something completely different. I know I was there, and I won't be afraid to go there again.'[9]

Most near-death experiences are similar to the one above in that the subject enters a pleasant place where he or she meets deceased relatives, and then comes to some kind of barrier which he does not cross. A significant minority of patients however report something very different, something much more 'hell-like' than 'heaven-like'. Rawlings reports a much higher incidence of unpleasant NDEs from patients who are questioned immediately after resuscitation than from those who are questioned after an interval of a few days, and suggests that this could be due to the need for the mind to suppress such highly disturbing material in order to protect itself. He cites a number of such cases. One man described seeing an empty sea of blue fire which he later identified with the lake of fire described in the last book of the Bible. A woman found herself in a dark room in which she could hear people moaning, and from the window of which she could see the grotesque face of a giant watching her. Another man described travelling through a long tunnel to an underground cave pervaded by an odour of decay and full of eery sounds; he called, 'Jesus, save me!' and saw a person in white who told him to live differently. He then found himself back in hospital. Rawlings' own research into NDEs was prompted by the experience of repeatedly resuscitating a man suffering successive heart attacks who each time he came round screamed that he was in hell, implored him to keep trying, and even insisted that he pray for him. All these people apparently responded to their experience by making a commitment of Christian faith; three of the four were not previously churchgoers.[10]

Research into the NDE

The near-death experience has been the subject of study for the last century or so. But it was given new impetus in 1975 by the publication of Raymond Mood's book *Life After Life*. Dr Moody reported the NDEs of 150 people who had recovered from serious accidents or been resuscitated, and offered the first analysis and discussion of the phenomenon. His book attracted an enormous amount of interest, and has inspired a new generation of investigators to study the near-death experience according to the standards of modern scientific research.

Most of this work has been done in America, where in 1978 a society was formed which was later named the International Association for Near-Death Studies. Some of the investigators have been psychiatrists such as Bruce Greyson and Ian Stevenson, who used questionnaires, interviews and medical records to establish that people who have NDEs are less, not more, likely to have had any psychic experiences.[11] Others have been pyschologists such as Kenneth Ring, who used modern sampling and testing methods to measure the frequency and distribution of the NDE and to examine any common elements in the medical history or religious belief of the subjects.[12] Yet others have been cardiologists who have used their close contact with people who have been resuscitated after a cardiac arrest to record and study their experiences. Michael Sabom documents a number of cases of patients who were able to describe with complete accuracy the resuscitation procedure carried out while they were clinically dead and 'out of the body'.[13] Fred Schoonmaker has interviewed over 2,300 survivors of life-threatening conditions, mostly in his own cardiovascular unit, and found that sixty per cent volunteered accounts of NDEs and a further eight per cent reported an NDE when encouraged to do so.[14] Most of the investigators did not, at the outset of their research, have any strong religious convictions, although some became convinced during its course that there must be a life after death, and at least one, cardiologist Maurice Rawlings, felt it necessary to embark on a serious study of the teachings of the major religions on the afterlife. This was his conclusion:

> After a laborious study of comparative theology in the sacred books of many religions, including the Torah and Talmud of Judaism; the Koran; the Vedas, Upanishads, Brahmanas of Hinduism; the Avesta of Zoroastrianism; the sayings of Confucius; the Agamas of Jainism; the Tripitake of Buddhism; the Kojiki of Shintoism; the Tao-te-ching of Taoism; and the Analects, I have discovered that the one book that is the most descriptive of the after-death experiences of resuscitated patients is the Christian Bible.[15]

Are there any natural explanations of the NDE?

Most researchers into the near-death experience have not limited themselves to the mere collecting of data. They have sought in a great variety of ways to find a hypothesis which would explain those data, and all kinds of theories have been put forward to explain the NDE in purely naturalistic terms. Such theories fall into three groups.

1. The NDE is caused by medical or physiological factors such as oxygen deprivation, the effect of pain-killing or other drugs, the malfunctioning of the central nervous system, fever and biochemical reactions in the brain.

2. The NDE is caused by psychological factors such as unconscious wishful thinking, hallucination, and self-protective devices.

3. The NDE is caused by religious or cultural factors; people experience what they expect to experience.

The problem with these hypotheses is that none of them successfully accounts for all the documented instances of the near-death experience; examples can be found to disprove each one. The findings of parapsychologists Karlis Osis and Erlendur Haraldsson are particularly important in this regard. Osis and Haraldsson sent questionnaires on the experiences of the dying to over 2,000 doctors and nurses in both America and India, and conducted a detailed computer analysis of the returns. They found that there was no correlation whatsoever between medical, psychological or religious factors and the occurrence or nature of a near-death experience. So, for example, patients treated with sedatives or drugs, and those suffering from illnesses normally associated with the presence of hallucinations were in fact less likely, not more likely, to have an NDE than other patients. And those who hallucinated while suffering from a particular medical condition reported seeing living persons, whereas near-death visions were invariably of deceased persons. Oxygen deprivation, stress, expectations of death or recovery, the presence of particular psychological states, adherence to Christianity or Hinduism, and other possible factors appear to have had no influence on either the occurrence or the non-occurrence of the NDE. The researchers were forced to conclude that there is no naturalistic explanation currently available to us which can account satisfactorily for the near-death experience.[16]

How do those who have a near-death experience interpret it?

Experts may be divided over the correct interpretation of the near-death experience, but those who have actually had one are in no doubt. This is the response of a lady who was struck by lightning:

> In the moment that I was hit, I knew exactly what had happened to me. My mind was crystal clear. I had never been so totally alive as in the act of dying. . . . At this point . . . I had what I call the answer to a question I had never verbalised to anyone or even faced: Is there

really a God? I can't describe it, but the totality and reality of the living God exploded within my being and He filled every atom of my body with His glory. In the next moment, to my horror, I found that I wasn't going toward God. I was going away from Him. It was like seeing what might have been, but going away from it. In my panic, I started trying to communicate with the God I knew was there.[17]

All researchers report that those who have had a near-death experience become absolutely convinced that there is a life after death, irrespective of what they believed beforehand. They dismiss attempts to explain the NDE in naturalistic terms as ridiculous, and show a changed attitude both to life and to the prospect of death, approaching it not with fear but with a peace and joy different from that normally experienced. This does not of course prove that the people they have met and the world they have glimpsed are really there; and it must also be remembered that a near-death experience is just that—the subject has not actually died. But nonetheless it is tempting to conclude that the most likely explanation of the near-death experience is that it does relate in some way to what happens when we finally do die.

Contacting the dead

There are many people in this country who firmly believe not only that we survive death but also that it is possible under certain circumstances to communicate directly with the spirits of individuals who have died. This is the practice known as spiritualism, and it has been the subject of a great deal of research over the last hundred years or so. This research is of the greatest importance, for it is often claimed that spiritualists really can and do contact the spirits of deceased persons, and therefore that we will survive death in some way.

Various methods of contacting the dead are used, but two are more common than others, and are widely practised today. These are mediumship and ouija.

Mediumship

Mediums are people 'believed to possess psychical abilities which they use to communicate with the personalities of deceased individuals'.[18] They may be divided into two main categories. Physical mediums claim to serve as a channel for the reception of messages from the dead in the form of physical phenomena such as raps, the tilting of tables or even apparent materialisations of the communicating spirit. Mental mediums operate by disassociating themselves from the normal state of waking consciousness in order to receive mental messages which they then relay verbally. This may be achieved by using an object such as a crystal ball, or a technique such as automatic writing. Sometimes mediums will appear to be temporarily possessed by the communicating spirit, who speaks through them.

Ouija

Ouija is, properly speaking, a form of mental mediumship. It differs in that it is usually practised by a group of people rather than a single medium, and in that these people may have no known psychic abilities. It consists of the letters of the alphabet arranged round a table or printed on a board, and a free-moving pointer or upturned glass on which the participants lightly place a finger. The pointer or glass spells out the message letter by letter.

The history of spiritualism

Spiritualism has an ancient pedigree. As long ago as the eleventh century BC Homer described how his hero Odysseus summoned the spirits of the dead with the help of the sorceress Circe, and spoke to many of them including his mother. In the ninth century BC Saul, the first king of Israel, used a medium to contact the spirit of the dead prophet Samuel. We know that a version of ouija, using a pendulum rather than a pointer, was practised as far back as the fourth century AD.[19]

However, any attempt to contact the dead is strictly forbidden in the Bible ('let no one be found among you . . . who is a medium or spiritist or who consults the dead'—Deuteronomy 18:10–11). This prohibition was obeyed in Christian Europe for centuries until spiritualist practices were suddenly revived in the mid-nineteenth century. The impetus was provided in 1848 in Hydesville, New York, when a family named Fox moved into a supposedly haunted house. Strange noises were heard at night, and the two children began to ask the spirit, which they nicknamed Mr Splitfoot, to respond to their questions with a certain number of raps. The spirit supposedly obliged, and the case became famous throughout the country. Within a few years hundreds of people were claiming to be able to communicate with the dead, and the practice grew rapidly in popularity on both sides of the Atlantic.[20]

Most of the early practitioners were physical mediums. Perhaps the most famous was D.D. Home, who was responsible for many phenomena including knocks and rappings apparently conveying messages from the dead, some of whom claimed to be friends and relatives of those present and gave information which Home could not easily have obtained himself. Another was Florence Cook, who seemed to be able to cause a deceased spirit named Katie King to materialise in front of those present, while herself sitting bound to a chair. Yet another was Eusapia Palladino, an illiterate Italian peasant who compromised her many apparently genuine feats of mediumship by obviously cheating on other occasions. A more recent case is that of Mrs Helen Duncan, a materialisation medium sentenced in 1943 to nine months' imprisonment under the 1735 Witchcraft Act.[21]

Of the mental mediums, the first to become famous was Mrs Leonora Piper, who on many occasions relayed convincing messages to her clients from their deceased relatives. Mrs Piper was also one of the mediums involved in the so-called 'cross-correspondences', alongside Mrs Alice Fleming, sister of Rudyard Kipling, Mrs A.H. Verrall, lecturer in classics at

Cambridge University, Mrs Winifred Coombe Tennant, JP and British delegate to the League of Nations, and others. Each of these mediums received apparently meaningless and fragmentary messages which, when put together, consisted of clear statements containing many complex classical allusions. The messages purported to come from three deceased psychical researchers: F.W.H. Myers, Edmund Gurney and Henry Sidgwick.[22]

Today spiritualism is flourishing. Spiritualist churches have been established throughout the country, and regular spiritualist meetings are held in many towns and cities. In an age when belief in traditional Christianity is declining, spiritualists claim to offer comfort to the bereaved in the form of continued contact with their loved ones. Some also practise spirit-healing—healing through the agency of mediums by contact with spirits 'on the other side', many of whom claim to be deceased doctors. There are now 70 million spiritualists worldwide.[23]

Ouija too has enjoyed a revival. In the late 1970s a ouija board was the most popular Christmas present in the USA,[24] and a recent survey of 80,000 schoolchildren in Britain showed that eighty per cent claim to have taken part in ouija sessions or spiritualistic seances.[25]

Research into spiritualism

The nineteenth-century revival of spiritualism was at first ignored by the scientific establishment. But its rapid growth soon began to arouse interest, and in 1882 a group of Cambridge academics founded the Society for Psychical Research (SPR). Its aims were to examine 'without prejudice or prepossession, and in a scientific spirit, those faculties of man, real or supposed, which appear to be inexplicable on any generally recognised hypothesis'.[26] Three years later a similar society was founded in America.

In the last hundred years the members of the SPR society, who have included many distinguished scientists, have examined the claims of spiritualists and mediums according to the rigorous standards of critical scientific research. As with the near-death experience, a large number of alternative explanations have been put forward, including telepathy, chance, the working of the subconscious mind and of course fraud. The SPR has uncovered many fraudulent mediums in particular. But for a significant proportion no plausible explanation has been found, other than what is happening is real—that is, that a disembodied spirit of some kind is responsible for the movement of the ouija board or the messages of the medium.

One of the foremost modern authorities on mediumship and survival is Professor Alan Gauld. In a 1977 article entitled 'Discarnate Survival', he summarises the various hypotheses which have been put forward to explain the spiritualist phenomena, examining each one in turn.[27]

1. The survivalist hypothesis

The survivalist hypothesis suggests that the true explanation for the messages received by mediums is that they are exactly what they seem to be—that is, the communications of deceased persons who have survived death and live on in some other place. This is the hypothesis adopted by spiritualists.

There are two main objections to this theory. First, why did the deceased not communicate with the living in this way until the middle of the nineteenth century? And why is the phenomenon not more common—surely every dead person must wish to reassure their loved ones of their continued existence? Secondly, why are almost all communications trivial, even when they are supposed to come from literary and intellectual giants? Have Plato and Shakespeare grown tired of philosophy and drama? Or have they lost the turn of phrase they had before? And why do different communications give contradictory information about the other world?

Gauld concludes that this hypothesis is not altogether satisfactory.

2. The super-ESP hypothesis

The super-ESP hypothesis suggests that the messages received by the medium are not sent by the spirits of deceased persons but rather that they are picked up by her from the minds of the living—present at the time or not—by means of ESP.

There are serious objections to this hypothesis too. It requires us to believe that it is possible to acquire information by mental contact not just with other persons present in the same room but with persons unknown to the medium and scattered all over the world, for there are documented cases where the medium conveyed information not known to anyone present but later verified by following up such contacts. There are also cases in which the medium has spoken in a language not known to her—occasionally in a language no longer in use. There are other cases in which the medium has produced obscure information which has proved to be correct only by checking with written records not generally available to the public.

The ESP hypothesis would seem to raise questions more complex than those it claims to solve, and Gauld concludes that it is too vague to command credibility.

3. The continuity hypothesis

The continuity hypothesis suggests that while some part of us survives death, it is less than our whole person. This would account for the banality of most communications while yet allowing accurate information to be conveyed.

The main objection to this hypothesis would seem to be the difficulty in defining exactly what part of a human being might survive independently of the rest. We might accept that a person has a spirit which might survive the death of his body—but what else could survive and communicate? The memory? The thoughts? And if so, how? This hypothesis too seems to raise more problems than it solves.

4. The evil spirit hypothesis

Gauld briefly mentions a fourth hypothesis which he does not investigate. This hypothesis suggests that mediums do indeed contact discarnate spirits, but that these belong not to people who have died but to impersonating evil entities. There is one significant objection to this theory: that nowadays we don't *believe* in evil spirits. But to reject an otherwise convincing hypothesis on the grounds that we think we know better is intellectually irresponsible; and there is a compelling amount of evidence to support it. This can be summarised as follows:

(a) Mediums, usually known under other titles, have traditionally been thought to contact evil and non-human spirits, both in the West and in other societies. There may have been few attempts by Western mediums to contact the dead between the ninth century BC and the mid-nineteenth century AD. But that is not to say that there was no mediumistic activity of the kind described above; there was, and plenty of it. The difference is that first the mediums were known under other names— priestesses and sorceresses in the classical age, witches in the medieval and modern period; and that secondly the messages received were believed to have come not from the dead but from non-human, and usually demonic, sources. Professor E.R. Dodds summarises:

> The two groups of pre-nineteenth century mediums about whom we have most information, the *chatochoi* [those held down or overpowered, and hence, derivatively, possessed] of the late Graeco-Roman period and the witches of the sixteenth and seventeenth centuries, while performing a number of the feats performed by modern mediums, perversely attributed them in the one case to the agency of non-human gods or demons, in the other to the agency of the devil.[28]

Phenomena similar to those produced by modern mediums, including spirit-healing, are also found in many non-Western societies, although again the medium is known under other names—shaman, witch-doctor. Here too the sources are believed to be non-human, and the shaman or witch-doctor must undergo lengthy training and elaborate initiation rites to enable him to fulfil his function safely and effectively.

So although mediumistic activity is common to all ages and all societies, modern spiritualists are alone in claiming that the spirits contacted are exclusively those of the dead.

(b) Spiritualist practices have been forbidden by both religious and civil authorities for thousands of years on the grounds that they are evil and dangerous. The Old Testament Book of Deuteronomy, dating back to the middle of the second millennium BC, states as follows:

> Let no one be found among you who . . . practises divination or sorcery, interprets omens, engages in witchcraft, or casts spells, or who is a medium or spiritist or who consults the dead. Anyone who does these things is detestable to the Lord (Deuteronomy 18:10–12).

The eighth century BC prophet Isaiah wrote:

> When men tell you to consult mediums and spiritists, who whisper and mutter, should not a people enquire of their God? Why consult the dead on behalf of the living? (Isaiah 8:19).

Why should spiritualism have been forbidden if it is either a meaningless or a harmless practice? It is indeed classed in these texts alongside witchcraft, sorcery and other evil practices. It is interesting that in both passages the prohibition is followed by the promise that God will send a prophet to teach man all he needs to know about life and death. Isaiah's words are particularly famous: 'For unto us a child is born, unto us a son is given . . . and he will be called Wonderful Counsellor, Mighty God, Everlasting Father, Prince of Peace' (Isaiah 9:6). Christians identify this prophet with Jesus Christ.

(c) If it is the case that some or all of the spirits contacted by mediums are evil in nature, we would expect to see harmful consequences for those involved. And this is precisely what we do see. Study after study, whether conducted by spiritualists, psychiatrists, psychic researchers or clergymen, has found that a remarkably high proportion of those who participate in genuine spiritualistic or occult practices later suffer some form of severe mental breakdown or physical illness.[29] One authority on the occult has stated quite categorically that 'the powers that mediums contact are not the dead, but evil entities, and they are very dangerous indeed'.[30] Rollo Ahmed, an expert on the occult, warns that 'the result [of many seances] is the moral degeneration of those who attend, accompanied by ill-health and mental troubles which they seek to have cured by "Healers"'.[31] Psychiatrist Dr Harmon H. Bro observes that most of those who engage in psychic activities such as these 'embark on a course of increasingly distraught behaviour, compulsive actions, alienation from friends and relatives and finally multiple-personality symptoms or suicide'.[32] Scores of such cases are described by Dr Kurt E. Koch in his books on counselling and the occult. Koch warns that even when a person seems to have received physical healing through mediumistic forces, he or she invariably suffers spiritual death.[33] The Revd George Bennett of the Divine Healing Mission goes further:

> I have known folk go to spiritist healers to receive what seems to be an almost immediate healing of some infirmity or other. The self-styled 'healer' has told them, or given them the impression, that departed spirits on the other side are benevolently working through them for the good of mankind. But, after a little while, the apparent healing has gone and they are now worse off than before. They have the added burden of mental and spiritual distress. They are sometimes in a frightful mess.[34]

The same risks are attached to ouija.

There is one further curious fact which lends support to the idea that the spirits contacted by mediums are not those of the dead: when asked directly about Jesus Christ, the spirits—even those purporting to belong to the staunchest Christians—are at best evasive and at worse abusive. This would be comprehensible if we were dealing with evil spirits, but is rather odd otherwise.

In the face of evidence such as this the Christian church has accepted the biblical prohibition and banned spiritualistic activity as evil and dangerous. The Roman Catholic Church offers the clearest guidance; its position is summarised as follows:

> Spiritism has been a sweet solace to many in most poignant hours of bitter sorrow and loss; therefore it is hallowed in their eyes by tenderest memories. They are woefully deceived. Hard as it may seem, we must get down to the bed-rock of fact. Spiritualism has been specifically condemned on no less than four occasions by the Holy Office, whose decree, 30 March, 1988, utterly forbids all Spiritualistic practices [even when] intercourse with demons [is] strictly excluded, and communication sought with good spirits only. Modern Spiritism is merely witchcraft revived. The Second Plenary Council of Baltimore (1866), whilst making ample allowance for . . . trickery of every kind, warns the faithful against lending any support whatever to Spiritism, and forbids them to attend seances even out of idle curiosity, for some, at least, of the manifestations must necessarily be ascribed to Satanic intervention since in no other manner can they be understood or explained.[35]

Conclusion

This brief survey of spiritualistic attempts to contact the dead would seem to lead to two conclusions. First, that there is a spiritual world with which we may interact at least on this side of the grave and very possibly on the other. And secondly, that to attempt to contact spirits from this world is highly dangerous and should under no circumstances be undertaken.

Apparitions

There is one further major phenomenon which until relatively recently was universally regarded as proof that death is not the end: ghosts—or, more accurately, apparitions, since not only the dead but also the dying and on occasion the living have been known to appear to others. During the nineteenth century it became unfashionable to admit to believing in ghosts, and this remains the case today. However, the last hundred years have seen the completion of a great deal of careful research in this area, and it is now possible to hold a more informed view.

The most common kind of apparition is the ghost. Ghosts are not usually dressed in the white sheets of common legend, but wear the clothes in which they dressed when alive. They may pass through doors and walls, and usually ignore the living. Hauntings are generally associated with a specific place, usually a house, and four out of five of them have been found to be linked with a tragic event or death.

Apparitions of the dying have been recorded many times. A typical case would be one in which a person appears to a close friend or relative many miles away at the precise time of his death, usually completely unexpectedly. The dying themselves may see persons who have died previously coming to greet them and escort them to the other world.

Apparitions of the living are also not unknown. They take two main forms. A person's double may be seen in one place while he himself is in another. And a person may have what is known as an 'out-of-the-body experience'; this is similar to a near-death experience except that the subject is in a state of normal health and that he may be seen, while out of the body, by another person far distant from the location of his real body.

Finally, there is the so-called poltergeist or 'noisy spirit', which may not be the spirit of a human being at all. Poltergeists differ from ghosts in that they are rarely seen, they have a direct physical effect on real objects, and they are normally associated with the presence of an individual rather than with a particular place.

Whatever the explanation for these phenomena, it has been demonstrated by reliable researchers beyond all reasonable doubt that they do occur.

The history of apparitions

All of the above have been recorded many times throughout the centuries. The earlier books of the Old Testament describe the dead as shadowy spirits living a half-existence in an underground world from which they occasionally emerge to appear to the living. The Roman writer Pliny the Younger tells the story of a philosopher named Athenodorus who rented a house in Athens on the cheap because it was reputed to be haunted. When the ghost appeared he followed it until it pointed to a place in the grounds. It turned out that a skeleton was buried there, and once this had been given a proper reburial the ghost ceased to appear.[36] An early instance of an apparition of a dying person is recorded in the life of the tenth-century saint Dunstan, who received a vision in his cell at Glastonbury of the murder of his friend King Edmund at his hunting lodge in Wales. A messenger later confirmed that the king had died at the time and in the circumstances seen by Dunstan.[37] And an example of an apparition of a living person can be found in the eighteenth-century accounts of the simultaneous presence of Cardinal Alphonsus Liguori celebrating mass and attending the distant deathbed of Pope Clement XIV in Rome.[38] Finally, poltergeists have been recorded in ninth-century Germany, twelfth-century Wales and eighteenth-century England.[39]

Research into apparitions

Serious research into these phenomena began in 1882 with the founding of the Society for Psychical Research, and for the most part was conducted by eminent academics prepared to risk ridicule for doing it. In 1886 three of the founding members of the SPR, F.W.H. Myers, Edmund Gurney and Frank Podmore, published the first full-length study on the subject of apparitions, *Phantasms of the Living*, and in 1903 Myers followed this with his mammoth *Human Personality and its Survival of Bodily Death*. The SPR has continued to investigate reported cases from that time to the present day. Recent studies have included Celia Green and Charles McCreery's *Apparitions* (1975) and Andrew MacKenzie's *Hauntings and Apparitions* (1982). Apparitions seen by the dying have been studied by Karlis Osis and Erlundur Haraldsson, and their findings are reported in *At the Hour of Death* (1977); and research on out-of-the-body experiences has been analysed by Susan Blackmore in *Beyond the Body* (1982), another in the SPR centenary series. Modern research into the poltergeist has been similarly thorough, important centres being located at Freiburg University in Germany, where psychologist Hans Bender has investigated many cases, and at the Psychical Research Foundation in Durham, North Carolina, under its director, parapsychologist W.G. Roll.[40]

Apparitions of the dead

Over the last hundred years the SPR has investigated many reported cases of ghosts, and some of these are discussed with the supporting evidence by MacKenzie in *Hauntings and Apparitions*. MacKenzie includes only the most carefully researched cases for which no alternative explanation can be found.

Perhaps the most remarkable of the cases he considers is the so-called Cheltenham ghost. This ghost, a tall lady dressed in black and with a handkerchief held to her face as if in grief, was frequently seen in and around the Despard family house in Cheltenham. In appearance the ghost was indistinguishable from a living person, and indeed she was often taken for a guest by visitors, even being seen walking in the garden in full sunlight. However, her behaviour was not like that of the average visitor: she would disappear suddenly and completely while in full view, appear in a room whose doors were closed, and pass through various devices such as strings attached across the stairs to trip her. Attempts to touch her failed. It has been suggested that she is Imogen Swinhoe, second wife of the first occupant of the house, who after an unhappy marriage separated from her husband in 1876. But what makes the case remarkable is that the ghost was seen by seventeen people and heard by over twenty, and that other sources confirm the details of the haunting. The reports cover the years from 1892 to 1944, and come from, among others, a doctor and a solicitor—professional people not normally given to flights of fancy.[41]

A more recent example investigated by the SPR and reported by MacKenzie dates from 1965, when a frail, ill little boy woke Mrs Stella Herbert in the middle of the night by kneeling at the side of her bed and clawing imploringly at her arm. Mrs Herbert was an Australian, visiting a compatriot friend on an English farm, and had no knowledge of the history of the house. The next day her host called on Margaret Minney, who had lived on the farm most of her life, and who in astonishment revealed that her brother Johnnie, who was as Mrs Herbert described, had been taken ill with meningitis in that room, and had died in 1921 at the age of five.[42]

Both these examples involve ghosts from the past who intrude upon the present. But there are other well-documented cases where it is the observer from the present who seems to intrude upon the past. MacKenzie reports the experience of Miss E.F. Smith, who one winter night in 1950 was forced to walk eight miles home in snow and rain after her car skidded into a ditch. She lived in the village of Letham, Angus, Scotland, and on her way witnessed a strange scene. She saw men in rough primitive dress carrying resin torches and skirting a lake apparently searching for bodies as if following a battle. Subsequent research suggests that she was seeing the aftermath of the battle of Nechtanesmere, which took place in 685 between Picts and Northumbrians. A particularly interesting fact is that the lake is no longer there, and Miss Smith did not know of its previous existence; yet the line of ground she indicated corresponded exactly to its shoreline.[43]

Apparitions of the dying

Parapsychologists have been able to investigate a number of examples of the appearance of a recently dead person to an acquaintance who did not know of the death. One of the most detailed is a case singled out by Eleanor Sidgwick in her 1923 analysis of 200 reports of apparitions (in the *Proceedings of the SPR*):

On the morning of 7 December 1918 Lieut. McConnel, aged 18, a trainee pilot, was unexpectedly asked by his Commanding Officer at Scampton, Lincolnshire, to fly a Camel aircraft to Tadcaster, sixty miles away. At 11.30 a.m. McConnel took leave of his roommate, Lieut. Larkin, saying that he expected to be back for tea. At Tadcaster aerodrome, in dense fog, McConnel apparently lost control of his plane, 'nose-dived', and crashed with the engine full on. A girl who saw the plane crash ran to the plane and found McConnel dead. The violence of the contact seemed to have stopped his watch, which registered 3.25 p.m.

Lieut. Larkin was reading and smoking in his room when he heard someone walking up the passage. The door opened with the usual noise and clatter which McConnel always made and Larkin heard his greeting, 'Hello, boy!' He half turned round in his chair and saw McConnel standing in the doorway, half in and half out of the room, holding the doorknob in his hand. He was dressed in his full flying clothes but wearing his naval cap—an unusual item of apparel. The two young men exchanged a few words, McConnel said, 'Well, cheerio!', closed the door noisily, and went out. Larkin did not have a watch, but was certain the time was between a quarter and half past three, because shortly afterwards a Lieut. Garner-Smith came into the room and it was then a quarter to four. Garner-Smith came to enquire whether McConnel was back because they planned to go to Lincoln that evening. Larkin replied, 'He is back, he was in the room a few minutes ago!' Garner-Smith then went off to search for McConnel. Larkin discovered that McConnel was dead when he overheard a group of officers discussing the crash in the Albion Hotel, Lincoln, that evening.[44]

Related to cases such as the one quoted above are those in which a dying person claims to see others who have died before him. A number of such cases were carefully examined by the physicist Sir William Barrett in his book *Death-Bed Visions* (London: 1926). Barrett found that the patient was clear-headed and rational at the time of the experience; that he believed the person or persons he saw had come to escort him to the other world; and that the experience brought him great peace. One example is given of a patient who was surprised to see her sister, whom she thought was alive; in fact the sister had died three weeks previously, but the news had been kept from the patient in order not to upset her.[45] Barrett's findings were confirmed by Osis and Haraldsson in their 1977 study of no fewer than 85,000 deathbed experiences in America and India.[46]

A more recent investigation focused upon a London hospital, where dying patients would report being attended by a particularly comforting middle-aged nurse dressed in a grey uniform. Nothing unusual—except that the nurses wore blue uniforms, and were unaware of any colleague in grey even when patients said she was actually present in the room with them; and that grey had been the colour of the uniform worn years previously. The physician who investigated these reports found that none of the patients had previously heard about the grey nurse, and that they always died shortly after she had attended them.[47]

Apparitions of the living

Apparitions of the living take one of two main forms: either the subject leaves his body and is seen in another place (as in the out-of-the-body experience or OBE), or he is seen in two places at once (he has a double). The first type is more common, although not all OBEs are witnessed by a third party.

One of the best attested examples of an OBE with witnesses is the Wilmot case, details of which were published in the *Proceedings of the SPR*. An account of the case is given by parapsychologist R. Crookall.[48] A ship on which S.R. Wilmot was a passenger encountered a violent storm as it sailed from Liverpool to New York. On the eighth day of the storm Wilmot dreamed that his wife appeared in his cabin, dressed in her nightclothes, hesitated on discovering that he shared it with another passenger, caressed him and left. When he woke, his fellow passenger remarked upon the lady's visit, and insisted that he had seen her. Upon reunion with his wife, she immediately asked whether he had received a visit from her on the night in question, and gave an accurate description of the ship, which she had never seen, including the cabin and its other occupant. She explained that as she lay awake worrying about him, it had seemed to her that she left the bed and travelled across the sea to seek him.

Crookall also reports a number of cases where a third party has claimed to observe the departure of a person from their normal body—always at the point of death. Typically the observer sees a kind of vapour or cloud leave the body of the dying person, rise above it and form itself into an exact duplicate of that body. The duplicate is sometimes attached to the physical body by cords, which may break or be broken by visiting figures who then escort the person, in his new body, away. In other cases the spiritual body just floats away or disappears, and the physical body in the bed is found to be a corpse.

Two things are particularly striking here. First, these accounts by third parties correspond closely to accounts given by those who have had a near-death experience. Secondly, the same thing was happening in the sixth century: several examples are given by Pope Gregory the Great in books two and four of his *Dialogues*—a work with which I doubt the modern witnesses were familiar.[49]

In a few cases an individual has been seen in two places at once by a number of people. A good example is given by Brian Inglis:

> The best known account relates to Émélie Sagée, a teacher at a school for young ladies in Livonia. During a period of over a year in the mid-1840s, she was frequently seen by her pupils inside their class room at the same time as they could 'see' her double outside in the school grounds. Sometimes while she was performing some action, such as writing with a chalk on a blackboard, her double would be seen to behave as if imitating her; but at other times the double acted independently—coming into a room for example, and sitting down, while Émélie could be seen by the girls walking outside.
>
> Émélie was highly regarded as a teacher, and although the stories of her 'bilocation' soon spread, and were accepted by the directors of the school, they were reluctant to get rid of her until parents, hearing about her, began to withdraw their daughters. She had often been sacked for the same reason from other schools, she lamented to the children; but there was nothing she could do about it. Investigating the tale, Robert Dale Owen claimed that in all his research into the subject he had not come across any example of the apparition of the living 'so remarkable and so incontrovertibly authentic as this'.[50]

Poltergeists

Poltergeists produce phenomena which might more naturally be attributed to the unbridled imaginings of a rebellious child bent on destruction. Researchers have found them to move objects—in a way which defies the laws of physics—to break crockery, to drag beds—and their occupants—around the room, to throw stones and ring bells, to light fires and pour water from ceilings, to interfere with electrical apparatus, to pinch and scratch, to open doors and windows, to rip up clothes, and perform a host of other irritating tricks. Although sometimes faked, a mountain of thorough research has been done into cases where fraud is simply not a plausible explanation.

Take a certain lawyer's office in Rosenheim, Germany, in the 1960s. First the telephone system went berserk, registering calls which had not been made. A complete overhaul brought no improvement, and the lawyer decided to sue. During the police investigation, neon tubes began to twist in their sockets and explode. The electricity company were called in, and blamed surges in the current. The office was connected to an independent generator—and the current continued to surge. Then pictures began to rotate on their hooks to face the wall, once caught in the act on a video. Filing cabinets began to move across the floor, requiring two policemen to replace them. Physicists were called in. At least forty disinterested people witnessed these events. Eventually parapsychologists were called in, and they linked the phenomena with the presence of a nineteen-year-old secretary. She left, and no further disturbances were recorded.[51]

Obviously the secretary cannot have been directly responsible for these events, in that she could not have caused them personally. And this is often so in poltergeist cases. The phenomena frequently occur in the presence of a particular person, who far from deliberately causing them is often extremely distressed by what is happening. A survey by parapsychologist W.G. Roll of poltergeist cases from 1612 to 1974 concluded that the typical agent is a person, often a teenager, suffering from severe emotional or psychological stress.[52] But it seems that some other agent must be involved too, for like the spirits contacted by mediums poltergeists respond to questions with raps, and it is hard to explain the defiance of the normal laws of physics shown by many poltergeist outbreaks.

Possible explanations for apparitions and poltergeists

Various hypotheses have been advanced to account for the occurrence of apparitions. These were grouped under five main headings in a survey published in the *Proceedings of the SPR* in 1956:[53]

(a) The apparition is not actually there, but is due to mental hallucination on the part of the observer; the hallucination is a response to the receipt of telepathic impulses from the spirit concerned.

(b) Apparitions are merely 'idea-patterns' produced by the subconscious of the observer, and have no objective reality.

(c) Apparitions are 'etheric images' created by a mental act, and remain imprinted on a place rather like images on a film or electromagnetic patterns on a tape.

(d) Apparitions are the 'astral' or 'etheric' bodies of the persons concerned. This is perhaps the commonest explanation; it is based on the assumption that in addition to our physical body we each possess some kind of spirit body which is independent of the physical one and survives when it dies. This spirit body is the one seen; it is merely the shadow of the person, not the person themselves.

(e) Apparitions are the spirits of the departed.

Of these theories, the first three suggest that when an apparition is seen there is no material presence; the apparition is in some way a product of the mind of the observer.

The last two hold that an apparition is really there. Most researchers opt for the fourth on the grounds that cases can be found which disprove each of the others. Identical hallucinations are not experienced by more than one person at a time; and yet many apparitions have been witnessed by a number of people whose testimonies agree. Similarly, several people are not likely to create the same subconscious image of an apparition, especially when they have no inkling that others have seen a similar thing and when identical reports may be years apart. The third hypothesis would certainly seem to explain some cases, such as the experience of Miss Smith, but fits less well with ghosts who respond to questions with raps or those such as Johnnie Minney who interact with the living. The fifth would also explain some cases, but fails to account for apparitions of the living.

Two main theories have been put forward to explain poltergeist phenomena.[54] The first suggests that these phenomena are unconsciously produced by the link person, and that they are in some way a projection of the uncontrolled psychic side of a person. The second suggests that the phenomena are produced by a spirit of some kind. These two hypotheses are not incompatible; as many of the phenomena are similar to those produced by mediums, it may be that the poltergeist agent is in some way acting as a temporary medium.

Conclusions

Whichever of these hypotheses one chooses to adopt as the most likely explanation for the phenomena discussed above, it seems clear once more that there is a spiritual world separate from the material world, in which the same physical laws do not apply. Those who have studied the subject are in no doubt about this. This was the conclusion of Professor Charles Richet, a distinguished French scientist who investigated many spiritistic phenomena:

> It has been proved that a whole world of powers, sometimes accessible, vibrates around us. We cannot even suspect the nature of those powers; we only see their effects. These effects are, however, so clear that we can assert the reality of the forces.[55]

Secondly, it seems clear that we may participate in this spiritual world despite the fact that we belong to the material one. And so why should we not continue to participate in it after we leave the material world? This was the conclusion of parapsychologists Osis and Mitchell to their study of out-of-the-body experiences:

> If an out-of-the body experience literally is what the term implies, that is that some part of personality is temporarily out of the body, then it would be of the utmost importance for research in survival after death. If there is something in us which can get out, perceive

and act apart from the body, this indeed would make it more plausible that one might also get out at the time of death and continue to exist in one way or another.[56]

So—do we survive death or not? A vast amount of research has been done, much of it recently, on the near-death experience, on spiritualism, and on apparitions—and indeed on many other aspects of paranormal experience. This research has amassed a large number of facts, and put forward a relatively small number of hypotheses to explain those facts. Let us remind ourselves, in the words of scientist Robert Crookall, that

> in scientific studies, the method of dealing with matters such as these is first to assemble the facts, then to classify them, then to suggest how they can best be explained. The hypotheses thus envisaged suggest new lines of enquiry or experiment . . . Hypotheses are never absolutely proved [on this side of the grave, that is]. Nevertheless, they may be of such a wide application, and may serve to explain such a diversity of facts, that they approach absolute acceptance.[57]

It is my view, and that of many others, that the hypothesis which most satisfactorily accounts for the existence of phenomena such as those we have looked at is the one which states that there *is* a spiritual world independent of the material one, that we may witness its existence now, and that we may reasonably expect to enter it at death; and that there are also other, non-human, spiritual beings or forces, some good, some bad, with whom we must reckon.

Notes

1. 'ESP in the Framework of Modern Science', in *Science and ESP*, ed. J.R. Smythies (London: 1967), p. 210.
2. Colin Wilson, *Man, Myth and Magic* (London: 1987).
3. J.D. Pearce-Higgins and G. Stanley Whitby (eds.), *Life,*

Death and Psychical Research: Studies on Behalf of the Churches' Fellowship for Psychical and Spiritual Studies (London: 1973), p. 211.

4. *Ibid*, p. 213.

5. For further information on early NDEs see C. Zaleski, *Otherworld Journeys: Accounts of Near-Death Experience in Medieval and Modern Times* (New York: 1987). Summaries of these and related texts are given in the appendix to my *Dante and the Medieval Other World* (Cambridge: 1990), which is concerned with the literary tradition built up around the NDE.

6. 'Life Revisited (Parallels in Death Experiences)', *Omega* 9, 1978–9, pp. 1–11.

7. C. Zaleski, *Otherworld Journeys*, p. 177.

8. F. Schoonmaker, 'Denver Cardiologist Discloses Findings after 18 Years of Near-Death Research', *Anabiosis* 1, 1979, pp. 1–2.

9. *Before Death Comes* (London: 1980), pp. 120–22.

10. *Beyond Death's Door* (London: 1979), pp. 102–07; 17–22.

11. 'The Phenomenology of Near-Death Experiences', *American Journal of Psychiatry* 137, 10 (Oct 1980), 1193–96.

12. *Life at Death: a Scientific Investigation of the Near-Death Experience* (New York: 1980).

13. *Recollections of Death: a Medical Investigation* (New York: 1982).

14. Study cited by S.J. Blackmore, *Beyond the Body: An Investigation of Out-of-the-Body Experiences* (London: 1982), p. 144.

15. *Before Death Comes* (London: 1980), p. 97.

16. K. Osis and E. Haraldsson, 'Deathbed Observations by Physicians and Nurses: A Cross-Cultural Survey', *Journal of the American Society for Psychical Research* 71 (July 1977) pp. 237–59.

17. Quoted by M. Rawlings, *Beyond Death's Door* (London: 1979), pp. 81–82.

18. R. Cavendish, *Encyclopaedia of the Unexplained* (London: 1974), p. 143.

19. *Odyssey* Book XI; 1 Samuel 28. The history of ouija is summarised by B. Inglis, *The Paranormal: An Encyclopaedia of Psychic Phenomena* (London: 1985), p. 228.

20. I. Wilson and R. Bruce, *Life After Death?* (London: 1987), p. 33.

21. For the history of mediumship see J.D. Pearce-Higgins, 'Trance Mediumship', in *Life, Death and Psychical Research* (London: 1973), and W.G. Roll, 'Mediums', in R. Cavendish (ed.), *Encyclopaedia of the Unexplained* (London: 1974), pp. 143–52.

22. The mediumship of Mrs Piper is discussed by A. Gauld, 'Discarnate Survival' in B.B. Wolman (ed.), *Handbook of Parapsychology* (New York: 1977), pp. 577–630; and by R. Kastenbaum, *Is There Life After Death?* (London: 1984), pp. 144–52. For the Cross-Correspondences see also B. Inglis, *The Paranormal* (London: 1985), pp. 223–24.

23. J. Richards, *But Deliver Us From Evil* (London: 1974), p. 67.

24. B. Inglis, *The Paranormal: An Encyclopaedia of Psychic Phenomena*, p. 228.

25. Study conducted by the Revd Peter Anderson and cited by J. Richards, *But Deliver Us From Evil*, p. 61.

26. B. Inglis, in his preface to A. MacKenzie, *Hauntings and Apparitions* (London: 1982), p. xi.

27. In B.B. Wolman (ed.), *Handbook of Parapsychology* (New York: 1977), pp. 577–630.

28. Quoted by Gauld, p. 610.

29. Various studies are cited by J. Richards, *But Deliver Us From Evil*, chs. 3–4. See especially pp. 41–2, 59.

30. Quoted by J. Richards, *But Deliver Us From Evil*, p. 77.

31. *The Black Art* (London: 1936), quoted by J. Richards in *But*

Deliver Us From Evil, p. 71

32. 'Dangers of Psychic Development', *Fate*, Feb–Mar 1971, quoted J. Richards, *But Deliver Us From Evil*, p. 42.

33. K.E. Koch, *Occult Bondage and Deliverance*, quoted J. Richards, *But Deliver Us From Evil*, p. 73.

34. *Spiritual, Psychic and Radiesthetic Healing*, quoted J. Richards, *But Deliver Us From Evil*, p. 74.

35. M. Summers, *The History of Witchcraft and Demonology* (London: 1926).

36. Pliny the Younger, *Letters*. See B. Inglis, *The Paranormal*, p. 186.

37. See J.D. Pearce-Higgins, 'Biblical Miracles' in *Life, Death and Psychical Research*, p. 132.

38. This and other examples are given by S.J. Blackmore in chapter 2 of *Beyond the Body* (London: 1982).

39. These and other examples are given by W.G. Roll, 'Poltergeists', in *Encyclopaedia of the Unexplained*, ed. R. Cavendish (London: 1974) p. 196.

40. A good outline of modern research into the poltergeist in the UK, USA and Germany is given by W.G. Roll in his article 'Poltergeists' above.

41. A. MacKenzie, *Hauntings and Apparitions* (London: 1982), ch. 3.

42. *Hauntings and Apparitions*, pp. 32–34.

43. *Hauntings and Apparitions*, ch. 10.

44. *Hauntings and Apparitions*, pp. 22–23.

45. Case discussed by R. Kastenbaum, *Is There Life After Death?* (London: 1984), p. 43.

46. See note 15.

47. P. Turner, '"The Grey Lady": a Study of Psychic Phenomena in the Dying', *Journal of the SPR* 40, 1959, pp. 124–29.

48. 'Out-of-the-body Experiences and Survival' in *Life, Death and Psychical Research*, eds J.D. Pearce-Higgins and G.S. Whitby pp. 71–72.

49. *Saint Gregory the Great: 'Dialogues'*, translated by O.J.

Zimmerman (New York: 1959). See for example II.34 (Scholastica), II.35 (Germanus) and IV. 16 (Romula).

50. *The Paranormal*, p. 170.

51. See F. Spedding, 'Physical Phenomena and Psychical Research', in *Life, Death and Psychical Research*, eds J.D. Pearce-Higgins and G.S. Whitby p. 46; and B. Inglis, *The Paranormal*, pp. 202–03.

52. 'Poltergeists', in *Handbook of Parapsychology*, ed. B.B. Wolman (New York: 1977), pp. 382–413.

53. Discussed by A. MacKenzie, *Hauntings and Apparitions*, p. 28.

54. Discussed by J.D. Pearce-Higgins, 'Poltergeists, Haunting and Possession', in *Life, Death and Psychical Research*.

55. *Thirty Years of Psychical Research* (London: 1923); quoted R. Kastenbaum, *Is There Life After Death?* (London: 1984), p. 80.

56. 'Physiological correlates of reported out-of-the-body experiences', *Journal of the SPR* 49, 1977, p. 525.

57. 'Out-of-the-Body Experiences and Survival', in *Life, Death and Psychical Research*, eds J.D. Pearce-Higgins and G.S. Whitby (London: 1973), p. 76.

4

REINCARNATION

We have seen that the history of the human race is a history of belief in life after death; that the major world religions all teach some form of survival beyond the grave; and that recent scientific research seems to confirm both the existence of a spirit world independent of the physical world, and our ability to participate in it.

If we assume therefore that on the basis of this historical, religious and scientific evidence we may expect to find ourselves in some sense still alive after we die, then a further obvious question arises: Do we have access to any reliable information on precisely what will happen to us?

There are two main places in which we may look for such information. Religions of the East teach that death is followed, after an interval, by rebirth into this world. Religions of the West (or, more precisely, of the Judaeo–Christian tradition) teach that death is followed, possibly also after an interval, by a new life in another world. Neither doctrine can be proved, as a matter of direct personal experience, on this side of the grave at least. And yet we are not compelled to confine ourselves purely to the realm of religious speculative philosophy; there is a considerable amount of scientific and historical evidence which may be brought to bear on this subject. The present chapter seeks to offer a critical examination of the Eastern doctrine of rebirth into this world—or, as it is popularly known, reincarnation.

The history of belief in reincarnation

The long history of belief in reincarnation is reflected in the confusing array of different technical terms associated with it within the English language alone. The word 'reincarnation' itself literally means 'becoming flesh again'. Less specific is 'transmigration', which means 'passing into another body'— human or otherwise. Also used are two words of Greek derivation, *metempsychosis* (migration of the soul into another body) and *palingenesis* (regeneration in another body).

The origin of the concept of reincarnation is unclear. We do however know that it goes back a long way; it was current in India by the seventh or eighth century BC, and in Greece by the sixth century BC. Even then its source was unknown; in the fifth century BC the historian Herodotus attributed it, incorrectly, to the Egyptians.[1] It is widely accepted today, not just in the East but increasingly in the Western world, and mostly among people who would not regard themselves as conventionally religious. A Gallup poll conducted in 1979 reported that no fewer than twenty-eight per cent of adults in Britain believe in some form of reincarnation. Similar figures have been reported in other countries.[2]

On the whole reincarnation has been rejected by the monotheistic religions of the West; Judaism, Christianity and Islam emphasise not reincarnation but resurrection—that is, the doctrine that not just the soul but the whole person will be raised again to bodily life. In the East, however, it is almost universal. In particular, it is a central doctrine of Hinduism, Buddhism, Jainism and Sikhism.

Reincarnation in the East

The oldest written reference to the doctrine of rebirth is found in the *Upanishads* of Hinduism. It is however far more complex a doctrine than is generally realised. In the West we tend to think of reincarnation as rather a comfortable concept: just as I have lived before, so will I live again. This is far removed from the teaching of Hinduism, and even further from that of Buddhism. For the Hindu, rebirth also means redeath, and redeath rebirth; it means to be locked into an endless cycle of suffering and illusion—definitely a vicious circle. The individual 'self' or jiva may live on in another body, but for the Hindu this self is not real; it is the eternal soul or atman which is real, immortal, and part of divine reality or Brahman. For the atman, reincarnation is reimprisonment, and peace is to be found only in release and permanent unity with Brahman. The strictest Hindu teaching states that the 'self' then ceases to exist, and the individual is no more. Later thought allows for some possibility of individual consciousness within Brahman. In the meantime the soul is bound, by the law of karma, to transmigrate into another body—which may be divine, human, animal or even insect.

Traditional Buddhist beliefs take us even further from our modern assumptions concerning the doctrine of reincarnation. Like his Hindu predecessors, the Buddha saw life as suffering, as something to be escaped rather than embraced. But unlike them, he taught that there is no such thing as the soul or atman, and no such thing as Brahman. I am nothing more than a temporary association of transitory factors, like bubbles moving on the surface of a stream; and the sea towards which I am moving, known to Hinduism as Brahman, is no more than a void. To fully understand this is to achieve release and, of course, extinction. And yet something binds me to the world, and to rebirth; that something is karma, the enduring consequence of my actions. So Buddhism teaches that 'there is nothing that transmigrates and yet there is rebirth'.[3] Rebirth may occur into any one of five states: gods, human beings, animals, ghosts, or inhabitants of hell. Enlightenment occurs only from the first two.

Rebirth is also a central tenet of the Jain faith. Jainism was founded at about the same time as Buddhism, again in India, by a man known as Mahavira. Today it has about 4 million followers. Jains believe that there is no divine being, that the soul will transmigrate repeatedly, but that release through enlightenment is ultimately possible. Transmigration is caused by karma, which is seen as a material substance which clings to the soul and binds it to life. The soul may be reborn into any form of existence, animate or inanimate, and because of this possibility Jainism teaches a policy of extreme non-violence towards any form of life.

The remaining principal religion of India is the Sikh faith, founded in the sixteenth century and followed today by about 16 million people. It was strongly influenced by both Hinduism and Islam. Like Muslims, Sikhs believe that there is a Creator God; and like Hindus, they hold that salvation is to be found in mystical union with him, and that while searching for this union the individual will be reincarnated many times.

Reincarnation in the West

Reincarnation also has a long pedigree in the West, although not a constant one. It was present in ancient Greece as one current among many different religious movements and philosophies, prominent in the mystery religions and the other-world myths of Plato. It passed into Roman thought to some degree, but never became dominant. In the year 480 Christianity was decreed to be the official religion of the Roman empire, and in the year 553 the concept of reincarnation was condemned by the church as incompatible with the Christian doctrine of resurrection. For centuries afterwards, reincarnation remained only a minority concept surfacing occasionally in various underground movements and sects.

This remained the case until modern times. It is no longer Christianity which dominates Western thinking, but science. And although science has made enormous strides forward in so far as our understanding of the physical universe is concerned, it has not provided answers to the questions which have traditionally been the preserve of religion. And so many people are again turning to religion—this time however not to the familiar teachings of Christianity, but to the doctrines and practices of Eastern religions. Reincarnation has burst into the popular consciousness of the West, although, as we shall see, in a very different form from that in which it is found in the East.

The New Age movement

Interest in Eastern religious thought was first expressed in the West in the late nineteenth century. Hindu and Buddhist texts were translated into English, and new religious societies founded to propagate them. The most influential were the Theosophical Society and the Anthroposophical Society, founded respectively by Madame H.P. Blavatsky and Rudolf Steiner. Hindu gurus began to travel to the West. More recently, Eastern practices such as yoga and transcendental meditation have become popular. And of course we now live in a multi-cultural society; one-third of the inhabitants of the city of Leicester, where I presently live, originate ethnically from the Indian subcontinent, and many of them are Hindus. Hinduism is taught in our schools and practised in our streets; it is no longer remote or unfamiliar.

The willingness of many people to return to the search for a religious worldview is however perhaps most commonly expressed in the increasing popularity of the New Age movement. This is more a network than a movement, in that it has no central organisation. It is held together instead by a number of shared assumptions. These may be summarised as follows: all is one; we are all one; the one is God; we are God. We attain unity with God through spiritual growth and, where necessary, successive reincarnations. This is similar to the teaching of Hinduism and Buddhism, and profoundly different from that of Judaism, Christianity and Islam.[4]

There are, however, some fundamental differences between the New Age and the traditional spirituality of the Eastern religions. Whereas Hinduism teaches that enlightenment may be achieved only after many lifetimes, and whereas Buddhism teaches that it may be obtained by following the highly demanding path of spiritual discipline laid down by the Buddha, practitioners of the New Age believe that thanks to modern, scientific techniques it is readily available to anyone who would seek it. There are many consciousness-changing techniques ('psychotechnologies') which may be employed, including meditation, yoga, chanting, mood-altering music, mind-expanding drugs, guided imagery, balancing and aligning 'energies', hypnosis, body disciplines, fasting, martial arts, mechanical devices that measure and alter bodily processes, and mental programmes (intensive seminars, psychotherapies).[5]

The range of sub-groups which make up the New Age movement is considerable. There are groups which seek to tap the alleged mystic properties of crystal. There are groups which offer 'growth seminars' to businesses and companies, promising increased personal productivity through exposure to New Age teaching. There are groups which explore areas traditionally regarded as occult—witchcraft, mediumship ('channelling'), faith-healing. There are groups which promote ecological issues, health foods, aromatherapy, relaxation techniques, world peace. There are political groups; the 1992 General Election in Britain was fought by a New Age political party, the Natural Law party. And there are groups which seek to rediscover the pagan practices of our ancestors—shamans and native American (Indian) cultures in the United States, for example, and druids and summer solstice festivals in Britain.

The New Age movement is thus a curious blend of Eastern spirituality and Western science, or, as some would say, pseudoscience. It teaches both enlightenment and reincarnation, but the meaning of these terms has been changed almost beyond recognition. Enlightenment now involves not the effacement of self, but rather the fulfilment of self; not release from the world, but rather self-actualisation within the world. It means not escape but success; not flight but a grasping of opportunity. Reincarnation likewise no longer means the unfortunate recasting of a transitory self or of a bundle of impermanent characteristics bound together by a law called karma into another round of wearisome life; it now means the opportunity to overcome death and enter once again into the fullness of life, with the complete preservation of the personality. I survive again to act another part. Indeed, there is a flourishing practice of 'past-life therapy', whereby any unresolved pain which I may be carrying with me from my past lives may be uncovered and dealt with in consultation with suitably experienced therapists. As one authority writes, 'New Age has simply recast the theory of reincarnation into the language of Western humanistic psychology, science, and technology.'[6]

Reincarnation: Is there any evidence?

It is clear that the doctrine of reincarnation has a long history and remains popular today. But why is it believed so widely? Is there any evidence to support it, or must it remain a matter of conjecture?

Because we now rely on science more than on religion, the most convincing arguments in favour of reincarnation, at least to the Western mind, would be empirical and scientific in nature. If such evidence could be found to support the doctrine of reincarnation it would be powerful indeed. And as with the phenomena we looked at in the last chapter, a great deal of scientific research has now been done into cases of people apparently able to recall previous lives. These cases fall into two categories. The first category consists of those people who are able to remember spontaneously events from their previous lives in the same way that they remember events from earlier in their present life. The second category consists of those who are able to recall such events in dreams or, more commonly, under hypnosis.

Spontaneous recall

The foremost researcher into cases of spontaneous recall of past lives is Dr Ian Stevenson, professor of psychiatry and director of the division of parapsychology at the University of Virginia. Stevenson is a thorough and balanced researcher who commands the respect of the academic community; he has been studying cases of possible reincarnation for over thirty years, and has written up his findings in a number of publications. In all he has examined over 1,300 cases from all over the world, although most of those which he has studied in detail have come from Eastern countries. His subjects are usually young children.[7] Stevenson gives the following summary of a typical case:

> The case usually starts when a small child of two to four years of age begins talking to his parents or siblings of a life he led in another time and place. The child usually feels a considerable pull back toward the events of that life and he frequently importunes his parents to let him return to the community where he claims he formerly lived. If the child makes enough particular statements about the previous life, the parents (usually reluctantly) begin inquiries about their accuracy. Often, indeed usually, such attempts at verification do not occur until several years after the child has begun to speak of the previous life. In some verification results, members of the two families visit each other and ask the child whether he recognizes places, objects, and people of his supposed previous existence. On such occasions the case usually attracts much attention in the communities involved and accounts reach the newspapers.[8]

Stevenson and his researchers have investigated many such cases at first hand, including some in which the families have not attempted verification themselves. Often the child has been able to recall information and recognise people with astonishing accuracy, and in a way which admits of no natural explanation. He or she may also possess personality traits, preferences, skills and even phobias known to have been characteristic of the deceased individual with whom identity is claimed. Occasionally a child may show birthmarks or physical deformities corresponding to injuries suffered at the time of death by the previous personality.

Stevenson has considered all manner of possible natural explanations for the cases he has studied. The most obvious is fraud, and he dismisses this on two grounds. First, the complexity of many of the cases would make pretence impossible to sustain under the kind of scrutiny applied by the researchers. Secondly, Stevenson finds insufficient motivation for deceit; many of the families concerned indeed attempt to keep their child's claims quiet. Another commonly preferred explanation is cryptomnesia—that the material being recalled consists of long-buried memories pertaining not to a previous life but to this one. This Stevenson discounts on the grounds that most of his subjects are very young children who have had no opportunity even to acquire such information, never mind forget it. Stevenson also considers various paranormal explanations, including ESP and inherited memory, but rejects these on the grounds that they could account only for a minority of the cases.

Faced with the inadequacy of these natural explanations, Stevenson considers two supernatural ones, each of which he regards as plausible. The first is possession—that the child in question is in fact possessed in some way by the spirit of a deceased person. The second, to which Stevenson on balance inclines, is reincarnation. Even he, however, states:

I would only here reiterate that I consider these cases *suggestive* of reincarnation and nothing more. All the cases have deficiencies as have all their reports. Neither any case individually nor all of them collectively offers anything like proof of reincarnation.[9]

Recall under hypnosis

The above cases all concern children who claim to recall a past life with no intervention or assistance. It has been found that adults can rarely do this, and so most research into adult recall has been done with the aid of hypnosis. Results from such research were being published as early as 1924, but most of the work has been done in the last twenty years.[10]

One of the best-known modern researchers in this field is Dr Helen Wambach, an American psychologist with additional experience in both psychotherapy and parapsychology. In 1978 Wambach published the results of a study of 1,088 past lives recalled under hypnosis, giving details of the methods used and information recalled by her subjects.[11] Typically she would be working with a group of people whom she would hypnotise, instruct to go back in their minds to one of five given historical periods and tell to remember their past lives on awakening. They were then questioned closely on a number of specific aspects of those past lives—occupation, clothing, food, skin and hair colour, landscape and climate, commerce and architecture, and others—so that the data they provided could be checked against historical records.

The majority of Wambach's subjects were highly responsive to this approach, some reporting as many as fourteen distinct past lives. It was found that those details which could be checked were correct in the vast majority of cases; that the past lives were appropriately distributed with regard to race, sex and social class for each time period; and that the number of lives recalled in each period was proportional to the estimated world population at that time. However, Wambach, unlike Stevenson, does not subject the results she has obtained to the scrutiny of possible alternative explanations, preferring to accept them uncritically as evidence for reincarnation. This leaves us, as we shall see, with certain difficulties.

Other researchers have also conducted large-scale studies into past-life recall under hypnosis. The work of hypnotherapist Arnall Bloxham is particularly well known, and was the subject of a BBC television programme in 1976.[12] Bloxham's methods differed from those of Wambach in that he conducted all his cross-examination while the subject was under hypnosis, working with each subject individually, and in that he tape-recorded the session. One of his best-known cases was that of housewife 'Jane Evans', whose past lives included identities as a Roman, Livonia; as a twelfth-century Jew, Rebecca; as a fifteenth-century French courtesan, Alison; as a sixteenth-century Spanish maid, Anna; as a seventeenth-century London seamstress, Anne; and as a nineteenth-century American nun, Grace. Not only was each of these lives recalled with an astonishing amount of historical detail, but Jane showed a complete identification with the experiences and emotions of her subjects. The Bloxhams found their findings with Jane and others so intriguing that they founded the Reincarnation Research Institute of Great Britain.

Jane's case and others like it are very striking. Jane cannot have been deliberately inventing her 'past lives'. But it is disappointing that in all these studies no attention seems to have been given to any possible explanations other than that of reincarnation. Could Jane's subconscious mind, for example, have had access to information gained through her schooling or reading but of which she had no conscious memory? A number of theories have been put forward by other authorities.

Alternative explanations for past-life recall

1. Psychological explanations

The most common explanation for the recall of apparent past lives under hypnosis is that of 'hidden memory' or cryptomnesia. Psychologists believe that while we have ready access to our conscious memories, these contain only a small proportion of the total information stored, and that indeed almost everything which we have seen, read or experienced is registered deep in our subconscious minds. Such subconscious memories have often been shown to be the source of the 'past lives' recalled under hypnosis.

One psychiatrist, Dr Reima Kampman, rehypnotised subjects who had previously produced accounts of 'past lives' under hypnosis, and cross-examined them about their sources—a simple test carried out by neither Wambach nor Bloxham. The results were striking—childhood experiences, books browsed in libraries and novels read years previously were identified as the material from which the 'past lives' had been constructed.[13]

Another researcher, Melvin Harris, has conducted a painstaking quest over many years for books that might have acted as sources for 'past lives', particularly those recorded by Bloxham. The life of Livonia recalled by 'Jane Evans', for example, has been found to derive from a historical novel entitled *The Living Wood* by Louis de Wohl. The life of Anna is taken from Jean Plaidy's *Katharine, The Virgin Widow*. The life of Alison appears to be traceable to *The Moneyman* by T.B. Costain. In all three cases the correspondences are detailed, and include idiosyncrasies and fictional elements particular to the novels only.[14]

There can therefore be no doubt that at least in many cases of 'past-life' recall, cryptomnesia is a sufficient explanation. In the words of Professor Ernest Hilgard, director of the Hypnosis Research Laboratory at Stanford University, 'New identities claimed during trance are not uncommon and very easy to produce. Invariably, they're related to long buried memories, and anybody who makes claims to the contrary has not based them on scholarly judgments.'[15] Cryptomnesia does not, however, as Stevenson points out, account for conscious 'past-life' recall in young children.

Other psychological factors may also play a part in 'past-life' recall. One such factor might be the subject's expectations of what the hypnotist wants—it is undoubted that Wambach in particular asked her subjects leading questions; and it has been known for hypnotised subjects to give details not only of 'past' lives when requested to do so but also of future ones! Fantasy may be another factor—as in normal dreams, when it is common for emotions and experiences to be recast in fictional settings. Others may include the rationalisation of fears (a fear of snakes is attributed to having been bitten by one in a past life) and cultural or religious conditioning. None of these is considered by Wambach.[16]

2. Psychic explanations

A number of what may be termed psychic or paranormal explanations for 'past-life' recall have also been put forward— telepathy (direct communication from one mind to another), extra-sensory perception (knowing something from information not gathered through the five senses), clairvoyance (seeing mentally what cannot be seen physically), and retrocognition (the ability to move backwards mentally in time and so obtain knowledge from the past). Wambach reports that her patients would often receive her next question telepathically before she had articulated it, and it has been suggested that the information used to construct a past life might also be gleaned by tapping into the minds of those present in some way. There are various examples of people suddenly finding themselves—while fully conscious—witnessing events which occurred many years or centuries previously, such as the case referred to in Chapter 3 of Miss Smith, who apparently witnessed the aftermath of a seventh-century battle while walking home one night.[17]

While factors such as these may play a part, however, they are unlikely to provide a total explanation either in the case of 'past lives' recalled under hypnosis or in the case of Stevenson's children, for two main reasons. First, Stevenson in particular has demonstrated that the information known to the child about the supposed previous personality often could not have been acquired from any one living source, so that the child would have to receive and amalgamate a complex web of factors from different people. And secondly, even allowing that ESP might conceivably account for the information received, it would not account for the complete self-identification of the subject with the supposed previous personality.

It has been suggested that memories can somehow be genetically inherited, and that the 'past lives' being recalled are in fact those of the subject's ancestors rather than his own; this however would not account for those cases (the majority) where there is no genetic link between the various personalities. Such transmission could alternatively be explained psychically—it has been suggested that the information is being withdrawn from the 'collective unconscious' (Jung's terminology) or the so-called 'akashic records' (occult terminology)—a pool of information in which the experiences of all people are somehow mingled, accessible to those able to enter an altered state of consciousness such as that experienced under hypnosis.

3. Occult or spiritual explanations

Past-life recall may in many cases be accounted for adequately in terms of psychological or psychic factors. Stevenson indeed regards these as sufficient to explain cases of past-life recall under hypnosis. He however accepts only two theories as plausible when it comes to the case of past-life recall in children. The first is reincarnation; the second is possession. He understands both in terms of the continued activity of the previous personality in question:

The difference between reincarnation and possession lies in the extent of displacement of the primary personality achieved by the influence of the 'entering' personality. Possession implies either a partial influence with the primary personality continuing to retain some control of the physical body, or a temporary (if apparently complete) control of the physical organism with later return of the original personality.[18]

It is clear from this definition that Stevenson views both reincarnation and possession in rather particular ways. By reincarnation he seems to mean that the personality of a deceased person somehow invades the body of a foetus or baby, completely displacing its natural occupant. This is not only different from the traditional Eastern concept of reincarnation; it is different from the common Western understanding of the term, according to which a person lives again in another body created, as it were, specially for him or her, rather than somehow ousting the natural owner. And by possession Stevenson means a less complete form of reincarnation, in that only a partial takeover of the new body occurs.

Of these two, Stevenson inclines towards reincarnation rather than possession as the more convincing explanation for past-life recall in children, although he does state that he does not regard any of the various arguments he advances as decisive.[19] One case in particular can really be explained only in terms of possession. This is the case of Jasbir, a three-and-a-half-year-old Indian boy suffering from smallpox. Jasbir lapsed into a coma and was presumed dead, only to wake up just before his own funeral claiming to be Sobha Ram, a twenty-two-year-old from a nearby village who died at about the same time. It is difficult to see how Jasbir can have been a reincarnation of Sobha Ram if he was born three-and-a-half years before Sobha Ram's death; on the other hand, none of the various psychological and psychic explanations of past-life recall seem to fit either, leaving some form of possession as the only plausible hypothesis.[20]

Stevenson defines possession as the partial or temporary displacement of one human personality by another. This, like his definition of reincarnation, runs directly counter to the traditional understanding of possession, according to which a person said to be possessed is taken over not by another, deceased human being, but by a non-human (and evil) spiritual entity. And it does seem that some of his cases are much more easily explained by a theory of occult possession than by one of human possession or reincarnation. Possession by evil spirits is in fact the explanation put forward to Stevenson by an orthodox Hindu swami, Sri Sri Somasundara Desika Paramachariya of southern India—who of course, as a Hindu, does believe in reincarnation. He wrote:

> All the 300 odd cases reported by you do not in fact support the theory of reincarnation. . . . They are all spirit possessions, ignored by the learned in south India.[21]

This hypothesis would seem to make a great deal of sense of a number of puzzling factors in cases reported both by Stevenson and by Wambach. And the swami is not alone in suggesting that some kind of spirit influence could be at work. This theory is supported by at least one regression therapist, who suggests that the 'past-life' personalities which emerge under hypnosis could also be possessions (in these circumstances temporary ones) by spiritual entities.[22]

If past-life recall is in fact to be accounted for in some cases at least by the influence of discarnate spiritual entities, in the same way that many authorities account for the experiences of mediums and spiritualists, then we would expect to see certain similarities between the two. This is indeed what we do see. Helen Wambach states that she 'could observe no essential difference between the mediumistic trance and the hypnotic trance'.[23] It is also notable that Wambach's research into past-life recall grew out of various occult activities—ouija, astrology, mediumship, automatic writing, table-tipping and communication with an entity named Ethan. Stevenson also remarks on the similarities between mediumship and past-life recall:

> Some sensitives or mediums also experience a kind of identification with the persons living or deceased about whom they received information. They may use the first person in describing the experiences of the person cognized.[24]

As one writer on reincarnation observed:

> There seems to be a shadowy nether world of overlapping personality manifestations common both to mediums in seances and to reincarnation experiences.[25]

We saw in Chapter 3 that one of the factors pointing to the involvement of evil entities in spiritualism is the presence of subsequent distressing symptoms in those who participate. This also appears to be a factor in some cases of past-life recall. Some of Stevenson's subjects showed disturbance similar to those frequently found in people who have engaged in occult activities, including mental illness and suicide. Sometimes this is true both of the subject in question and of the previous personality—Emilia Lorenz and her brother Paulo, in whom she was said to be reincarnated, made repeated attempts to commit suicide; both were eventually successful. Their mother had attended spiritualistic meetings before Paulo's birth and received communications which purported to be from Emilia announcing her intention to return. Another of Stevenson's subjects was later diagnosed as suffering from schizophrenia, of which the cause is not yet understood. Could it be that some at least of what is diagnosed as schizophrenia might also be due to possession?[26]

There are dangers also for hypnotic subjects. Some have been so traumatised by their experiences that they have refused to co-operate further with the researcher; this is true of a number of

Bloxham's subjects, including 'Jane Evans'. But this is not the limit of the danger. Stevenson warns that

> in a few cases the previous personality has not gone away when instructed to do so, and the subject in such cases has been left in an altered state of personality for several days or longer before restoration of his normal personality.[27]

There are other factors which also make the possession hypothesis more convincing than the reincarnation hypothesis. First, if reincarnation were occurring we would expect to see some discernible karmic pattern in the cases of those subjects who are able to recall a succession of past lives. That is, each life should be directly affected by the actions of the previous life; successive reincarnations should take the subject nearer to, or further from, enlightenment according to the karma inherited. No such pattern is apparent. Secondly, if reincarnation were occurring we would expect to find, as indeed Wambach claims to do, that the cause of death would in most cases be natural, following the death statistics for the population as a whole. Stevenson did not find that this was so:

> In a large percentage of the cases from all countries so far studied, the deceased person whose life the child claims to remember died in some violent manner—through accidents, murder, suicide or war. . . . This incidence of violent death far exceeds that of the general population in the areas where the cases occur.[28]

This provides a striking correspondence with what has been found to be the pattern in the case of ghosts, as we saw in Chapter 3.

Finally, it is interesting to note that the theory of possession by evil spirits has a long pedigree, and is an accepted phenomenon in many religious cultures, including Hinduism and many of the religions of pre-literary societies. One of the major functions of witch-doctors and shamans in such societies is in fact to deal with the evil spirits which may be afflicting people.

Possession has also been known to Christians through the ages. There is for example an account in the Bible of a boy brought to Jesus by his father, who explains that he is 'possessed by an evil spirit that has robbed him of speech. Whenever it seizes him, it throws him to the ground. He foams at the mouth, gnashes his teeth and becomes rigid' (Mark 9:17–19). Jesus commanded an evil spirit to come out of this boy, who suffered a convulsion and fell apparently lifeless to the ground. Jesus took him by the hand and helped him up. Today such a boy would be regarded as an epileptic—a disease which in two cases out of three has no known cause. Could some modern cases of epilepsy in fact be caused by possession?

On another occasion Jesus cast a whole group of evil spirits out of a man who had been possessed by them and through whom they had spoken (Mark 5:1–20). Modern psychiatry would diagnose this man as suffering from multiple personality, a disorder which is well documented but which again is little understood. Multiple personality is of course another of the explanations which has been put forward for the past-life personalities adopted by the hypnotised subjects we have been discussing.

Conclusions

Reincarnation, at least in its Western form, is an attractive doctrine. It holds out the possibility of another life of the kind with which we are familiar, and banishes the fear of extinction or simply of the unknown. It is plausible, not least perhaps because it connects with common experiences such as *déjà-vu*, but also because it is believed so widely in the East, and Eastern spirituality is becoming increasingly fashionable in the West.

However, attractive as the doctrine of reincarnation may seem, it nonetheless remains the case that there is no hard evidence to support it, and indeed there are a great many other explanations which plausibly account for the cases of apparent reincarnation which have been uncovered. We must therefore conclude that, although reincarnation cannot be firmly disproved, there is no solid basis for believing in it.

Notes

1. Reincarnation receives its first full mention in India in the *Brihadaranyaka Upanishad*, and in Greece in the teachings of Pythagoras. See also Herodotus, *History*, II.123.
2. The poll was conducted for *The Sunday Telegraph* and reported on 15.4.79. A 12 nation poll issued in February 1969 produced figures ranging from 10% to 26%; at that time the UK registered 18%.
3. See L.E. Sullivan (ed.), *Death, Afterlife and the Soul* (New York: 1987), p. 141.
4. Critiques of the New Age movement are R. Chandler, *Understanding the New Age* (English edition, Milton Keynes: 1989); and D.R. Groothius, *Unmasking the New Age* (Illinois: 1986).
5. Techniques listed by R. Chandler, *Understanding the New Age*, p. 32, quoting M. Ferguson, *Aquarian Conspiracy: Personal and Social Transformation in the 1980s*.
6. R. Chandler, *Understanding the New Age*, p. 18. Reincarnation in New Age thinking is also discussed by M. Albrecht, *Reincarnation: a Christian Critique of a New Age Doctrine* (Illinois: 1982, first published 1947).
7. Stevenson has published many papers in scientific journals. His full-length studies have included *Twenty Cases Suggestive of Reincarnation*, first published in 1966, and *Cases of the Reincarnation Type*, published in 1980. An overview of his work is given by S. Cranston and C. Williams in *Reincarnation: a New Horizon in Science, Religion and Society* (New York: 1984), ch. 4.

8. Stevenson, *Twenty Cases Suggestive of Reincarnation* (Second edition, Charlottesville: 1974), pp. 16–17.

9. *Twenty Cases.*

10. One of the earliest studies was A. de Rochas, *Les vies successives* (Paris: 1924).

11. H. Wambach, *Reliving Past Lives: The Evidence Under Hypnosis* (London: 1978).

12. The book accompanying the television series was J. Iverson, *More Lives Than One? The Evidence of the Remarkable Bloxham Tapes* (London: 1976). Bloxham's work is also discussed by I. Wilson, *Reincarnation? The Claims Investigated* (Harmondsworth: 1982).

13. Kampman's research is discussed by I. Wilson, *Reincarnation*, pp. 114–16. It was first published in R. Kampman, *Hypnotically Induced Multiple Personality* (Oulu: 1973).

14. Harris's research is discussed by I. Wilson, *Reincarnation*, pp. 233ff.

15. *San Francisco Examiner*, 17 March 1977, p. 24.

16. These possibilities are discussed by Stevenson in *Twenty Cases*, p.3, and in the October 1976 newsletter of the American Society for Psychical Research.

17. For retrocognition see the appropriate section in B. Inglis, *The Paranormal: An Encyclopaedia of Psychic Phenomena* (London: 1985).

18. Stevenson, *Twenty Cases*, p. 374.

19. Stevenson, *Twenty Cases*, p. 381.

20. Jasbir's case is discussed in Stevenson, *Twenty Cases*.

21. Quoted in Lynn de Silva, *Reincarnation in Buddhist and Christian Thought* (Colombo: 1968), p. 49.

22. Quoted by M.C. Albrecht, *Reincarnation*, p. 72.

23. H. Wambach, *Reliving Past Lives* (London: 1978), p. 49.

24. Stevenson, *Twenty Cases*, p. 321.

25. Albrecht, *Reincarnation*, p. 76.

26. For a personal testimony see L. Alexander, *To Hell and Back* (Tring: 1985).

27. Quoted Cranston and Williams, *Reincarnation*, p. 107.
28. *Reincarnation*, p. 63.

5
THE TEACHING OF THE PROPHETS

Introduction

Both Eastern and Western religions teach that man lives on after death. They do not however agree about the nature of his new life. If we cannot subscribe, through lack of evidence, to the Eastern doctrine of reincarnation into a further life in this world, can we commit ourselves any more wholeheartedly to the Western idea of a continuation of our present life in another world?

It is not surprising that the religions of East and West (remembering that I use the term Eastern as shorthand for religions of Indian origin, and the term Western to designate religions of the Judaeo-Christian tradition) have arrived at different conclusions concerning life after death. The Eastern religions have developed gradually in the consciousness of a people, expanding and refining their teaching with the passing of the centuries, starting with something quite primitive and slowly building up a whole complex philosophy of life and death. The Western religions, by contrast, are based on specific teachings given at specific times by specific men who claimed to have them from God. These men are known as prophets, and they are the founders and guides of Judaism, Christianity and Islam.

This major difference between Eastern religion and Western religion, between what has developed and what has been revealed, rests upon a difference in the way the nature of God is understood. If by God we mean, as does the Hindu or the Buddhist, everything that is, a ground of being, or a void—in short, a reality which is impersonal—then religion can only grow and develop as we seek to understand and reunite ourselves with that reality. If, on the other hand, by God we mean a personal being, someone who created man and interacts with him, someone in whose image man is made, then we can expect him to reveal himself to us, and to do this through particular people whom he has chosen for the purpose. It is on this second assumption that the teaching of the Jewish, Christian and Muslim religions is based.

These differences in belief between the 'developed' and 'revealed' religions have produced radically different responses to the question of life after death. The teaching of Hinduism and Buddhism in this regard is centred in the doctrine of reincarnation, which we examined in the last chapter. The teaching of Judaism, Christianity and Islam is centred in the revelations given through the prophets, and it is with the prophetic tradition that we will be concerned in the present chapter.

What is a prophet?

In the first century AD the Greek philosopher Philo defined a prophet as follows:

> A prophet does not utter anything whatever of his own, but is only an interpreter, another suggesting to him all that he utters; he is enraptured and in an ecstasy; his own reasoning power has departed and has quitted the citadel of his soul, while the divine spirit has entered in and taken up its abode there, playing the instrument of his voice in order to make clear and manifest the prophecies that the prophet is delivering.[1]

At the most basic level, therefore, a prophet is a spokesman for God. His function is to reveal the will of God to man. He is a crucial figure in any revealed religion. Jews believe that God appointed a whole series of prophets, beginning with Moses in about the sixteenth century BC, to speak to their nation and mould its history. The words of these prophets are handed down in the scriptures. Christians believe that the Hebrew (early Jewish) prophets were succeeded by Jesus, although they believe Jesus to have been more than a prophet in the normal sense of the word. Muslims believe that the Hebrew prophets and Jesus were succeeded by Muhammad, who brought God's word to the Arab people.

But prophecy is not unique to Judaism, Christianity and Islam. Zoroastrianism was founded in the sixth century BC by the prophet Zoroaster. We know that prophecy was common in the ancient world; the Hebrew prophet Elijah on one occasion had to compete with 450 prophets of the Canaanite god Baal and 400 prophets of the god Asherah.[2] The ancient Greeks had prophets and prophetesses who were believed to speak on behalf of various divinities; indeed, Michelangelo painted some of them alongside the Hebrew prophets on the Sistine Chapel ceiling.

The major prophets of Judaism, Christianity and Islam

The first person described in the Hebrew scriptures as a prophet is Abraham (Genesis 20:7), to whom God gave the covenant promises of land and descendants. But the first prophet in the full sense of the word is usually reckoned to be Moses, to whom God spoke many times, giving him detailed messages for his people. Moses' key prophetic experiences were his initial calling, in which God spoke to him from out of a burning bush (Exodus 3), and his receiving of the Ten Commandments on Mount Sinai (Exodus 20). His role was to be to lead the Israelites out of Egypt and into the land they had been promised; he is also traditionally regarded as the author of the first five books of the Old Testament.

Other prophets followed Moses. They include Samuel, Nathan, Elijah and Elisha, all of whom lived in the tenth and ninth centuries BC. They are known as the Former Prophets, and their stories are recorded in the books of Samuel and Kings. After them came a succession of prophets whose messages have survived in the books named after them. They lived between the eighth and fifth centuries BC, and are commonly known as the Latter Prophets. There are fourteen of them: Amos, Hosea, Isaiah, Micah, Zephaniah, Jeremiah, Nahum, Habakkuk, Ezekiel, Joel, Obadiah, Haggai, Zechariah and Malachi. In addition there is the prophetic book of Jonah, written in the fourth century BC.

The messages of these prophets were all concerned with the relationship between God and his people. They called for faith in God alone and for obedience to his laws; they promised blessings and uttered dire warnings; they demanded national repentance and foretold the destruction and restoration of the kingdom. The last of the Hebrew prophets, Malachi, announced the arrival of a 'messenger' who would be sent to prepare the way for the coming of God. Four centuries later a new prophet appeared in Judah, called John—whom we know as John the Baptist. John's message was simple. He called upon the people to change their ways, proclaiming that 'the kingdom of heaven is at hand' (Matthew 3:2). He announced the imminent arrival of one mightier than himself, who would be the agent for the outpouring of the Spirit of God. Finally, he identified Jesus of Nazareth as this man, and made the staggering claim that he was no less a person than the Son of God himself (John 1:34).

Jesus was accepted as a prophet by many Jews, and is regarded as such by Muslims as well. But there were a number of major differences between Jesus and all other prophets, both earlier and later. First, it was claimed that Jesus was not merely a spokesman from God but that he was God himself. Secondly, it was claimed that he was restored to life on this earth two days after having been put very unpleasantly and thoroughly to death.

And thirdly, it was claimed that the many Old Testament prophecies of a new kingdom, of an ideal king, of a day of judgment, and of destruction and restoration all found their fulfilment in the life, death and future glory of this man. These claims are so astonishing that we cannot do them justice here, and so Chapter 6 will be devoted to the question of the identity and authority, or otherwise, of Jesus.

There have been other prophets since Jesus. Much of the writing of Paul and John in the Christian New Testament is prophetic, and it includes material relating to death and the life to come. The founder of Islam, Muhammad, was a prophet; he lived from about AD 571–632. Other more recent prophets have founded sects; the most notable of these is Joseph Smith, the nineteenth-century founder of Mormonism, and we will look at him as our main example of a modern prophet. Prophecy on a lesser scale, in terms of its effects on others, remains a recognised occurrence within the Christian church today.

The prophets of Judaism

A prophet was a man with a personal relationship with his God. God spoke to him directly, beginning with a specific and clear announcement to him that he was to be sent to speak to the people. God's call to the Hebrew prophets is recorded in the Old Testament. Moses heard God speak to him from out of a burning bush. Isaiah saw a vision of the Lord sitting on a throne surrounded by angels, and was told to go and speak to the people. Jeremiah heard God say he was appointing him a prophet to the nations.[3] The men chosen for the most part held no special status in society; Amos was a sheep farmer, Jeremiah 'only a youth', Ezekiel a member of a family of priests.

A prophet's calling signalled a revolution in his life. He had had a particular experience of God, perhaps in the form of a vision or audition (hearing, audibly, the words of God). He was commissioned to deliver a message from God to a people; he had, as the scripture usually puts it, been sent. He entered into a new, spiritual relationship with God in which God spoke to him regularly and directly. When Moses' authority as God's spokesman was challenged, God replied: 'With him I speak mouth to mouth, clearly, and not in dark speech; and he beholds the form of the Lord' (Numbers 12:8). Jeremiah claims to have stood in the council of the Lord, to have perceived and heard his word, to have given heed to his word and listened (Jeremiah 23:18).

A true prophet was not therefore either self-appointed or appointed by others; he was appointed directly by God himself. Indeed, he was often highly reluctant to take on the task. Moses complained that he was not eloquent. Jeremiah said he was too young. Jonah just said he wouldn't; when told to travel east to Nineveh to deliver God's word to the Assyrian people, he immediately set sail west towards Spain. This reluctance was often born out of understandable fear; unpopularity, persecution and even death were the usual reward of a Hebrew prophet. Jeremiah grew so tired of the opposition he encountered that he resolved to speak no more; only to find that 'if I say, "I will not mention him, or speak any more of his name," there is in my heart as it were a burning fire shut up in my bones, and I am weary with holding it in, and I cannot' (Jeremiah 20:9).

The major task of a prophet was to deliver a message. The central message of the Hebrew prophets was always the same: that God had chosen his people and expected them to obey his commandments. The unpopularity of many of the Hebrew prophets stemmed from the fact that instead of announcing God's love they found themselves compelled to express his wrath; instead of promising blessing they were required, by the disobedience of the people, to warn of punishment. In their messages there is a constant tension between election and rejection, salvation and judgment, and it is in this tension that the Christian and Muslim faiths alike were to find the roots of their doctrine of life after death.

For the Hebrew prophets, however, the message was focused primarily on the present; prophecy was not essentially about the future. They called for reform, for a change of direction, for a return to the God-given values of the past. Their task was not so much to predict the future as to shape it. This they did not only by their words but also through their lives. In the obedience of the prophets the people were to find the model for their own obedience. Sometimes it was even more specific than this; the prophet Hosea was commanded to marry and remain faithful to a prostitute, in order that he might represent to the people God's faithfulness to them even in the face of their own disloyalty.

A prophet was a man who could not be ignored. He was acting as the spokesman of God, having been specifically appointed to his office by God and given direct instructions as to what he should say. But of course everything depended on whether or not he in fact was what he claimed to be, and the Hebrew scriptures do lay down criteria for distinguishing between true and false prophets.[4] A false prophet, whether sincerely mistaken or deliberately deceiving, can be identified by three factors. First, his messages contain errors. That is, they contradict established teaching, for example by calling people to other gods; or they fail to be borne out by subsequent events. Secondly, the prophet himself is found not to live a godly lifestyle. He cannot preach obedience to the people if he does not demonstrate it in his own life. And thirdly, his message is convenient to himself rather than inconvenient—in other words, he has something to gain. We have seen that the genuine Hebrew prophets had very little to gain, and were generally reluctant to take on the task at all.

We saw in Chapter 2 that Judaism is, and always has been, primarily concerned with this life rather than with the next. This has been true also of its prophets. There are only two instances in the prophetic literature in which it is clearly taught that man will be restored to full life from the shadowy underworld to which he had traditionally been believed to go after death. The first comes from the book of Isaiah, and states that the dead of Israel will be raised again to life on this earth:

> But your dead will live; their bodies will rise.
>> You who dwell in the dust, wake up and shout for joy.
> Your dew is like the dew of the morning;
>> the earth will give birth to her dead (Isaiah 26:19).

The second comes from the book of Daniel:

> At that time shall arise Michael, the great prince who has charge of your people. And there shall be a time of trouble . . .; but at that time your people shall be delivered, every one whose name shall be found written in the book. And many of those who sleep in the dust of the earth shall awake, some to everlasting life, and some to shame and everlasting contempt (Daniel 12:1–2).

It is also the case that the prophets were concerned with the life of the community rather than the life of the individual, and so when they did speak of the future they spoke of the future of that community. Some, such as Amos, Zephaniah and Jeremiah, spoke of a Day of Judgment, the Day of the Lord. Others, such as Isaiah, Haggai and Zechariah, spoke of restoration. Ezekiel, Isaiah again and Joel spoke of a new kingdom which would be established by God on earth. This kingdom would be ruled over by a divinely appointed king, and characterised by the outpouring of the Spirit of God on all people. These events were expected to happen in history, but they have often been interpreted eschatologically—that is, as referring to an afterlife.

If the Hebrew scriptures are historically accurate the prophets have an overwhelming claim to speak with the words of God. Many of their prophecies were apparently fulfilled, they lived irreproachable lives and they had little to gain personally from their words. But unfortunately these stories are incapable of historical verification. They can be proved neither true nor false. Most of them survive in forms dating from generations after the events, and there are no independent sources against which they can be checked. Indeed, the Hebrew scriptures do not even claim to be purely historical in nature; they are the record of God's dealing with a people, and cannot be read on a purely historical level.

Nonetheless, the Hebrew prophets have left us with a powerful message which must either be taken as a whole or rejected. To reject it would be to recognise the Jewish people as a people of genius who have expressed their pain and their hopes in a collection of extraordinary and beautifully written stories, but to say that those stories have been mythologised to a degree which makes them unreliable as the word of God. To accept the message, on the other hand, would be to hold that the words of the prophets are true, and that those which have not yet been fulfilled can be expected to come to pass. This is the stance taken by both Jews and Christians. Jews look for the fulfilment in this life of those prophecies which are outstanding, expecting a Messiah and waiting for the establishment of a Jewish nation on earth. Christians regard some of these prophecies as already having been fulfilled—Jesus is seen as that promised Messiah, ushering in the new kingdom—and look forward to the final fulfilment of others not in this life but in the next. They base this belief on the teaching of the New Testament, of which the historical accuracy is not subject to the same degree of doubt, as we shall see in Chapter 6. But both Jews and Christians alike regard the Hebrew prophecies as the revealed word of God.

Islam and the prophet Muhammad

A prophet is a spokesman sent by God with a particular message at a particular time to a particular people. Muslims believe that God spoke to the Arab people through the prophet Muhammad, whom they regard as the successor to the Hebrew prophets and to Jesus. They believe that the message brought by Muhammad is recorded in the *Quran*, just as the message of Moses was recorded in the Jewish Law, that of David in the Psalms and that of Jesus in the Gospels. All these prophets are accepted by Muslims as genuine, but Muhammad is regarded as the final and greatest prophet. He is seen as a spokesman in the most literal sense, the *Quran* having been given to him by God in precisely the form in which we now have it, with no input from the prophet himself.

Like the Hebrew prophets before him, Muhammad received a personal revelation in which he was commissioned to speak the words he would be given. This occurred as he was meditating one night in a mountain cave near Mecca; a figure appeared before him and commanded, three times, 'Recite!' Like others before him, Muhammad protested that he had nothing to say, and like others before him he was overruled.

> Recite in the name of your Lord who has created, Created man out of a germ-cell. Recite for your Lord is the Most Generous One Who has taught by the pen, Taught man what he did not know! (*Quran* 96).

Muhammad later identified the figure as the angel Gabriel. Over the next twenty-two years he received a large number of these messages. Initially written down on scraps of leather, camel bones and other materials, they were later gathered together to form the book now known as the *Quran*.

The primary message revealed to Muhammad and presented in the *Quran* is one of reform. The *Quran* states that the revelations given to the Jews and to Jesus have been distorted, and that God spoke through Muhammad to correct what have become corrupt scriptures: 'People of the Book, now there has come to you Our messenger making clear to you many things you have been concealing of the Book, and effacing many things' (*Quran* 5.16).[5] In preaching this message Muhammad was calling the people away from false practices such as polytheism and idolatry, and back to the original faith of their father Abraham. Islam was therefore not a new faith, but the restoration of the true faith.[6]

Muhammad was undoubtedly a deeply religious man and a gifted charismatic leader to whom the Arab people in particular, and through them world civilisation as a whole, owe a great debt. But how sure can we be that he was a true prophet, speaking with the authority of God? If we are to stake our lives on his message, as millions do, can we be absolutely sure that we will not do so in vain?

Much ink has been poured out in an attempt to discredit both Muhammad and his message. It has been claimed that he was an impostor. It has been suggested that his messages arose from his subconscious mind. He has been thought to be, variously, an epileptic, suffering from hysteria or some other mental condition, and the victim of spirit possession—a possibility which even he himself considered at the beginning.[7] But it is now generally accepted, even by non-Muslim scholars, that Muhammad's visionary experiences were genuine, in the sense that they did correspond to something real. Moreover, his experience was undoubtedly similar in many respects to that of the Hebrew prophets. Like them, Muhammad was an ordinary man who received a call which he had neither sought nor expected, who was spoken to directly by God, and who was required to act as a spokesman bringing a message of reform to his people.

But there are also a number of ways in which Muhammad differed from the Hebrew prophets, and these may give us cause for hesitation. First, he had an enormous amount to gain personally from the exercise of his office. The Old Testament prophets were usually reluctant and often persecuted; Jesus was put to death. None of them desired or achieved worldly authority. Muhammad on the other hand rose from the status of humble trader to become the self-appointed spiritual and political leader of the entire Arab people, consolidating his power by military conquest and the imposition of a system of taxation—the autocratic head of a theocratic state. And it is notable that as he did so, the divine messages gradually altered in both form and content, losing the exalted poetic style of the early revelations:

The Koran became a kind of newspaper, publishing the orders of the day to the troops, passing judgement on domestic affairs and explaining the ups and downs of the conflict. Moreover Allah's style altered in consequence. Even in Mecca the disjointed verses of the early days—terse and abrupt to the point of considerable obscurity, full of striking poetic images—had become . . . much longer, more pedestrian and more precise. The narrative could not retain the lyrical style. But in Medina, alongside fragments which still recall the happier Meccan flights, we find a great many more endlessly long-drawn-out laws, exhortations, protestations and proclamations, often painfully prosaic and cluttered with repetitions and stylistic errors.[8]

So whereas the earlier revelations might be understood as supernaturally revealed messages, this becomes increasingly unconvincing as an explanation of their origin as time goes on. There are, for example, many long accounts of the stories of the Hebrew patriarchs and prophets. In the words of one commentator, 'We are confronted by the fact that Muhammad sought (at this stage, at least) to satisfy the natural demand for some miraculous evidence of his Prophetic claims, by ascribing exclusively to divine revelation his knowledge of stories which correspond in such detail with the Talmud that of their essentially Jewish origin there can be little doubt.'[9] This large-scale borrowing from previous scripture is not found in either the Hebrew prophets or the New Testament, although it is characteristic of the *Book of Mormon*.

So it seems that some revelations were included in order to reinforce Muhammad's spiritual authority. Other passages have the effect of backing up his military and political decisions. Still others were strikingly helpful to him at a personal level:

personal . . . problems were sometimes solved by a divine revelation of the most convenient kind: it was thus that he was granted the right, unlike other believers, to have more than four wives and dispensed from the normal obligation to divide his time equally between them; that he escaped criticism when, in defiance of Arab custom, he married the divorced wife of his adopted son; that he was absolved from his oath to have nothing more to do with his concubine Mary and extricated from the trouble caused thereby among his several wives; and that his wives were bidden to veil themselves, were threatened with a double punishment for unchastity, and were forbidden to remarry after his death.[10]

The second scriptural test of a prophet is whether he lived a godly lifestyle, and it would seem that by the standards of his predecessors Muhammad did not. The prophet Hosea was called to remain faithful to a prostitute wife. Jesus remained celibate, and insisted on the highest standards of sexual morality:

> You have heard it was said, 'You shall not commit adultery.' But I say to you that every one who looks at a woman lustfully has already committed adultery with her in his heart. . . . It was also said, 'Whoever divorces his wife, let him give her a certificate of divorce.' But I say to you that every one who divorces his wife, except on the ground of unchastity, makes her an adulteress; and whoever marries a divorced woman commits adultery (Matthew 5:27–32).

These scriptures must presumably have been among those reckoned by Muhammad to have been subject to corruption, because his own life in no way reflects them. He had at least ten wives. He divorced several of them on the grounds of unco-operativeness or age. He took concubines, on one occasion creating havoc in the harem by sleeping with one of the concubines on the designated night and in the hut of one of his wives. The resultant storm was quietened only by a revelation from Allah, who reassured the prophet: 'Allah has given you absolution from such oaths,' and who through Muhammad threatened the wives, 'If he divorces you, perhaps his Lord will give him instead better wives than yourselves' (*Quran* 66.1–5). This apparently had the desired effect. But it does seem that

Muhammad was not a model of sexual propriety.

The third test of a prophet concerns his message. Is it in harmony with established teaching, and is it borne out by subsequent events? Here too we have a problem. Muhammad was clear that he was the successor to the Hebrew prophets and Jesus. He was equally clear that the revelations from God to these earlier prophets had become distorted in the transmission. But he was less clear about what exactly it was that the Hebrew prophets and Jesus had taught. In particular, he thought that the gospel was a book revealed to Jesus in the same way that the *Quran* had been revealed to him. He believed that Christians worshipped a family Trinity consisting of God, Mary and Jesus. He taught that Jesus had foretold the coming of another prophet—himself—when Jesus was in fact referring to the Holy Spirit. The Holy Spirit, or Spirit of God as the Hebrew prophets knew him, is replaced in Muhammad's theology by the archangel Gabriel, the intermediary through whom his own revelations were brought. On other points he expressly contradicted the New Testament (always on the grounds of corruption), teaching that Jesus had not been put to death and had not therefore been raised to life again; that, in short, he was not the Son of God as claimed but only a prophet. Similar points could be made of his understanding of the Hebrew scriptures.[11]

Muhammad's teaching on life after death is also interesting in this respect. It seems to contain little that is original, and to consist largely of a rather literalistic and over-simplified version of many passages in the Hebrew and Christian scriptures. A good summary of Muhammad's many references to the afterlife is provided by Rodinson:

One day the Hour would come. At first Muhammad had believed it to be imminent. Then it seemed further off, yet not too far. The Hour, in other words the Day of Resurrection, the Day of Judgement, would come quite unexpectedly. There would be a great clamour, a fearful din, a sound of enormous trumpets. The sun and the stars would be darkened, walls would swell and boil and the earth tremble. Then the dead would rise from their graves, where perhaps they had already had a foretaste of the fate in store for them. Then Allah would sit in judgement with his angels around him. Considerations of wealth or kinship or social position would no longer count. Each would play his part, a little book in his hand with, inscribed in it, the reckoning of his virtues and his sins. Neither the angels nor the prophets would be able to intercede unless Allah permitted. There would also be a weighing in a celestial balance. The basic criterion for the judgement would be faith. Those who had believed in Allah and in his Prophet and had acted in accordance with this faith would be rewarded. The rest, the unbelievers, whatever their deeds, would be punished.

The description of the state of the dead after the judgement occurs somewhat belatedly in the Koran. The damned were to go to Gehenna, in other words the Fire. Angels would be assigned to torture them. The wretched sufferers would be loaded with chains and iron collars, and jets of fire and molten bronze would be turned on them. When their skins were burned they would be replaced by new ones. Sometimes it would be terribly cold. They would drink foul water and some a boiling drink, and eat the fruit of the *zaqqum* tree which was particularly bitter. All this would devour their entrails. They would beg in vain for the blessed to sprinkle a little water on them from their celestial dwellings. The blessed would mock them and refuse, with all the sadistic satisfaction of privileged people who are conscious of their own rectitude, and, as usual in such cases, who consider their privileges well deserved.

The blessed would receive their reward in the Garden of Eden, also called paradise. Then they would enjoy the peace, tranquillity, joy and satisfaction of praising Allah unceasingly. But there would be other more material delights. Lying on couches in the shade of orchards and vines, dressed in green garments, made of satin and brocade, adorned with silver bracelets, they would watch youths, eternally young, moving among them, offering them dishes of meat and especially fowls, fruit and cups of delicious but innocuous wine. Streams and springs would give forth exquisite coolness which would make the blessed forget the relentless sun and scorching dryness of their native land. For wives they would have women who were good, beautiful, amorous and seductive, dwelling in a pavilion, ever virgin, ever young, with modest looks and shapely breasts, and huge gazelle-like eyes of a beautiful black.[12]

This has many elements in common with the Judaeo-Christian teaching on life after death. But it reads much more like an account of the popular Jewish and Christian writings on life after death than a restatement or even reinterpretation of traditional doctrine, and it certainly does not appear to contain any new revelation. We are reminded of the anonymous Jewish descriptions of heaven and hell of the last centuries BC and the early centuries AD, and the popular texts and paintings of the early Christian Middle Ages. Rodinson does indeed suggest that the teaching of the *Quran* on this subject is in fact derived from early poetic or popular Christian material.[13]

What, therefore, are we to conclude? This much is sure:

Muhammad was a complex man, full of contradictions. He was fond of his pleasures, yet indulged in bouts of asceticism. He was often compassionate, yet sometimes cruel. He was a believer, consumed with the love and fear of his God, and a politician ready for any expedient. Without any great gift of eloquence in ordinary life, he was able for a short period to produce, from his unconscious, phrases of disturbing poetic quality. He was cool and nervous, brave and timid, a mixture of cunning and frankness, forgiving and at the same time capable of terrible vindictiveness, proud and humble, chaste and sensual, intelligent and, in certain things, oddly stupid. But there was a power in him which, with the help of circumstances, was to make him one of the rare men who have turned the world upside down.[14]

Can we be sure that this power was from God? Perhaps it was, originally. But there is much in the *Quran* that is explicable more easily in human than divine terms; and too much that is worryingly convenient to Muhammad himself. As for the teaching on life after death, it seems little more than a rather naive version of the Jewish and Christian teaching. So although Muhammad may well have been a prophet, there is little to convince us that he was a reliable one.

Mormonism and Joseph Smith

Judaism, Christianity and Islam are the major world religions founded on the teachings of prophets. But there are others too. One of the best known is the Mormon religion. Mormonism is like Islam in that it grew out of both Judaism and Christianity, although it is much more recent than any of these religions. It is based on the *Book of Mormon*, which Mormons believe to have been revealed to Joseph Smith, prophet and founder of Mormonism, in the nineteenth century. Mormonism is prominent throughout the West, although most of its members live in the United States. It is particularly interesting from our point of view because of its proximity to our own times and the relative abundance of historical information from which we may assess the prophetic claims of Joseph Smith.

Joseph was born in 1805 in the American state of Vermont. His family were among the pioneer farmers moving inland to settle new areas for the first time, clearing land and establishing townships. When Joseph was eleven the family moved to Palmyra in New York state. The new communities were strongly religious, rival denominations competing to establish themselves, and from the age of about twelve Joseph began to take an interest in religious matters. At the age of fifteen he received a vision and was filled with the Holy Spirit. Three years later he had another vision, in which an angelic being called Moroni informed him that God had a work for him to do, and that he would find buried on a nearby hill a book written on gold plates together with two seerstones necessary for its translation. On the appointed day Joseph dug up these plates and began to translate them. His translation appeared in the year 1830 as the *Book of Mormon*—Mormon being the military leader of the

Nephites, a Jewish people who were supposed to have migrated from Palestine to America in about 600 BC. The book also contains segments apparently written by Moroni, Mormon's son, and is said to date from the fourth century AD.

The Mormon religion was founded by Joseph and others at about the same time that the *Book of Mormon* was published. Other churches were condemned, said to be lost in false teachings; only in the *Book of Mormon* was the fullness of the gospel of Jesus Christ represented. The authority of the Bible was however upheld, although in Joseph's retranslation. Mormonism is therefore essentially a Christian religion, although it differs from Christianity in a number of important respects, as Bushman points out:

> What distinguished Mormonism was not so much the Gospel Mormons taught, which in many respects resembled other Christians' teachings, but what they believed had happened—to Joseph Smith, to Book of Mormon characters, and to Moses and Enoch. . . . The core of Mormon belief was a conviction about actual events. The test of faith was not adherence to a certain confession of faith but belief that Christ was resurrected, that Joseph Smith saw God, that the Book of Mormon was true history.[15]

The validity of Mormonism would therefore seem to hinge on the authority of Joseph Smith as its prophet and founder. This has always been a matter of fierce debate. Joseph undoubtedly presented himself as a spokesman from God in much the same way as Muhammad; both claimed to have received a definite call, to have experienced visions, and to have been given a message in written form. Joseph's teaching on life after death, like Muhammad's, is not dissimilar from that of Christianity, but it is not a matter with which he is greatly concerned, and there are relatively few references to it.[16]

However, a closer scrutiny seems to suggest that there is grave reason to doubt the genuineness of Joseph Smith and the message of the *Book of Mormon*. It is clear that prior to the founding of the Mormon church Joseph was a man with something of a reputation as a good-for-nothing. Over ninety contemporary testimonies concerning his character were collected in 1834 by E.D. Howe from other Palmyra residents, and they are mostly extremely negative. Joseph and his family are said to be 'destitute of moral character and addicted to vicious habits', 'lazy and intemperate and worthless men, very much addicted to lying'.[17] Another account describes Joseph as lazy and dirty, but with a warm personality, a fertile imagination and the gift of the gab.[18]

One of the activities which appears to have got Joseph into the most trouble was his practice of money-digging. By all accounts superstition and occult practices of one kind or another were rife at the time, and Joseph seems to have exploited his neighbours' credulity by offering to locate buried treasure with the aid of a seerstone. He was twice charged with deception and brought to trial for these activities, although he denied any part in them. Later, after the establishment of the church, Joseph founded a bank and printed money; this likewise led to criminal charges being brought against him.

Joseph's personal morality appears to have been no more impressive than his public morality. He claimed to have received a revelation from God giving permission for 'plural marriage'— which meant not only polygamy but also extra-marital affairs. He instituted a 'spiritual marriage' ceremony, which legitimised sexual relations between himself and at least forty-five women, some of whom were single, some married. Furthermore, when his first wife Emma objected to this practice, he received a revelation in which she was warned that she would be destroyed. Polygamy subsequently became a matter of strained debate in the Mormon church, and it was eventually condemned.

Judged by his character, it would therefore seem doubtful whether Joseph had the credentials of a true prophet. The same applies when we consider whether he had anything to gain by his message. The Mormon church moved from New York state to Ohio and then to Illinois, where a new town named Nauvoo was founded. Joseph was appointed its mayor. As head of the Mormon church and Mayor of Nauvoo, he began to lay plans for the establishment of a Mormon state. In 1844 he convened a 'Council of Fifty' to rule over this state; one of its responsibilities would be to crown him its king. He also planned to run for the United States presidency. These plans were never realised. Opposition to Joseph grew, finding a voice in the *Nauvoo Expositor*. Joseph ordered its destruction, with the result that he was charged with criminal damage, released on bail, attacked by a mob and shot dead.[19]

The third test of a prophet is the nature of the message itself, and Mormonism ultimately stands or falls on the authenticity of the *Book of Mormon*. Here too we are on shaky ground. Joseph claimed to be translating from characters inscribed on ancient gold plates. Where are the plates? Nobody but Joseph was allowed to see them, and Joseph claimed to have returned them to the safe keeping of Moroni. What were the characters? The only expert to whom a copy of some of them was submitted dismissed them as meaningless.[20] How were they translated? Apparently by the magical use of a seerstone. What is the literary quality of the text? Very poor—the manuscript was delivered without punctuation, and the book reads like an inferior imitation of the Bible. In addition, large chunks of the Authorised Version of the Bible are quoted almost word for word, which is odd given that the *Book of Mormon* is said to date from the fourth century, and the Authorised Version known to date from the seventeenth. Are there any other possible sources? Yes—an extended study has recently drawn close parallels between Joseph's work and a book entitled *View of the Hebrews* by Ethan Smith, published in 1823 in Poultney, Vermont.[21] Furthermore, no archaeological evidence has been uncovered to date confirming the historical events recorded in the *Book of Mormon*. This is again in contrast with the Hebrew and Christian scriptures, both of which are amply supported by archaeological findings.

Conclusions

Judaism, Islam, Christianity and Mormonism are all founded upon and sustained by the teaching of prophets. The credentials of the Hebrew prophets are hard to uncover because of the very great difficulty of assessing their characters and messages at a distance of up to 3,000 years; but at the same time there is nothing to suggest that they were not true prophets. They were concerned mainly with the revelation of God's will for the Jewish people, and had little to say directly about life after death. However, they often spoke of judgment, punishment and restoration; this was initially interpreted within a purely historical timescale but latterly understood also in terms of an afterlife. And they announced the coming of a divinely appointed King and the founding of a new kingdom, thus paving the way for the advent of Jesus, who claimed to have come in fulfilment of these prophecies.

We have more information about Muhammad than about the Hebrew prophets. Muhammad seems to have had much in common with his predecessors in that he was responding to a genuine call from God and experiencing, at least initially, genuine visions. But it is much harder to accept the authenticity of the later visions, and Muhammad's own credentials as a prophet became increasingly dubious as time went on. In particular, his wielding of political power and the moral quality of his personal life cast shadows over his unwavering claims to speak with the words of God. In contrast to the Hebrew prophets, he had much to say about life after death; but most of it reads like little more than a corrupt version of the Christian teaching.

Joseph Smith, the prophet of Mormonism, is the easiest to assess because he lived so recently, and there is a wealth of secondary material about him and the church he founded. His credentials as a prophet are very strained indeed; to accept him as God's spokesman and the *Book of Mormon* as God's word requires us to turn a blind eye to an enormous quantity of evidence which would suggest that Joseph was little more than an able opportunist. He had very little to say about life after death, and again what he did say is derived from the Christian teaching on the subject.

It seems therefore that a search for information about life after death within revealed religion but outside the New Testament provides us with very little to get hold of. The prophets of Judaism, Islam and Mormonism are either of dubious credentials or offer little original material. So it is to Christianity that we must now turn, and the next chapter will examine the character and teaching of Jesus, who claimed to be not only a prophet but the unique Son of God.

Notes

1. Quoted by J. Lindblom, *Prophecy in Ancient Israel* (Oxford: 1962), p. 29.
2. 1 Kings 18.
3. Exodus 3; Isaiah 6; Jeremiah 1.
4. See, for example, Deuteronomy 13:1–5, 18:21–22; Jeremiah 29:9–40; Ezekiel 12:21–14,11.
5. See also *Quran* 5.47, 5.20, 9.30–31, 5.16. Discussed by J. Esposito, *Islam: The Straight Path* (Oxford: 1988), pp. 21–22.
6. J. Esposito, *Islam: The Straight Path*, p. 15.
7. N. Anderson, *The World's Religions* (Leicester: 1975), pp. 96–97.
8. Rodinson, 1971, p. 217. See also J. Lindblom, *Prophecy in Ancient Israel*, p. 13.
9. Anderson, 1975, p. 97.
10. Anderson, 1975, p. 98. See *suras* 33.49, 33.51, 33.36–8, 66.1–5, 33.53, 33.30.

11. Discussed by Anderson, 1975, pp. 100–01 and Rodinson, 1971, pp. 132–33, 185–88, 238–39.

12. M. Rodinson, *Mohammed* (translated by A. Carter, London: 1971), pp. 243–44.

13. Rodinson, 1971, pp. 244–45.

14. Rodinson, 1971, p. 313.

15. R. L. Bushman, *Joseph Smith and the Beginnings of Mormonism* (Urbana: 1984), pp. 187–88. Also discussed by D. Persuitte, *Joseph Smith and the Origins of the Book of Mormon* (Jefferson, Carolina and London: 1985); and J. Shipps, *Mormonism: The Story of a New Religious Tradition* (Urbana and Chicago: 1985).

16. M.C. Burrell and J. Stafford Wright, *Some Modern Faiths* (Leicester: 1983), p. 58. References in the *Book of Mormon* to the afterlife occur as follows: judgment (I Nephi 12, 14; 2 Nephi 12–13, 27; Alma 41), resurrection (Mosaiah 15–16), heaven and hell (Alma 40), the New Jerusalem (3 Nephi 21), the Messiah (2 Nephi 2, 10).

17. D. Persuitte, *Joseph Smith and the Origins of the Book of Mormon* (Jefferson, Carolina and London: 1985), pp. 35–36, quoting E.D. Howe, *Mormonism Unvailed*.

18. Persuitte, 1985, p. 14.

19. R.L. Bushman, *Joseph Smith and the Beginnings of Mormonism* (Urbana: 1984), pp. 69–76, 160–62.

20. Persuitte, 1985, pp. 74–76.

21. Persuitte, 1985.

6

WHO WAS JESUS?

They were all filled with awe and praised God. 'A great prophet has appeared among us,' they said. 'God has come to help his people.' This news about Jesus spread throughout Judea and the surrounding country.

(Luke 7.16)

From the very beginning Jesus was regarded as a prophet, and he referred to himself as such. But he was also, from the very beginning, regarded as much more than a prophet; he was regarded as the Christ, the Saviour promised in the Hebrew scriptures, come to rescue Israel and establish God's kingdom on earth. And he claimed to be more even than that; he said he was no less than the Son of God. These are claims which go far beyond those made either by or on behalf of the Hebrew prophets, Muhammad and Joseph Smith. And so if it was important to examine their credentials before committing ourselves to their teaching, it is doubly necessary to look carefully at the credentials of Jesus. Could he really have been all these things?

There are various factors which would suggest that Jesus was who he claimed to be. His teaching was radical and profound, and he had a lasting impact on the whole of Western society. He performed many miracles. He was, as one of his followers put it after his death, 'powerful in word and deed before God and all the people' (Luke 24:19). But the most striking evidence that Jesus offered in demonstration of his identity was his resurrection. The early church was founded on the belief that Jesus had been crucified, had died, had been buried, and had bodily walked out of the tomb, alive, two days later. For many, this statement has become a familiar formula which is repeated almost automatically in church every Sunday. But to pause over it even for a moment is to realise that its claims are simply staggering. Jesus died. Jesus rose from the dead. Jesus has power over death. The first Christian writers, the authors of the New Testament, did not present the life, death and resurrection of Jesus as just a story, as a legend, or even as something which is in some vague and ethereal sense spiritually true. They presented it as fact. They claimed that it literally happened. These are claims which have not been made about any man either before or since. And if they are true, Jesus is the only person in human history to speak with any real authority on the subject of life after death. But are these claims true? Is there any evidence to support them?

Can we be sure Jesus really existed?

Let us begin with perhaps the most basic questions of all: Did Jesus even exist? Was he an identifiable person living in an identifiable place at an identifiable time, or is he merely a legend?

It cannot be doubted that the answer to these questions is 'yes'. There was a real man called Jesus, and we know a great deal about him. We have two main kinds of evidence. First, the historical existence of Jesus is well documented by first-century Jewish and Roman writers, most of whom were not sympathetic to his cause. In particular we have the writings of the Jewish historian Josephus (c. AD 37/8–100+) and the Roman historian Tacitus (c. AD 55–117). Tacitus, referring to the Christians executed by Nero, states that

> Christus, the founder of the name, had undergone the death penalty in the reign of Tiberius, by sentence of the procurator Pontius Pilate,

and the pernicious superstition was checked for a moment, only to break out once more, not merely in Judaea, the home of the disease, but in the capital itself, where all things horrible or shameful in the world collect and find a vogue (*Annals* XV.44).

The Jew Josephus was, as might be expected, less hostile. There are as many as eight references to Jesus in an early version of his *Jewish War*, which covers the period 170 BC to AD 73. He refers to Jesus' miracles, to his large following and to the popular belief that he would free the Jews from Roman rule. He also records that Jesus was taken by the Jewish authorities to Pilate, who found him innocent of their charges but was subsequently bribed to order his execution. He even discusses the claim that Jesus rose to life after his crucifixion, saying that he personally felt unable to decide where the truth lay.[1] In a later work, the *Jewish Antiquities*, Josephus refers to Jesus in these words:

> Now there was about this time Jesus, a wise man, if it be lawful to call him a man, for he was a doer of wonderful works—a teacher of such men as receive the truth with pleasure. He drew over to him both many of the Jews and many of the Gentiles. He was the Messiah; and when Pilate, on the accusation of the leaders amongst us, had condemned him to the cross, those that loved him from the first did not forsake him, for he appeared to them alive again the third day, as the divine prophets had foretold these and ten thousand other wonderful things concerning him; and the tribe of Christians, so named after him, are not extinct to this day.[2]

Other pagan writers mention Jesus, most particularly Pliny the Younger (AD 61/2–c.113), who in a worried letter to the emperor Trajan describes the early Christian community meeting together to recite 'a form of words to Christ as God', and Suetonius (c. AD 70–c.160), who mentions 'followers of Chrestus' in his *Life of Claudius* and 'the Christians, a class of men addicted to a novel and mischievous superstition' in his *Life of Nero*. We also have a number of quotations from early writers whose works are lost, preserved in the books of various third-century Christian authors; and some clear but disparaging references to Jesus in early Jewish writings.[3]

On this basis it is universally accepted by historians that a man named Jesus lived in Palestine, that he was called the Christ (the ancient Jewish term for the Saviour whose coming was promised in their scriptures), and that he was put to death in Jerusalem by Pontius Pilate during the reign of the Roman emperor Tiberius (who ruled from AD 14–37).

However, helpful though these writings are in establishing the historical existence of Jesus, they give little idea of his life and teaching. For this we must turn to the Bible, which gives a much more detailed account. The Bible is divided into two parts, the Old and New Testaments. The Old Testament contains the sacred scriptures of the Jewish people, and was written long before the birth of Jesus. We have seen that it is filled with promises given through many prophets that a saviour would be sent to establish God's kingdom and rescue his people. Isaiah in particular spoke of a man who would come as a servant, to be rejected, despised and put to death, but through whom the people would be rescued from their state of guilt and placed in a glorious new kingdom. Jesus was both identified by others and acknowledged by himself to be this man. The circumstances of his birth, life and death as recounted in the New Testament were exactly as foretold in the Old Testament. Jesus' coming was therefore not unannounced; it had been expected for centuries.[4]

The second part of the Bible is known as the New Testament. It contains four gospels, which give accounts of the life, death and resurrection of Jesus; the Book of Acts, a record of the lives and teaching of the early apostles, the main event of significance being the conversion and commissioning of Paul; a number of letters, mostly from Paul, to the early churches concerning matters of doctrine; and one prophetic book, the Book of Revelation. None of it is written by Jesus himself. It differs from the Old Testament in that it is mostly straightforwardly historical and didactic in character, whereas the Old Testament contains many kinds of writing. It was created during the period which followed Jesus' death. Even without the supporting evidence of the Roman and Jewish writings discussed above, the nature and detail of the New Testament documents is such that alone they offer overwhelming proof that Jesus was a real man who lived and died in Palestine 2,000 years ago. Indeed, it would have required such expertise and ingenuity on the part of the writers of the New Testament to invent the gospel story, from a multitude of sources and with astonishing historical accuracy and internal consistency, that the men who did so would be as remarkable as the Christ they describe. Moreover, many of the statements made in the gospels can be checked against other early records, archaeological findings and general knowledge of the period gleaned from alternative sources. When such checks have been made the New Testament has always been found to be accurate.

What does the New Testament tell us about Jesus?

The basic facts about the life of Jesus as given in the New Testament are these. We can be certain that Jesus was born in the few years which preceded the year now reckoned as nought. Luke tells us his birth occurred while Augustus Caesar was Roman emperor (which we know to have been from 27 BC to AD 14). More precisely, Luke and Matthew both state that he was born during the reign over Judah of Herod the Great, which ran from 37 to 4 BC, and Luke adds that this was while Quirinius was governor of Syria (he was appointed in 6 BC). Jesus must therefore have been born some time between Quirinius' appointment in 6 BC and Herod's death in 4 BC.[5]

We are also told where he was born. Both Luke and Matthew state that this was in Bethlehem in Judea. Luke explains that Joseph and Mary had journeyed to Bethlehem from their home in Nazareth, in the province of Galilee, in order to comply with Caesar's decree that everyone return to their native city to enrol in a census; Jesus was born while they were there.[6]

Jesus is said in the New Testament to have been brought up in Nazareth, where he lived with his parents and brothers and sisters, and where he was trained as a carpenter in his father's workshop. He left Nazareth at the age of about thirty; Luke says that this was in the fifteenth year of the reign of the emperor Tiberius, and Matthew that it was at the time of the arrest of John the Baptist by Herod Antipas; this places the date at about AD 28.[7]

He spent the next three years or so travelling from place to place teaching that a new era in history was about to begin. He told his hearers that they should follow his new way of life, and promised that those who did would live on after death. Many people believed him, and followed him—partly because of the extraordinary authority and quality of his ethical teaching, and partly because of the many remarkable miracles he performed. It is recorded that on at least three occasions he brought a dead person back to life; one of them, Lazarus, had already been placed in the tomb. He explained to his closest followers that he was the incarnation of God, God come to earth as a man, and that this was the explanation for his extraordinary powers.[8]

The religious leaders of the time were deeply offended by Jesus' teaching, much of which was critical of them, and alarmed by the popular support he was attracting; they therefore plotted to kill him. The opportunity came in Jerusalem on the occasion of the annual Jewish Passover festival. Jesus was betrayed by Judas, one of his disciples. He was arrested and taken before the Jewish supreme court of justice. Failing to find any evidence against him, the high priest asked him whether he was the Christ, the Son of God. We do not know the exact wording of his answer, because the gospel accounts give slightly different versions. According to Mark, he said, 'I am.' Matthew and Luke give a slightly weaker response, but all three report that his reply caused the court unhesitatingly to declare him guilty of blasphemy for equating himself with God, and to condemn him to death.[9]

The Jews were not permitted to impose a death sentence without the consent of the Roman procurator, who in this case was Pontius Pilate. Jesus was therefore taken before Pilate, who examined him and stated that he could find no evidence against him. This incensed the Jews, who insisted that 'we have made a law, and by that law he ought to die, because he has made himself the Son of God' (John 19:7). Eventually Pilate, fearing a popular uprising, gave reluctant permission for Jesus to be put to death by crucifixion. This occurred some time after the year 30 (John refers to three Passover festivals during the period of Jesus' public ministry, which began in about 28) and before the year 36 (when Pilate ceased to be procurator of Judea). Most scholars regard AD 30 as the likely date.[10]

Jesus was crucified on a hill outside Jerusalem at nine o'clock on Friday morning, the day before the Passover festival began. He died six hours later and was removed from the cross that evening. A Jew named Joseph of Arimathea asked Pilate for permission to remove the body temporarily to his own private tomb, so that proper burial could be given two days later, after the Sabbath. Pilate agreed, but ordered a guard of soldiers to be placed at the site. On Sunday morning some of Jesus' women followers went to the tomb to prepare his body for burial. They found the tomb empty, and were told by a stranger that Jesus had risen. Before long they and the eleven disciples had all seen the resurrected Jesus with their own eyes.[11]

According to Luke and John Jesus visited the disciples many times over the next forty days, giving convincing proofs that he was alive. He performed further miracles, and stated again that he was the Christ, and that his death and resurrection were foretold in the Jewish scriptures. He instructed them to tell the world what he had taught them. He also appeared publicly, and according to the Apostle Paul was seen by up to 500 people at once.[12]

If these accounts present a true picture of what really happened 2,000 years ago, then they contain profound implications for us today. Jesus claimed to be the Son of God, the promised Saviour sent to rescue mankind from death and to restore us to a relationship with his Father. He spoke frequently about death and what lies beyond it. And he reappeared alive on the third day after his execution, not just to prove his divine identity but also to demonstrate his power over death and fulfil his promises. No other teacher, prophet or religion has offered evidence of this kind before or since. If Jesus really rose from the dead, then his teaching on life after death deserves the most serious consideration. It means that there must be answers to questions like, 'Why do we have to die?', 'What is life after death going to be like?' and even, 'How should we live our lives on earth?' And it makes perfect sense of the scientific, psychic and spiritualistic evidence which suggests so strongly that there is a supernatural or spiritual world which exists independently of the physical world, and which otherwise remains unexplained.

Are the New Testament documents authentic?

We have established that Jesus was a real man who lived and died in Palestine 2,000 years ago. We have looked at the accounts of his life given in the New Testament. It is significant that those accounts *claim not only to be factual but also to be written by people who were there at the time or who knew those who were.* If they are true, we can be absolutely certain that there is a life after death and that we do know something about it. But is the New Testament reliable? When was it written, who by, and how do we know it hasn't been changed over the centuries?

When was the New Testament written?

Had they occurred in our time, the events of Jesus' life, death and resurrection would have been recorded in writing immediately. Two thousand years ago, however, there was no national press. News spread by word of mouth, and only later was it committed to writing. It is therefore surprising that the interval between the events and the writing was quite short. There is broad agreement among scholars concerning when most of the New Testament reached its final form: the earliest part is known to date from about twenty years after the death of Jesus, and the whole to have been essentially complete after fifty to seventy years. Some authorities argue for even earlier dates than these, and one very thorough recent study suggests that the entire New Testament had been written by AD 70, less than forty years after Jesus' death.[13] The details we have of Jesus' life and teaching are therefore not just reconstructions and guesses made generations after his death; they go right back, in black and white, to within living memory of the events themselves.

The methods by which these conclusions have been reached are complex. One set of clues is provided by the relationship between the New Testament documents and the known historical events. For example, it seems certain that the gospel of Mark was written after the death of Peter in AD 64–65, and before the end of the Jewish War of AD 66–70; scholars therefore postulate a date of AD 65–70. We also know that Matthew and Luke relied on Mark as a source, and that their gospels must therefore have been written after his. Paul's travelling ministry is recounted by Luke in the Book of Acts, along with many references to historical events and named officials which we can date from other writings; these enable us to estimate probable dates for his letters. Most of the New Testament documents can be approximately dated in this way.[14]

Another set of clues to the date of the New Testament is provided by the fact that many of its books are cited in the writings of a group of early Christians now known as the Apostolic Fathers. These men wrote between the years of about 90 and 160, were familiar with most of the books of the New Testament, and regarded them as authoritative. The New Testament must therefore have been in circulation for some time before this.[15]

Further evidence for the date of the New Testament comes

from the fact that we have a large number of early copies of it. Some of these are fragmentary, some whole. They include eighty-six papyri recovered from cities buried in the Egyptian desert, 3,064 early Greek manuscripts, and 2,205 lectionary manuscripts written for church use.[16] The oldest of all these, datable by the style of its handwriting to about AD 130, is a small papyrus fragment discovered in Egypt about sixty years ago and now in the John Rylands Library in Manchester. On each side is a portion of the gospel of John, which is thought to have been written in Ephesus, on the present Turkish coast, between AD 90 and 100. The discovery that a copy or partial copy of it was to be found in Egypt only forty years later offers convincing confirmation of its early date. The earliest complete New Testament manuscript is the *Codex Sinaiticus*, now in the British Museum, which dates from about AD 350.[17]

The authors

The New Testament was not only written soon after the death of Jesus; it was written by the men who were closest to him or who knew those who were.[18]

During the period of his public ministry Jesus chose twelve disciples. They travelled with him, shared in his ministry and received his teaching, and were eventually commissioned by him to carry on his work. Two of them, Peter and John, are among the authors of the New Testament. Another writer, Paul, claimed to have met Jesus after his resurrection and to derive his teachings directly from him. Two more, James and Jude, are traditionally identified with the brothers of Jesus. Two of the books are of unknown authorship. The remaining three authors—Mark, Matthew and Luke—derived their information from these men and in all probability from the other disciples.

The books

The earliest gospel is that of Mark. It is generally accepted that Mark was writing in around AD 65, possibly in Rome, and that his main direct source was Peter. He may however have been writing partly from his own experience of events (Mark 14:51–52), and we know that with his parents he was involved from the beginning with the church in Jerusalem (Acts 12:12, 25).

The second gospel in the New Testament is that of Luke, a doctor who was a close associate of Paul. He also knew both Mark and James the brother of Jesus, and may have met Peter and Philip, another of the twelve disciples. In addition to the gospel, Luke also wrote the Book of Acts, which records the establishing of the international church in the first thirty years after Jesus' death. His testimony therefore covers the period from the birth of Jesus to about AD 60. The gospel is generally thought to date from about the year 80, and the Book of Acts from between AD 60 and 80.

The third gospel is that of Matthew, which must have been written somewhere between AD 70 and 115; most modern scholars estimate the date at about the year 85. Tradition has held the author to be Matthew the disciple of Jesus, but this is not now generally thought to have been the case—although it is possible that the disciple Matthew was in some way the source.

The last gospel is that of John. Debate has raged over the identity of this John, but the commonly accepted view, and the one implied in the text, is that he was John the disciple of Jesus, and an eye-witness of the events he describes. He was the last survivor of the twelve, and probably composed his gospel towards the end of the first century AD. Three of the New Testament letters are also by John, and the Book of Revelation is generally ascribed to him. This is the only prophetic book of the New Testament. Much of it is obscure and difficult to interpret, but it has generally been taken to describe the Second Coming of Jesus, the end of the world, the Day of Judgment and the creation of a new heaven and a new earth. It is therefore particularly important as a source of information on life after death.

The gospels are not the earliest of the writings to come down to us in the New Testament. These are found among the letters of Paul, written between AD 48 and his death in 64/5. Paul was a Roman Jew who persecuted the early church until his own encounter with the resurrected Jesus, after which he spent the remainder of his life building up Christian communities in many different places. We know that Paul visited Jerusalem on several occasions, and spent time there with Peter, John and James (recorded in Galatians 1:18–2:10 and Acts 15:1–29). The earliest of these visits took place only three years after Jesus' death. He was therefore personally acquainted with those who had known Jesus best, and able to report their accounts of his life, death and resurrection. However, Paul also repeatedly claims that his teaching—which includes some important passages on life after death—was given to him directly by Christ (see for example Galatians 1:11–12).

Important letters were also written by Peter (shortly before AD 64), James (the date is uncertain) and Jude (probably about AD 80). In addition the New Testament contains the Letter to the Hebrews, of unknown authorship, and a second letter bearing the name of Peter but not thought to be by him.

It is clear therefore that the New Testament was written by, or based on the teaching of, Jesus' closest followers. It covers the historical period beginning with the birth of Jesus and ending in about AD 60, and was mostly written between the dates of about AD 48 and the close of the first century. While modern scholarship is divided over many matters of detail, it is united in its acceptance of these basic facts.

The gap between the events and the writing

The New Testament writers claimed historical accuracy. Luke, for example, begins his gospel like this:

> Many have undertaken to draw up an account of the things that have been fulfilled among us, just as they were handed down to us by those who from the first were eye-witnesses and servants of the

word. Therefore, since I myself have carefully investigated everything from the beginning, it seemed good also to me to write an orderly account for you (Luke 1:1–3).

But can we be sure that his claim was justified? Despite the early date of the New Testament writings, there was nonetheless a gap of twenty years or so between the crucifixion and the first of them, and of thirty to seventy years between the crucifixion and the gospels.

This is a question which has been the subject of much study. It is now known that in addition to the testimony of eye-witnesses, the gospel writers had at their disposal a number of carefully transmitted records of Jesus' life and teachings, both oral and written. The study of the oral tradition is known as form criticism. Form critics have identified various types of short oral units which have been transposed into the final gospels, particularly those of Matthew and Luke (the two who were not eye-witnesses and therefore most dependent upon earlier accounts, including that of Mark). An example would be the account of the crucifixion. These units were often poetic in form; it seems even that some of Jesus' original teaching may have been delivered in verse, a device which would aid accurate transmission.[19]

The study of the written tradition is known as source criticism. No written sources for the New Testament survive, but source critics have shown that a number of earlier writings, now lost, must have existed. The most important is known merely as 'Q', and both Matthew and Luke draw heavily upon it; it is envisaged as a record of the sayings of Jesus in Aramaic, the language in which he spoke. Matthew had another source or sources known as 'M', and Luke a source or sources known as 'L'.

So the gospel writers were not writing after a gap; their work was the culmination of an uninterrupted tradition, preserved both in carefully composed oral units and in written form, and must have been consistent with it. And we know that it was accepted by the many eye-witnesses still alive at the time of its writing. A simple analogy would be the case of a veteran of the Second World War, writing a careful account now, some fifty years after the events themselves, relying either on his own memory, like John, or on a careful study of the many authoritative histories which have been written since the events he describes, like Luke. We would be inclined to trust his account on its own merits. But if his account were corroborated by living eye-witnesses and confirmed by the previous studies of the subject which are available to us, I think we would be well satisfied with its accuracy. This was precisely the situation when the four gospels were written.

Is what we read today the same as what they wrote?

We have in our possession 5,355 manuscripts of the New Testament in whole or in part, ranging in date from AD 130 to the Middle Ages. These manuscripts have been subjected to a great deal of critical study. By comparing them and tracing the relationships between them, experts are able to eliminate the inevitable minor variations and reconstruct the originals from which they must have derived with great accuracy. This branch of study is known as textual criticism, and it has now been established that 'the variant readings about which any doubt remains among textual critics of the New Testament affect no material question of historic fact or of Christian faith and practice'.[20] The New Testament we have is the New Testament as originally written.

It is interesting to compare the process of textual criticism as applied to the New Testament with that applied to contemporary classical texts. About 100 years before the New Testament was composed, Julius Caesar wrote a history of the Gallic War. No scholar today doubts the authenticity, date or textual accuracy of this book. And yet the manuscript tradition for Caesar's *Gallic War* is far weaker than that of the New Testament. Instead of the 5,355 New Testament manuscripts, we have only nine or ten of the *Gallic War*. The oldest New Testament fragment dates from

100 years after the events it describes; the oldest manuscript of Caesar's book dates from 900 years after the events it describes. All that remain now, as for many other classical works, are late copies of copies of copies which for one reason or another survived. And yet because even as many as nine or ten manuscripts can be compared and arranged in relationship to one another—rather as on a family tree—textual critics are able to reconstruct the original text with a high degree of confidence. There is therefore little room for doubt that the New Testament we read in our Bibles today is virtually identical to that which was written in the seventy years which followed the crucifixion.[21]

How do we know they were telling the truth?

So it is clear that what we read today about Jesus is the same as was originally written by his followers in the years after his death. But how do we know that they were telling the truth? Is it possible that the story told in the gospels is a fabrication, loosely wrapped around the man named Jesus whom we know to have been executed by order of Pilate? Or, perhaps more plausibly, that it is based on real events but that these became greatly exaggerated in the telling?

All a fabrication?

There are a number of reasons why the New Testament writers are most unlikely to have been making it all up. It is not just that they had little to gain by insisting on the truth of their story; they had a very great deal to lose. This is what happened to Peter.

Peter was living with his wife, brother and parents and earning his living as a fisherman when he first met Jesus. To follow him meant to leave home, family and business with no promise of any return. When Jesus was arrested Peter, fearing for his life, denied three times that he knew him. However, after witnessing the resurrection, he became one of the leaders of the early church in Jerusalem (Mark 14:66–72). There followed thirty years of persecution. He was imprisoned in Jerusalem by the Jewish authorities as soon as he began to teach that Jesus was raised from the dead, and was later imprisoned again and flogged (Acts 4–5). He was eventually condemned to death by Herod Agrippa (Acts 12), and executed in Rome by Nero, probably in AD 64–5.

James and John fared little better. James was executed by Herod Agrippa (Acts 12), John imprisoned and flogged alongside Peter, exiled to the island of Patmos during the reign of the emperor Domitian, and possibly also executed.[22]

But the apostle who had the most to lose was Paul. Paul was Jewish, brought up a Pharisee and educated in Jerusalem under a famous teacher. He also enjoyed the considerable privilege of Roman citizenship. Known as a persecutor of the first Christians, he was at the time of his encounter with Jesus engaged in a mission under the authority of the high priest to arrest those at Damascus (Acts 9 and 22). In espousing the cause of Christ he exchanged a secure position and bright future for a life of hardship and danger. He began his teaching in Damascus, where he escaped from a plot to kill him only by being let down from the city walls in a basket at dead of night (Acts 9). He was driven out of Antioch (Acts 13), dragged before the magistrates, beaten and flogged in Philippi (Acts 16), taken before a tribunal in Corinth (Acts 18) and arrested in Jerusalem by the Jews (Acts 22). He was sent to stand trial in Rome (Acts 24–27), where he was eventually executed. Paul himself said that only the truth of his witness justified this lifestyle, for on all other counts it would be folly: 'If Christ has not been raised, then our preaching is in vain and your faith is in vain . . . If for this life only we have hoped in Christ, we are of all men most to be pitied' (1 Corinthians 15:14–19). He, like them, chose to carry on to the last. Why, if not because he believed in it?

But even if we disregard the question of what motivation these men and other New Testament writers might have had for persistently propounding a pack of lies, it still seems inconceivable, given the nature of their teaching, that they could have been deliberately deceitful. Their writings contain the highest ethical instruction ever known to man. They condemned violence and dishonesty, and insisted on love, truth and humility. Peter taught that God demands truthfulness: 'Whoever would love life and see good days must keep his tongue from evil and his lips from deceitful speech' (1 Peter 3:10). Paul taught that God demands love:

> If I speak in the tongues of men and of angels, but have not love, I am a noisy gong or a clanging cymbal. . . . . If I give away all I have, and if I deliver my body to be burned, but have not love, I gain nothing. Love is patient and kind; love is not jealous or boastful; it is not arrogant or rude. Love does not insist on its own way; it is not irritable or resentful; it does not rejoice at wrong, but rejoices in the right (1 Corinthians 13:1–6).

James taught that God demands that we treat others well: 'Let every man be quick to hear, slow to speak, slow to anger, for the anger of man does not work the righteousness of God' (James 1:19).

We could go on for many pages. The ethical teaching of these men was simply extraordinary in its depth and complexity; it was completely unlike anything which had gone before, and has certainly not been paralleled since. Could it have come from the pens of conmen? Then what conmen they must have been! As the French philosopher Rousseau remarked, 'It is more inconceivable that several men should have united to forge the Gospel than that a single person should have furnished the subject of it. The Gospel has marks of truth so great, so striking, so perfectly inimitable, that the inventor of it would be more astonishing than the hero.'[23] The idea that the disciples were deliberately fabricating the story they told is simply unbelievable.

Were they exaggerating?

So it seems most unlikely that the New Testament could be a deliberate fabrication. But could it perhaps be an exaggerated account of a true story, changed over the period of time which elapsed between the events and the writing, amplified in the telling and retelling?

This hypothesis appears attractive at first sight, but less convincing on reflection. First, as we have already established, the 'gap' between the death of Jesus and the writing of the New Testament was in fact not a true gap at all; it was filled with both written and oral accounts on which Matthew and Luke in particular drew extensively. Secondly, there were many witnesses still alive at the time of writing of the New Testament who could have spoken out against distortions of the truth; instead the teaching of the disciples was accepted as genuine and the church grew rapidly. And thirdly, we have much archaeological and historical evidence to confirm the accuracy of many details in the New Testament.

Take for example an event described by John: 'Now there is in Jerusalem near the Sheep Gate a pool, which in Aramaic is called Bethesda and which is surrounded by five covered colonnades' (John 5:2). Here lay many invalids, hoping for a cure; Jesus healed one of them, a man who had been a cripple for years. Now we know that people did visit such sanctuaries for healing during this period. We also know that a Byzantine church was built on the site traditionally said to be that of the pool, and a medieval church on top of that. But it was not until 1888 that excavations located twin pools (the name means 'the place of the two outpourings') and solved the mystery of the puzzling layout of a pool surrounded by five colonnades; there were two rectangular pools with colonnades on each side, joined by a causeway, or fifth colonnade. John had accurately described a real place.[24]

Or take Luke's painstaking writing in the Book of Acts. As he records the travels of the early Christian leaders he notes the

names and titles of the local officials, all different, all accurate—
legates, proconsuls, praetors, lictors, politarchs, stratopedarchs,
tetrarchs; all correctly named and all correctly addressed for the
locality and date in question, even where earlier or later changes
in administrative status of a province caused changes in the titles
of the officials within it. Experts on ancient seamanship have
regarded Luke's account of the voyage and shipwreck of Paul
(he was with him) as remarkable for its nautical accuracy, and
historians of the period have paid tribute to the care with which
he describes the different atmospheres in the various cities
visited—Jerusalem, Antioch, Philippi, Athens, Ephesus.

In short, Luke's historical trustworthiness is widely accepted.
Sir William Ramsay, the classical archaeologist and historian
who spent many years studying Asia Minor and the Greek East,
stated that in his view 'this author should be placed along with
the very greatest of historians'.[25] Is it conceivable that Luke and
the other New Testament writers, whom we are satisfied were
writing sincerely, would have got all the unimportant details
right—but the essential claims wrong? That they would have
recorded with impeccable accuracy numerous minutiae—but
unwittingly exaggerated the main events which were the subject
and purpose of their writings?

What could they have exaggerated?

How might we further assure ourselves that such exaggeration,
however unlikely, did not happen? One way of examining this
possibility is to take a specific story and look for those elements
which might have been susceptible to alteration.

John recalls an occasion on which a man blind from birth was
healed by Jesus (John 9:1–41). It is too long to quote here, but
the essence of the story is this: Jesus anoints with clay the eyes of
the blind man, instructing him to wash in a nearby pool. The man
does so, and finds that for the first time in his life he can see. The
Pharisees are furious, and cross-examine both the man and his
parents in order to disprove the miracle. All insist that the man

was born blind. The man himself states his belief that Jesus is from God.

Is this what really happened, or has John—who was almost certainly there at the time—exaggerated things? In this story it is not hard to find elements which he could have misremembered. For example, Jesus could have touched the man's eyes rather than anoint them with clay. The debate with the Pharisees could have occurred on another occasion. The miracle could have occurred at another time or in another place than that recalled. But if the man was not blind, and was not made to see, then there is no story left. The incident simply cannot have occurred.

It is quite interesting to repeat this experiment yourself. Think back to an event which occurred many years ago, and consider how you might have exaggerated it in your memory. You are likely to find that you cannot vouch for all the details, but that you are quite sure of the main event. To the best of my memory, twenty-eight years ago my parents took me down to the Thames in Greenwich to watch the Queen knight Francis Chichester on his return from single-handedly sailing round the world. It was a grey day. My brother and I waved small plastic Union Jacks. The Queen knighted Chichester on board his yacht, Gypsy Moth IV. Now, I would not swear to all the details. Perhaps only my mother took us. Perhaps it was actually raining. Perhaps he had not just arrived back but had been back for some time. But I am completely sure of the main event: I saw the Queen knight Francis Chichester in Greenwich.

So when John tells us he saw Jesus heal a man from blindness, he was not exaggerating—either a blind man was made to see, or he wasn't. The details could have been changed over the years; but not the main point.

The story of the healing of the blind man is not of course the only extraordinary event recorded in the New Testament. Jesus is said, among other things, to have raised three people from the dead, to have had the power to quieten storms and turn water into wine, to heal the sick and deliver the oppressed, and finally to have been raised from the dead himself. It might be possible to find an alternative explanation for one or two of these things; but for all of them? Together they constitute a most powerful body of evidence to suggest that something quite unique, and unparalleled in human history, was happening.

Could they have been mistaken about the resurrection?

But perhaps there is one more possible explanation. If the New Testament writers were not lying or exaggerating, could they perhaps have been mistaken? And most particularly, could they have been mistaken about the one event which is crucial: the resurrection of Jesus? On the face of it the case for the resurrection is strong, because there were so many witnesses. We know that Jesus' closest followers claimed to have seen him and talked to him after his death. But many others did too. This is what Paul wrote to the church at Corinth some time between AD 52 and 57—that is about twenty years after the crucifixion:

> What I received I passed on to you as of first importance: that Christ died for our sins according to the Scriptures, that he was buried, that he was raised on the third day according to the Scriptures, and that he appeared to Peter, and then to the Twelve. After that, he appeared to more than five hundred of the brothers at the same time, most of whom are still living, though some have fallen asleep. Then he appeared to James, then to all the apostles, and last of all he appeared to me also (1 Corinthians 15: 3–8).

Paul is saying that more than 500 people saw Jesus appear after his death, and that most of these are still alive. His implication is clear: 'If you don't believe me, go and ask them.' A modern court would not easily be persuaded to reject the testimony of 500 witnesses with no apparent motivation for perjury. Peter and John were telling the same story within a few weeks of the resurrection: that Jesus was the Son of God, the promised

Saviour, and that he had been raised from the dead. They were speaking not in Corinth, but in Jerusalem itself, the very place where Jesus had been executed, and where their audience was least likely to be deceived by fanciful tales of unsubstantiated wonders. Luke tells us in Acts 4 that when Peter and John preached this message many believed it, and that the total number of converts stood at about 5,000.

But is there perhaps some other explanation for what had happened which would fit the facts equally well, without requiring us to believe that Jesus had really been raised from the dead? Several suggestions have been put forward.

Hallucination?

It has been argued that those who apparently witnessed Jesus fully alive after his death could have been suffering from hallucination.[26] We have all read about people who see and hear things which are not there. But research shows that hallucinations occur only in certain clearly defined circumstances, none of which apply in this case.

First, a hallucination is a private experience. In the words of the most comprehensive recent study, 'Hallucinatory and related perceptual appearances are essentially private and subjective. That is, at the instant in time at which the experience occurs, no other person shares the same experience.'[27] This makes it impossible that the twelve disciples and 500 witnesses mentioned by Paul could have been suffering from hallucination.

Secondly, hallucinations usually occur in association with specific medical and mental conditions—schizophrenia, alcoholic psychoses, hypothyroidism, delirium, hyperventilation and others. Paul's 500 witnesses are most unlikely all to have been schizophrenics and alcoholics, and Peter and John must have been in good mental and physical health to assume the key roles they held for years afterwards.

Thirdly, the minority of hallucinations not accounted for by illness nonetheless conform to predictable patterns: they occur under certain conditions (which may be environmental, such as deprivation of water, or psychological, such as stress); they occur in persons with particular predisposing characteristics; they have positive consequences for the subject; and they conform to the expectations and assumptions of the subjects, rather than challenging these. None of these patterns is present in this instance.

We cannot therefore accept that the resurrection appearances are explicable in terms of hallucination.

A ghost?

Another possible explanation for the appearance of Jesus after his death is that the witnesses were seeing a ghost or other non-physical apparition. And indeed this was the initial reaction of the disciples: 'Jesus himself stood among them and said to them, "Peace be with you." They were startled and frightened, thinking they saw a ghost' (Luke 24:36–37). And they had reason—he appeared unexpectedly in rooms with shut doors, and disappeared as mysteriously as he had come. However, according to Luke, Jesus himself addressed this issue—and I have been unable to find any examples of ghosts who could speak in the case studies cited in Chapter 3. Jesus said to the disciples:

> 'Why are you troubled, and why do doubts rise in your minds? Look at my hands and my feet. It is I myself! Touch me and see; a ghost does not have flesh and bones, as you see I have.' When he had said this, he showed them his hands and feet. And while they still did not believe it because of joy and amazement, he asked them, 'Do you have anything here to eat?' They gave him a piece of broiled fish, and he took it and ate it in their presence (Luke 24:38–42).

John also records that on another occasion the risen Jesus appeared on the beach where the disciples were fishing, and then also ate fish (John 21); and that he allowed the doubting Thomas to touch his wounds to prove that they were real (John 20:24–29).

Apart from his physical solidity and ability to speak and eat, the risen Jesus displayed other characteristics not shared by any of the documented cases of ghosts. Most important of these was his ability to interact with the environment. One morning he appeared on the beach from which the disciples had spent a night unsuccessfully fishing, and told them where to cast the net; it came up heavy with fish (John 21:3–8). John says that Jesus 'did many other signs in the presence of the disciples' (20:30). He also told the disciples to tell the world about him, and promised that they too would have the power to perform miracles—which, according to the episodes recounted in the Book of Acts, they did.

It would therefore seem quite clear that the disciples and other witnesses of the post-mortem appearances of Jesus could not have been seeing a ghost.

Not really dead?

A ghost cannot speak, eat and interact with its environment. But a living man can. Could it be that Jesus was not dead, but had survived the crucifixion in some way? That he had been mistakenly taken down from the cross while still alive—not dead but merely unconscious—and had recovered in the cool of the tomb? This explanation of the resurrection appearances was first propounded by Venturini in the eighteenth century, and has since been put forward a number of times, notably by a heretical Muslim sect called the Ahmadiya who claimed that after he had recovered and appeared to the disciples and others, Jesus travelled north to Damascus where he met Paul, and then on to India to spread his message there.[28]

The theory that Jesus was not dead seems initially plausible. There are, however, a number of major difficulties which arise on careful consideration of its implications. First, it fails to account for some of the details given in the gospel accounts of the crucifixion and resurrection. If Jesus had not died, the problem of how he was able to eat fish and converse with his followers would be solved. But then how could he have appeared in rooms where the doors were closed (John 20:19, 26)? How could he have vanished into thin air (Luke 24:31)? What did the disciples mean when they said he was carried up into heaven (Luke 24:51)?

Furthermore, how could he have got out of the tomb? Even if he had survived six hours on the cross and a further two whole days with no food and water, would he have had the strength, wounded as he was, to unwrap himself from tightly bandaged grave-cloths, roll back a stone the size of a door and tiptoe out without disturbing a guard of Roman soldiers? And were the disciples so naive that they would not have noticed that he had not died? The improbability of it all was summarised by D.F. Strauss more than a century ago:

> It is impossible that a being who had stolen half dead out of the sepulchre, who crept about weak and ill, wanting medical treatment, who required bandaging, strengthening and indulgence . . . could have given to the disciples the impression that he was a Conqueror over death and the grave, the Prince of Life, an impression which lay at the bottom of their future ministry.[29]

This hypothesis would therefore seem to resolve only a small number of issues, at the cost of raising a much thornier set of problems. However, there is one additional factor which makes it seem not just unlikely but inconceivable.

On the evening of the crucifixion soldiers were sent to take down the bodies of Jesus and the two men crucified alongside him. The two other men were not dead, and so the soldiers broke their legs to finish them off. Jesus was found to be dead, and so his legs were not broken. But the soldiers did make absolutely sure that he was truly dead. According to John, 'one of the soldiers pierced Jesus' side with a spear, bringing a sudden flow of blood and water' (19:34). Now if you cut the flesh of a living person it bleeds. If, however, you cut the flesh of a dead person, what is released is not blood but blood and pus; the body fluids separate after death. The soldier tested, and found Jesus to be dead.

What happened to the body?

We know that the body of Jesus was laid in a rock-hewn tomb owned by Joseph of Arimathea. A guard of Roman soldiers was placed outside. On Friday night the body was there. On Sunday morning apparently it was not. What had happened to it?

The prime suspects were not the disciples, and indeed it was to prevent them from stealing the body and claiming that Jesus had risen as he foretold that the guard was placed at the tomb. But if the disciples did nonetheless succeed in removing it, then they must have known that Jesus had not been raised from the dead, and the message they preached would have been a deliberate fraud. We have already seen that this is scarcely credible in view of the circumstances.

Perhaps the Jewish or Roman authorities took the body. But both had grown increasingly uneasy as more and more people in Jerusalem joined the original followers of Jesus. The Jewish leaders were so determined to stamp it all out that they imprisoned and flogged Peter and John; the Romans feared insurrection and regarded the Christians and their talk of a Saviour and a King as a threat. The easiest and most effective way to eliminate the Christian movement would have been to produce the body. They couldn't.

Perhaps the Roman guard took the body. But would a group of Roman soldiers have enjoyed reporting to their bosses that a dead man had disappeared from the tomb they were guarding? It would be more than their lives were worth; and we do know from Matthew that they escaped punishment only by promising to swear that it was the disciples who had stolen it (28:11–15).

Perhaps someone else took the body—tomb robbers, Joseph of Arimathea or some other sympathiser. But there would seem to be no motivation for such an action; and there still remains the problem of the guard.

Perhaps the body was still in the tomb. This seems very unlikely when we remember that the disciples were teaching that Jesus had been raised from the dead, within a few weeks of his death, and a few hundred yards from the spot where he had been buried. How much attention would have been paid to them if the body were still in the tomb? Everybody must have been talking about the fact that it had disappeared leaving only the cloths in which it had been wrapped.

There seems to be no reasonable explanation for the disappearance of the body other than that Jesus really had risen from the dead.

What happened next?

If we are to conclude that Jesus did rise from the dead, then such a conclusion should be compatible with what we know of subsequent events. And so it is. Indeed, it seems to be the *only* explanation which is compatible with subsequent events.

The disciples

When Jesus was arrested and taken to the Jewish high priest, Peter followed 'at a distance' (Matthew 26:58). When the court recommended that Jesus be executed, Peter not unnaturally began to fear for his life. Such was his terror that when two serving women and some passers-by (note, a couple of cleaners and some people out walking the dog, so to speak—not the authorities) asked him three times in succession whether he had not been one of Jesus' companions, he denied even knowing him. It is hard to believe that this is the same man who a few weeks later was taken before the same court for teaching that Jesus had been raised from the dead, and that there he declared roundly that 'there is salvation in no one else, for there is no other name under heaven given among men by which we must be saved' (Acts 4:12). What could have accounted for such a transformation, if not that Peter had met the risen Jesus, as indeed is recorded in Luke 24:34 and 1 Corinthians 15:5?

The other disciples too were changed from a dispirited bunch who according to John had all gone home (John 20:10) into determined co-workers with Peter and James, prepared to sacrifice their lives if necessary.

Likewise Paul. Paul had not known Jesus before his death, and had become one of the foremost persecutors of the early Christians. What could account for his sudden metamorphosis into a travelling preacher, subject to the same persecution to the death which he had handed out to others, other than the event which Paul himself says accounted for it—his meeting with the risen Jesus near Damascus (Acts 22:4–10)?

The church

It has been said of the resurrection of Jesus that 'we are here at one of the turning points of world history: no belief in the resurrection, no Christian church'.[30] And it is at the church that we must look next.

At the time of Jesus' death the band of his committed followers numbered eleven. In addition there were people scattered throughout Palestine who had listened to his teaching, witnessed his miracles and experienced his healing. These people were with few exceptions Jews, and had remained Jews; Jesus at the point when he was crucified had made no attempt to form a new religion. This position contrasts sharply with the beginnings of other major world religions. By the time Muhammad died, for example, he had become the most powerful man in Arabia, and almost the whole peninsula had been converted to Islam. By the time the Buddha died, he had become a famous and much-respected figure, with followers spread over a wide geographical area, and was buried in the manner of a king.[31] Jesus, by contrast, died the death of a common criminal, leaving only eleven discouraged disciples and none of the organisational structures which sustained Buddhism and Islam after the death of their founders. And yet from this apparently hopeless beginning sprang the Christian church—a church now flourishing in five continents, numbering billions of members, and growing faster than any other religious movement. How could this have happened?

The answer again must lie in the resurrection. During the six weeks after Jesus died he was seen alive many times. Shortly after these appearances ended, Peter began to preach the good news that Jesus had risen from the dead, and had thereby proved himself to be the promised Saviour of mankind in exactly the way he had said he would. And there in Jerusalem, where the tomb was known to be empty, 3,000 people believed Peter's message (Acts 2:41). Peter's second sermon produced 2,000 more believers (Acts 4:4). By the end of the century there were Christian communities in more than forty towns and cities all over the Roman empire. By the middle of the second century there were churches in almost every province and beyond. By the year 300 Christians were in the majority in parts of Roman Africa and Asia Minor. In 312 the emperor Constantine himself became a Christian. [32]

This rapid expansion would have been surprising, given the fact that its founder had been put to death before it even began, even if it had occurred in a conducive atmosphere. It is the more astonishing, then, given that it did in fact take place in the face of implacable persecution. The Jewish leaders had always felt threatened by the thought of the following that Jesus might attract among their people. But as the church began to expand, the Roman authorities too began increasingly to fear the Christians as threats to the security of the empire, and began to subject them to the fiercest of punishments. This is how Tacitus describes the emperor Nero's treatment of them in AD 64:

First, then, the confessed members of the sect were arrested; next, on their disclosures, vast numbers were convicted . . . And derision accompanied their end: they were covered with wild beasts' skins and torn to death by dogs; or they were fastened on crosses, and, when daylight failed were burned to serve as lamps by night. Nero had offered his Gardens for the spectacle, and gave an exhibition in his Circus . . . Hence, in spite of a guilt which had earned the most exemplary punishment, there arose a sentiment of pity, due to the impression that they were being sacrificed not for the welfare of the state but to the ferocity of a single man (*Annals* XV xliv).

Christians were still being put to death at the beginning of the third century. Tertullian describes the martyrdom of five Christians in the year 203 in Carthage for refusing to perform sacrifices to the emperor. Despite repeated opportunities to change their minds, and in the face of entreaties from their families, they upheld their Christian convictions. Their punishment was to be thrown to wild beasts in a public amphitheatre.[33] This does not seem to have been particularly unusual.

The persecution of Christians continued until the conversion of the emperor Constantine. Since then Christianity has had its good periods and its bad periods. But always there has been expansion. Today the expansion is greatest in Asia and Africa. One historian has postulated that 'on the most sober estimate . . . by the end of the 20th century Africa south of the Sahara will be in the main a Christian continent'.[34] Millions are becoming Christians in South Korea. Things are happening in Latin America. Had Christianity depended on the eleven discouraged disciples of an executed man, it could scarcely have spread so far and so fast in the face of this persecution.

The Holy Spirit

Without the resurrection, then, it is inconceivable that the early church could have grown as it did. And yet even with the resurrection, it still seems hard to account for the rapid and recent spread of Christianity in societies so very different from the one in which it arose. And indeed Christians believe that there was, and still is, a further factor at work. Wherever Christianity spreads, people assert not just that Jesus of Nazareth was resurrected from the dead 2,000 years ago, but that in their experience he is still alive today, and that he is present not in physical but in spiritual form—a form that is still able to perform miracles and change lives. This presence is known as the Holy Spirit.

During the six weeks after Jesus died he was seen alive many times. Then one day he told his followers that they would not see him again, and that they were to remain in Jerusalem until they received the Holy Spirit. The Holy Spirit, he said, would fill them with power, and they would become his witnesses 'in Jerusalem and in all Judea and Samaria and to the end of the earth' (Acts 1:8). That is, belief in Jesus would spread throughout the world, as indeed it has been doing.

On the Day of Pentecost, the Jewish harvest festival, Jesus seemed to return to the disciples, not physically but spiritually. It was as if a violent wind filled the house where they all were. Suddenly those uneducated disciples became able to speak in foreign languages which they didn't even understand, to the astonishment of Jews from many different nations who heard them relate the works of God in their own tongues. They were given power to preach the gospel (which means 'good news'), heal the sick and perform other miracles.

Peter preached in Jerusalem that day. The 3,000 people who became Christians also experienced the Holy Spirit coming upon them. From that day to this all those who place their faith in Jesus have received this same blessing. Some have been able to speak in another language. Some have healed the sick. Some have found the love of God flowing through them. A Christian today is not simply one who believes in Jesus; he is one whose life has been changed by Jesus through the anointing of the Holy Spirit.

That is why it is common for Christians to say that they have been 'born again', or that Jesus is alive. By that they don't simply mean that they believe the resurrection of Jesus to be an historical fact; they mean that the living Jesus is part of their everyday experience. In some Christians the experience appears to be profounder and more developed than in others, but all Christians have discovered this spiritual life to some extent. This, and not only the fact that Jesus was raised from the dead, is what sustains the growth of the Christian church.

This is the unique claim of Christianity, and it is what distinguishes it from all other world religions. To be a Christian is not to belong to a particular class, race or culture, as is the case with so many other religions. There is certainly nothing particularly English about being a Christian—Christianity began in the Middle East, not in Cheltenham. To be a Christian is this: to believe that Jesus was and is the Son of God, to live according to the implications of that belief, and above all to enter into a relationship with him through the presence of the Holy Spirit. That relationship is one which Jesus promised would not be broken through death:

> I am the resurrection and the life; he who believes in me, though he die, yet shall he live, and whoever lives and believes in me shall never die (John 11:25–6).

Notes

1. Josephus: *The Jewish War*, translated with an introduction by G.A. Williamson (Harmondsworth: 1959, revised edition 1970), pp. 396–401. Some scholars doubt the authenticity of these passages, but for no clear reason other than the implications of what they contain. They certainly do not read as if written by a Christian. See also F.F. Bruce, *The New Testament Documents* (Leicester, InterVarsity Press, 1943), pp. 108–12.

2. xviii.3.3. *Flavius Josephus: Selections from his Works, with an introduction and notes by Abraham Wasserstein* (New York:1974), p. 181.

3. References given by N. Anderson, *Jesus Christ: the Witness of History* (Leicester: 1985), pp. 20–22. See also F.F. Bruce, *The New Testament Documents*, chs 9–10.

4. Jesus' claims to be the Christ: Matthew 16:13–17; John 3:17, 5:18–47, 14:1–14; Mark 14:61–62. The major Old Testament prophecies of the crucifixion of Christ are Isaiah 53 and Psalm 22.

5. Biographical details for Augustus, Herod and Quirinius are given under the appropriate headings in *The Interpreter's Dictionary of the Bible*, ed. G. A. Buttrick (Nashville: 1962). For Herod see Luke 1:5 and Matthew 2:1. Contemporary sources: Josephus, *Jewish War* and *Antiquities*. For Quirinius see Luke 2:2. Contemporary sources: Tacitus, *Annals* 3.21, 48.

6. Matthew 2:1; Luke 2:1–7. Census discussed in article 'Quirinius', *Interpreter's Dictionary*, and by F.F. Bruce, *The New Testament Documents*, pp. 86–87.

7. Jesus' early life: Mark 6:3; Matthew 13:55–56; Luke 4:16. Beginning of his ministry: Luke 3:21, 4.23; Matthew 4:12–17; Mark 1:14. John the Baptist: Josephus, *Antiquities* 18.v.2.

8. New era: Mark 1:14; Luke 4:16–21. New way: John 14:6. Eternal life: John 3:16, 11:25–26. The three dead people were the son of the widow of Nain (Luke 7:11–17); Lazarus (John 11:1–44); Jairus' daughter (Luke 8:40–56). Jesus as Son of God: John 5:19–47, 10:22–38; Mark 14:61–62.

9. The plot to kill Jesus is first recorded in John 11:45–57; see also Mark 14:1–2; Luke 22:2 and Matthew 26:3–5. Accounts of Jesus' arrest and trial are given in Matthew 26–27; Mark 14–15; Luke 22–23; John 18–19.

10. John refers to three different Passover festivals (2:13, 6:4, 11:55) covering at least AD 28–30. See F.F. Bruce, *The New*

Testament Documents, pp. 11–12.

11. The accounts of the crucifixion and resurrection are given in Matthew 27:27–end; Mark 15:16–end; Luke 23:26–end; John 19:17–end.

12. John 20–21; Acts 1:3; 1 Corinthians 15:16.

13. Summaries of the research on this point are given by F.F. Bruce in *The New Testament Documents*, and G. Johnston, 'New Testament Forms', in *A Companion to the Bible* ed. H.H. Rowley (2nd ed., Edinburgh: 1963). See also J.A.T. Robinson, *Redating the New Testament* (SCM Press: 1976).

14. For Mark see the article in *The Interpreter's Dictionary of the Bible*; for Paul's letters see G.R. Beasley-Murray, 'Introduction to the New Testament', in *A Companion to the Bible*, pp. 97–111.

15. See F.F. Bruce, *The New Testament Documents* p. 18, and G.R. Beasley-Murray, 'Introduction to the New Testament', pp. 120–22

16. An outline of the manuscript tradition is given by L.W. Hurtado, 'How the New Testament has come down to us', in *The History of Christianity* ed. T. Dowley (Tring: 1977), pp. 89–92. For more detail see N. Turner, 'The Transmission of the Text', in *A Companion to the Bible* ed. H.H. Rowley (Edinburgh: 1963), pp. 163–81; also F.F. Bruce, *The New Testament Documents*, pp. 14–20. For the discovery of the papyri see J. Romer, *Testament* (London: 1988), pp. 181–87.

17. See F.F. Bruce, *The New Testament Documents*, pp. 17–18; and J. Romer, *Testament*, pp. 183–84.

18. For background information on the various books and authors of the New Testament see F.F. Bruce, *The New Testament Documents* and G.R. Beasley-Murray, 'Introduction to the New Testament'. Good summaries are given in *The History of Christianity*, ed. T. Dowley and *The Word Illustrated Bible Handbook* ed. P. Blair (Milton Keynes: 1988).

19. Research on form and source criticism is outlined by F.F.

Bruce, *The New Testament Documents*, G.R. Beasley-Murray, 'Introduction to the New Testament', and G. Johnston, 'New Testament Forms'.

20. F.F. Bruce, 1943, p.20.

21. See F.F. Bruce, *The New Testament Documents*, pp. 16–18.

22. Apart from details recorded in the New Testament, other early historians record the lives and deaths of the apostles. The most reliable of these is Eusebius. Summaries of the information we have can be found under individual entries in F.L. Cross and E.A. Livingstone (eds), *The Oxford Dictionary of the Christian Church* (Oxford: 1974). See also F.F. Bruce, 'The History and doctrine of the Apostolic Age', in *A Companion to the Bible* ed. H.H Rowley (Edinburgh: 1963), pp. 495–522.

23. Quoted by N. Anderson, *Jesus Christ, The Witness of History*, p. 39.

24. For the archaeology see F.F. Bruce, *The New Testament Documents*, ch. 8; J. Romer, *Testament*, pp. 161–63; and J. Gray, 'Biblical Archaeology', in *A Companion to the Bible* ed. H.H. Rowley (Edinburgh: 1963), pp. 246–80.

25. See F.F. Bruce, *The New Testament Documents*, pp. 80–92; J. Gray, 'Biblical Archaeology', pp. 271–72. Ramsay quoted by Bruce, p. 43.

26. Discussed by N. Anderson, *Jesus Christ*, pp. 140–44.

27. P.D. Slade and R.P. Bentall, *Sensory Deception: a Scientific Analysis of Hallucination* (London: 1988), p. 16.

28. See N. Anderson, *Jesus Christ*, pp. 84–85, 130.

29. *Life of Jesus* (London: 1864), p. 412.

30. J.A.T. Robinson, 'Resurrection in the New Testament', *Interpreter's Dictionary*, IV, p. 48.

31. See *An Illustrated History of the World's Religions* ed. G. Parrinder (Feltham: 1983), pp. 266–71 (Buddha) and p. 469 (Mohammed).

32. See T. Dowley (ed.), *The History of Christianity*, pp. 65–68.

33. J. Robinson (ed.), *The Passion of S. Perpetua* (Cambridge: 1891). See also P. Dronke, *Women Writers of the Middle Ages* (Cambridge: 1984), pp. 1–13.
34. Stephen Neill; see A.C. Thiselton, 'An Age of Anxiety', in *The History of the Christian Church*, ed. T. Dowley p. 616.

7
THE DEATH OF JESUS

Death is the ultimate problem confronting humanity. Each one of us sooner or later must face the fact that we are to die, and that we have very little power over when it will happen. Indeed, as one writer has put it, 'What we call living can just as accurately be called dying.'[1] And yet something within us cries out that this does not seem right; death seems unnatural, an intrusion into the way things should be, a hurdle which by some means or other must be overcome. This is why mankind has always believed in an afterlife; this is the *raison d'être* of every religion; this is the reason why every attempt to enforce atheism on a people sooner or later fails. We saw in Chapter 3 that many scientists, the least given in modern society to flights of fancy, to superstition and to wishful thinking, are now convinced that life cannot be explained in solely material or physical terms, and that there is a spiritual dimension to human existence of which we must take account. And if we have a spirit which exists independently of the body before death, why should it die when the body dies?

Man's conviction that death is not part of the natural order of things has been expressed in many ways and at many times. The writer of the Book of Ecclesiastes, which is thought to date from between the third and fifth centuries BC, remarked of God that 'he has set eternity in the hearts of men'. And it is true that we never seem to feel quite at home in time. It flies; it crawls; we are so bad at measuring it that we carry it around on our wrists, and then resent its relentless ticking by. Sometimes it seems to stand still, and we catch a glimpse of timelessness. Sheldon Vanauken suggests that it is this kind of experience which demonstrates that we were meant to live not in time but in eternity:

> It suggests that we have not been or will not always be temporal creatures. It suggests that we were created for eternity. Not only are we harried by time, we seem unable, despite a thousand generations, ever to get used to it. We are always amazed at it—how fast it goes, how slowly it goes, how much of it is gone. Where, we cry, has the time gone? We aren't adapted to it, not at home in it. If that is so, it may appear as proof, or at least a powerful suggestion, that eternity exists and is our home.[2]

This is instinctively grasped by young children, who have no concept of either the passage of time or the certainty of death. Death is an idea which has to be learned slowly and in stages, starting at the age of two or three, and which is remarkably difficult to explain. It continues to seem an outrageous and intolerable proposition to many adults. I am always struck by the optimism of the US Declaration of Independence, drawn up in 1776, which states that life is not just natural but actually a human right: 'We hold these truths to be self-evident, that all men are created equal, that they are endowed by their Creator with certain inalienable rights, that among these are life, liberty and the pursuit of happiness.'

The cause of death

If death is the fundamental problem of the human condition, and if it is unnatural, then it must have, or have had, a cause. Something somewhere must have gone wrong. This proposition effectively forms the starting point and subject matter of most religions and religious philosophies. All of the major world religions offer some kind of explanation for the existence of death and some kind of strategy for dealing with it. The strategies vary, but the explanations are remarkably similar. They can be summarised in the statement that there is something wrong in the relationship between man and God (whatever is meant by God).

The Christian Bible, in both the Old and New Testaments, teaches that the responsibility for this problem lies with man; the word used to explain and describe it is sin (which comes from the Latin word for 'guilty'). In common with the other major world religions, Christianity holds that the consequence of the distance which has arisen between man and God is death. But whereas Hindus and Buddhists believe that death is followed by reincarnation, Jews, Christians and Muslims hold that it is followed by judgment. Only the New Age thinking suggests that man is fundamentally good and that there is no problem—an attractive doctrine, because it frees us from any responsibility, but one which simply does not account either for the evidence of history or for our experience of the present.

Why did Jesus die?

Most biographies have something to say about the death of their subjects, but they rarely give more than a page or two to it. By contrast the gospel writers in the New Testament devote about a third of their entire narrative to describing the events which led up to and surrounded the death of Jesus. Indeed they make it clear that death was the very purpose of his life—Jesus came in order to die.

At first sight it seems very hard to understand why Jesus should have died at all. Death is the direct consequence of sin; more particularly, it is the judgment of God on sin. Jesus, the Son of God, was without sin. So why did he die? And furthermore, what purpose could there possibly have been to his death?

The Christian teaching on this matter is well known, if little understood. Jesus died to save us from sin. And because the Christian teaching is that sin is the cause of death, this means that Jesus died to save us from death. These are the concepts we will examine in this chapter. We will look first at the nature of sin, then at the connection between sin and death, and finally at the sense in which Jesus' death is said to save us from sin and death.

Sin

We are all familiar with the word 'sin', but much of its true meaning has been lost. This is partly because of our second-hand knowledge of Christian teaching, and partly because the concept itself is a complex one—no fewer than five different Greek words are translated in the New Testament by the word 'sin', and they all have slightly different meanings.

The simplest way of looking at sin is as a series of isolated actions. This is how the Old Testament most commonly understands it. Sin is a breaking of the laws given to man by God, most particularly of the Ten Commandments. These can be divided into sins against God (worshipping other gods, worshipping idols, swearing, not keeping the Sabbath) and sins against people (not honouring your parents, committing murder or adultery, stealing or telling lies, and envy). Jesus summarised the Ten Commandments in the dual injunction to love God and to love others (Matthew 22:37–39). Sin in its broadest sense therefore consists of saying or doing things which offend against God, and saying or doing things which hurt other people. We have all done this to a greater or lesser degree, and we all know we have. The problem is that we have difficulty persuading ourselves that it really matters. The philosopher Kierkegaard put it like this:

Most people really believe that the Christian commandments (for example to love one's neighbour as oneself) are intentionally a little too severe—like putting the clock ahead half an hour to make sure of not being late in the morning.[3]

The Christian teaching (and also the Jewish and Islamic teaching) is that sin *does* matter. The fact that we have committed sins, breaking God's commandments, has the effect of separating us from the presence of God. This is the very reason why for most of us God seems remote and inaccessible— we fail to keep his commandments, and thereby create a great barrier between us and him:

> Your iniquities have separated you from your God; your sins have hidden his face from you, so that he will not hear (Isaiah 59:2).

And it is scarcely surprising that this should be so, for it is after all sin in this sense that separates human beings from one another. Infidelity, verbal or physical abuse, deceit, envy and workaholism all result in the breakdown of relationships between people. These same sins cannot be expected to foster closeness to God.

Another way of looking at sin is to see it in terms not of breaking a law but rather of a condition. This is how Jesus most commonly referred to it. Seen like this, sin is not so much about externals (such as murder) as internals (such as anger). Jesus once said:

> What comes out of a man is what defiles a man. For from within, out of the heart of man, come evil thoughts, fornication, theft, murder, adultery, coveting, wickedness, deceit, licentiousness, envy, slander, pride, foolishness. All these evil things come from within, and they defile a man (Mark 7:21–22).

The Apostle Paul expressed his own frustration at being unable to shake free from this condition in these words:

> I am unspiritual, sold as a slave to sin. I do not understand what I do. For what I want to do I do not do, but what I hate I do. . . . I know that nothing good lives in me, that is, in my sinful nature. For I have the desire to do what is good, but I cannot carry it out. For what I do is not the good I want to do; no, the evil I do not want to do—this I keep on doing (Romans 7: 14–19).

Sin is everything in me I don't like. Sin is being impatient, being shy, being afraid, being envious, being resentful. Sin is hurting others when I don't really want to, and failing to help them when I do want to. Sin is paddling my own canoe, relying on myself not God, protecting myself, trying to get my needs met independently from God. Sin is being chained to my own needs, chained to my feelings, chained to my negative thoughts, chained to my desires. It is a state in which I am trapped. Like Paul, Jesus compared it to slavery: 'Everyone who sins is a slave to sin' (John 8:34).

A third way of looking at sin is to see it not as a condition which affects the individual but as a disease which afflicts the whole of the human race—a disease of which individual sins are merely the symptoms. This is most clearly explained in theological terms by Paul, who traces it back to the story of Adam and Eve in the Garden of Eden. God created man and woman, and forbade them to eat of the tree of the knowledge of good and evil. The serpent persuaded them to do so. The immediate consequence was alienation from God, the source of life; the eventual consequence was death. 'The wages of sin is death,' Paul wrote in Romans 6:23. This is commonly referred to as original sin; the whole human race is said to suffer from its consequences, and the final consequence is death.

We are tempted to dismiss this story as unworthy of serious consideration. Debate over whether or not it is to be interpreted as literally true tends to obscure the fact that it is actually very subtly written. God is the Creator. He created a spiritual and a physical universe. He created spiritual and physical beings.

Some of those in the spiritual realm chose to rebel against him, chief among them the devil, Satan, the serpent, the deceiver, the father of lies—there are various biblical names for him. He is the personification and source of evil. The description of the eating of the fruit from the tree is a description of man's first acquaintance with evil. Evil is destructive. It brings death. It is a principle which infects the entire universe and which has infected us. We live, as Jesus' disciple John puts it, in darkness. Darkness, that is spiritual darkness, covers the world. To be in the dark is to be afraid, uncertain, lost; to lack meaning and purpose; to suffer in any of the myriad ways in which life brings us suffering. It is in this darkness that the powers sometimes contacted by mediums and in the pursuit of other occult activities are found; and it is in this darkness that we die.

Judgment

So far we have looked at the problem of sin and death largely from man's point of view. We find ourselves to be separated from God. But the Christian teaching is that God also has a perspective on the human condition. The word used in the Bible to describe the connection between sin and death from God's point of view is not separation but judgment. Death is the judgment of God on sin. If we go back to the story of Adam and Eve—which some Christians choose to take literally but which many prefer to take theologically, as a poetic description of the human condition—we find that when Adam and Eve chose to disobey God and eat from the tree of the knowledge of good and evil, they were immediately judged by God and banished from the garden. This deprived them of their close relationship with God, but it also ultimately deprived them of life itself; they became subject to death. This is explained in the story in terms of a second tree in the garden, the tree of life. When they were banished from the garden Adam and Eve lost their right to eat the fruit of this tree, and this ensured that they would one day die. They were judged by God, separated from the only source of life, and became subject for the first time to death. So sin led to separation and judgment which led to death.

But why, we might wonder, does sin matter so much? The answer lies in the holiness of God. God is holy—that is, God is pure, perfect and undefiled in a way which we can scarcely comprehend. God cannot tolerate sin any more than light can tolerate darkness; the two simply cannot mix. His natural response to sin is deep sorrow and righteous anger. If I compare myself with my fellow men and women I do not feel I should be the object of such sorrow and anger; I feel I've managed quite well really, par for the course, better than most—I'm not Nero, or Hitler, after all. But if I compare myself with a holy and perfect God I fall miserably short. Isaiah saw him in a vision, and reacted with the anguished cry, 'Woe to me, for I am a man of unclean lips' (Isaiah 6:5); he instantly recognised his own sin. Paul explained that 'all have sinned and fall short of the glory of God' (Romans 3:23).

Sin will therefore be followed by death. But the Bible teaches that death will not be the end. It will be followed by a day of universal judgment (a second judgment), and then, for those still found to be separated from God by sin, by a second death. This second death is called hell. We will look in more detail at the Last Judgment and hell in the next chapter.

There is one further point to be made. The law of sin and death, as Paul calls it, does not only affect the spiritual part of the created universe; it affects the physical part too. Just as we live under God's judgment, so does the whole earth. Instead of the perfection of the Garden of Eden, we now dwell in a flawed cosmos which is moving towards destruction. Floods, disasters and accidents of all kinds occur in a world which Paul describes as 'in bondage to decay' (Romans 8:21). This is not just a theological truth but a scientifically proven fact. We know, from the second law of thermodynamics in particular, that the entire universe is moving towards chaos and disintegration.[4] It is interesting, as we shall see in the next chapter, that this chaos and disintegration was foretold 2,000 years ago by the writer of the Book of Revelation, the last book of the Bible.

The meaning of the cross

The New Testament teaches that Jesus came for a purpose, and that the purpose was to save mankind. The prophets of the Old Testament had frequently foretold the coming of a Saviour, a Messiah, who would rescue the people and establish God's kingdom on earth. John the Baptist taught that this man was coming, and Jesus claimed to be him. He began his life of teaching with the following statement—a quotation from the prophet Isaiah:

> The Spirit of the Lord God is upon me,
>   because the Lord has anointed me
> to bring good tidings to the afflicted;
>   he has sent me to bind up the brokenhearted,
> to proclaim liberty to the captives,
>   and the opening of the prison to those who are bound;
> to proclaim the year of the Lord's favour (Luke 4:18–19).

Jesus came to bring freedom to man. He came as God's solution to the problem of the human condition, to rescue man from his bondage to sin. He achieved this not by his teaching, or by his miracles, but by his death—and in particular by his death on the cross.

The cross has always been crucial (the word 'crucial' comes from the Latin word for 'cross') to the Christian faith. It was crucial for Paul, who recognised that looked at from a purely human perspective it didn't seem to make much sense; 'for the message of the cross is foolishness to those who are perishing, but to us who are being saved it is the power of God' (1 Corinthians 1:18). The cross is the jewel which glitters at the centre of Christianity, priceless beyond measure. It is, however, like a jewel not only in its preciousness, but also in its many facets. The cross is like a cut diamond; it can be viewed from many angles, through any one of its faces. It speaks in different ways in different historical periods and to different cultures. The central message does not change, but the perspective from which we look at it may. This is reflected in the many different statements about the cross which we find in the New Testament.

Perhaps the most basic way of looking at the cross is to see it as both a sign and a promise: a sign of victory over death and a promise that we may share in that victory. Paul compared Jesus' resurrection to the firstfruits of a harvest:

> Christ has indeed been raised from the dead, the firstfruits of those who have fallen asleep. For since death came through a man, the resurrection of the dead comes also through a man. For as in Adam all die, so in Christ all will be made alive (1 Corinthians 15:20–22).

He puts it more simply when he writes that God raised Jesus from the dead to show us that he can raise us from the dead too:

> And if the Spirit of him who raised Jesus from the dead is living in you, he who raised Christ from the dead will also give life to your mortal bodies through his Spirit, who lives in you (Romans 8:11).

Jesus himself promised that he was going to heaven to prepare a place for us:

> In my Father's house are many rooms. . . . I am going there to prepare a place for you. And if I go and prepare a place for you, I will come back and take you to be with me that you also may be where I am (John 14:2–4).

So the Christian belief is that just as Jesus survived death, so through him can we. Jesus is the only person in history to have even claimed this power, never mind substantiated it in such a dramatic way.

Secondly, the cross represents a victory over sin. We find ourselves estranged from God, and the cross reconciles us to God. It is God's sign of forgiveness, God's statement that our failures are no longer important because Jesus has paid the price for them. This is the sense in which Jesus died to save us from our sin. We should have died, for we have sinned, and we are separated from God and under the judgment of God. That is the human condition in which we all share. Instead, Jesus died as a substitute for us. He took God's judgment on himself on behalf of mankind. This is why it is so important to realise that Jesus was both man and God; as a man he took the full force of God's judgment; as God, he deflected it from man. And this is why he cried out on the cross, 'My God, my God, why have you forsaken me?'—meaning not, why are you letting this happen; but why aren't you there, why am I cut off from you, the source of life; why am I suddenly in this darkness, this horror, instead of being in light; *where have you gone?*

This is how three different New Testament writers put it:

We implore you, on Christ's behalf: be reconciled to God. God made him who had no sin to be sin for us, so that in him we might become the righteousness of God (2 Corinthians 5:12).

For Christ died for sins once for all, the righteous for the unrighteous, to bring you to God (1 Peter 3:18).

Just as man is destined to die once, and after that to face judgment, so Christ was sacrificed once to take away the sins of many people, and he will appear a second time, not to bear sin, but to bring salvation to those who are waiting for him (Hebrews 9:27–28).

On the cross therefore Jesus died as our representative, taking on himself the full force of the judgment of God on human sin, suffering on our behalf in order to set us free. In Christ I now find myself to be both 'righteous'—that is, innocent—and 'justified'—that is, acquitted.

After his death, Jesus was judged for the life he had lived. It was found to be perfect, and he was therefore released from death and raised to eternal life. And because we have now been set free from the prison of sin by his death on our behalf, we too may be judged perfect and raised to eternal life:

> Therefore, there is now no condemnation for those who are in Christ Jesus, because through Christ Jesus the law of the Spirit of life set me free from the law of sin and death. For what the law was powerless to do in that it was weakened by the sinful nature, God did by sending his own Son in the likeness of sinful man to be a sin offering. And so he condemned sin in sinful man, in order that the righteous requirements of the law might be fully met in us, who do not live according to the sinful nature but according to the Spirit (Romans 8:1–8).

This does not of course mean that when we come to the Day of Judgment our lives will be found to have been perfect in the same way that Jesus' life was perfect. What it does mean is that as we have already been forgiven, acquitted and justified, our shortcomings will be overlooked. The cross was about man's sin. The Day of Judgment, for those who have accepted Jesus' victory on their behalf, will be about his perfection.

So the cross is a victory over death, and a victory over sin. A third way it can be looked at is as a victory over evil—which is of course the source of sin, and therefore of death. This is the biggest, and for me the most meaningful, way of looking at the cross. Man is deceived, cut off from God, floundering in darkness. The whole world is infected by this darkness, and vibrates with the influence of hostile powers. Everything is sullied, everything is unsatisfactory, everywhere there is pain and suffering and unfulfilled longing. Jesus came into the world to release us from this darkness by conquering the evil which is its source:

> Since the children have flesh and blood, he too shared in their humanity so that by his death he might destroy him who holds the

power of death—that is, the devil—and free those who all their lives were held in slavery by their fear of death (Hebrews 2:14–15).

The cross stands out against this black background like light cutting through darkness, a living demonstration that there is another way, a better way, and that through Jesus we may enter another realm—a realm of light and love, of freedom and meaning. Jesus came, in his own words, as a light to the world, so that no one who believed in him should stay in darkness. His story is a story of the encounter between the forces of darkness— most particularly Satan himself—and the light of God. During his life on earth Jesus was tempted by Satan, but resisted; he freed one person after another from the grip of evil; and finally he overcame Satan's attempt to destroy him on the cross. And it is through the cross that we find forgiveness for sin and release from the power of evil over us. Satan may still tempt us, but the power of the Holy Spirit sent by Jesus is available to us, and we may like Jesus resist him. Evil may still afflict us, but we may now appeal directly to God who will enable us to cope with whatever situation we find ourselves in. This is what was achieved on the cross.

Let us summarise. Jesus, the Son of God, was—in contrast to all other members of the human race—free from sin. Sin is spiritual death, and its eventual consequence is physical death. Jesus was spiritually alive, in full communication with God and perfect in his keeping of God's laws. When put to death on the cross and brought under judgment he therefore did not remain dead. This he demonstrated by physically leaving the tomb. But the cross was more than just a demonstration of Jesus' identity— although it was that. It was a watershed for the whole human race. It was the means by which we can all have spiritual life, and therefore immunity from death. The cross was a victory over death and sin and evil. Consider the following passage:

For God so loved the world that he gave his one and only Son, that whoever believes in him shall not perish but have eternal life. For God did not send his Son into the world to condemn the world, but to save the world through him (John 3:16–17).

In practice, for the Christian being 'saved' means three things. First through the cross the power of evil is broken and we are set free to live a different quality of life now—a life in which we are not enmeshed in sin and trapped in darkness, and in which we are not, in the words Jesus quoted from Isaiah, afflicted, broken-hearted, captive and imprisoned. In this new life we are fully restored to a close relationship with God; we become able to speak to him and listen to him in prayer, and we have access to his healing power.

Secondly, we are set free from sin, both our past sins and the principle of sin within us. Through the cross we find forgiveness for our failures, inadequacies and shortcomings; through the cross we are freed from our slavery to our own needs, feelings, negative thoughts and desires.

Thirdly, through the cross we are set free from death, by the promise that when we do die Jesus will raise us up in some way (which we cannot fully understand) and give us a new life, just as he was raised himself before the eyes of so many people. The cross is not therefore just something abstract. It is indeed a victory over evil, over sin, and over death. But it is more. The cross is an experience. I may travel along the path Jesus travelled now, today; I do not have to wait until I die. And I may therefore enter into eternal life now; I do not have to wait until the Day of Judgment. Paul wrote:

I have been crucified with Christ and I no longer live, but Christ lives in me. The life I live in the body, I live by faith in the Son of God, who loved me and gave himself for me (Galatians 2:20).

Eternal life begins now

So, how, exactly may we benefit from what Christ accomplished on the cross? How do I myself actually get hold of that victory? What is the mechanism by which I personally may benefit from Jesus' resurrection? How, in other words, does it work?

The situation we inherit is this. We are separated from God. God is the source of life. We are therefore separated from the source of life. Where there is no life there is death. We are therefore doomed to die. We suffer death in two stages: spiritual death, which we are all already experiencing, and physical death, which is the inevitable consequence of spiritual death. This is the problem of the human condition.

Jesus taught that there is one way, and one way only, out of this predicament: to accept that he really did die on my behalf and to believe in him. He has overcome death, and has the power to save us from death. We have a choice: we may choose life, or death. It is entirely up to us. Jesus said that

> whoever believes in the Son has eternal life, but whoever rejects the Son will not see life, for God's wrath remains on him (John 3:36).

He also said:

> My Father's will is that everyone who looks to the Son and believes in him shall have eternal life, and I will raise him up at the last day (John 6:40).

All we have to do is recognise that we are lost, cut off from God, and struggling with sin; that we fall far short of what God intended us to be, and that if we ask him to he will act to save us. This is what Jesus meant when he urged people to repent. The word 'repent' literally means 'think again'. We are to change the direction of our thinking and thus of our lives.

It is however important to understand what Jesus meant by belief. Belief for the Christian is something active; it is not merely a matter of intellectual acceptance. A Christian is not just someone who believes in his head that Jesus was the Son of God, or even that he came to earth to save mankind—it is often said that even the devil believes that. Christian belief implies much more than this. First of all it implies trust—a Christian does not just accept Jesus as the Son of God; he or she is prepared to stake the whole of life on that being true. Secondly, it implies commitment; a Christian is a person for whom commitment to Christ is stronger than any other commitment. And thirdly, belief implies obedience; a Christian is one who seeks in every area of life to obey Christ as he speaks through the Bible, through prayer, and through other people. Christianity is therefore not only about head belief; to be a Christian involves the whole of life—spirit, mind, will, emotions and body. This is what Jesus meant by belief, and this is the kind of belief which brings true freedom.

In order to receive this freedom, and to know without doubt that we have received it, one further thing is required. We must ask for it. When we do this something quite extraordinary happens. We are 'born again'—an overquoted and misunderstood phrase, but nonetheless one which corresponds to a real experience. This is how Jesus explained it to the Pharisee Nicodemus:

> 'I tell you the truth, no one can see the kingdom of God unless he is born again.' 'How can a man be born when he is old?' Nicodemus asked. 'Surely he cannot enter a second time into his mother's womb to be born!' Jesus answered, 'I tell you the truth, no one can enter the kingdom of God unless he is born of water [baptism] and the Spirit. Flesh gives birth to flesh, but the Spirit gives birth to spirit. You should not be surprised at my saying, "You must be born again." The wind blows wherever it pleases. You hear its sound, but you cannot tell where it comes from or where it is going. So it is with everyone born of the Spirit' (John 3:3–8).

The Spirit to which Jesus is referring is the Holy Spirit, and it is through the Holy Spirit that our relationship with God is restored. The Holy Spirit is a person, whom Jesus described as 'the Comforter', and whom he sent to us to give us spiritual life—that is, to restore us to a state of union with God. When we receive the Holy Spirit we cease to be spiritually dead and become spiritually alive; we are born again in our spirit. The immediate consequence of this is that we enter into a relationship with God. In particular, it means that we can talk to him in prayer, and hear him speaking to us. The barrier is gone. Paul describes the Holy Spirit as a 'deposit guaranteeing our inheritance' (Ephesians 1:14), a proof that we have been set free from the law of sin and death and that as our spirits have been restored to life, so one day our bodies will be. The Holy Spirit is a first instalment of what is to come, a guarantee that the rest will follow.

This means instant freedom from the law of sin and death. Furthermore, it is not just a theoretical freedom; it is a freedom which we can know and experience every day. It means being, for the first time in your life, free to be the person God intended you to be. It means having the assurance that God loves you. It means having a purpose in life and a promise of life after death. It means finding you have the resources to cope with whatever life flings at you. It is like coming out of a cage. This is the heart of the Christian life, and it starts now. An excellent description of this new life is given by the Apostle Paul in chapter 8 of his letter to the Romans. He makes a number of points.

1. As soon as we receive the new life we are released from the consequences of sin and death. The question 'Have I been good enough?' is no longer necessary; as Paul says, 'There is now no condemnation for those who are in Christ Jesus, because through Christ Jesus the law of the Spirit of life set me free from the law of sin and death.'

2. By this new life we are given power to live without sin. This does not however come automatically. If we choose to believe in Christ, we are born again spiritually and thus freed from sin. But we still have to decide which way to live; if we consciously seek to live in the power of our new relationship with the Holy Spirit, we will not be dragged back down into sin. But if we do not do this then the power will go and the old habits take over again:

> Those who live according to the sinful nature have their minds set on what that nature desires; but those who live in accordance with the Spirit have their minds set on what the Spirit desires. The mind of sinful man is death, but the mind controlled by the Spirit is life and peace (Romans 8:5–6)

This means that in practice the Christian life consists of learning to listen to the voice of the Spirit and then seeking the Spirit's help to obey.

3. We can confidently expect that when we die we will be raised from the dead:

> And if the Spirit of him who raised Jesus from the dead is living in you, he who raised Christ from the dead will also give life to your mortal bodies through his Spirit, who lives in you (Romans 8:11).

4. The new life is characterised by a new relationship with God; we become the children of God, and we may have the same relationship with God that Jesus had. This means we can speak directly and personally with him. We can hear him speak directly and personally to us as his children, loving us, guiding us and directing our lives:

> Those who are led by the Spirit of God are sons of God. For you did not receive a spirit that makes you a slave again to fear, but you received a Spirit of sonship. And by him we cry, 'Abba [Daddy], Father.' ... Now if we are children, then we are heirs—heirs of God and co-heirs with Christ (Romans 8:14–15,17).

5. For the time being we must continue to live in a spoiled world dominated by sin, although never in the same defeated way as before. But one day this world will end, to be replaced by a new world order which will be altogether different:

> I consider that our present sufferings are not worth comparing with the glory that will be revealed in us. The creation waits in eager expectation for the sons of God to be revealed. For the creation was subjected to frustration, not by its own choice, but by the will of the one who subjected it, in hope that the creation itself will be liberated from its bondage to decay and brought into the glorious freedom of the children of God (Romans 8:19–21).

6. The Spirit helps us to relate to God, even when we are at a loss:

> We do not know what we ought to pray for, but the Spirit himself intercedes for us with groans that words cannot express (Romans 8:26).

7. God loves us, and we have nothing, nothing whatever, to fear:

> If God is for us, who can be against us? He who did not spare his own Son, but gave him up for us all—how will he not also, along with him, graciously give us all things? Who will bring any charge against those whom God has chosen? It is God who justifies. Who is he that condemns? [And later:] I am convinced that neither death nor life, neither angels nor demons, neither the present nor the future, nor any powers, neither height nor depth, nor anything else in all creation, will be able to separate us from the love of God that is in Christ Jesus our Lord (Romans 8:31–34, 38–39).

If I believe in Jesus, I will be restored to a relationship with God through the Holy Spirit, whom he promised to send to anyone who asked for him in his name. If I have the Spirit, I have life, for the Holy Spirit breathes life into my spirit. If I have life, I will be freed from the consequences of physical death; my body will still die, but my spirit will remain alive.

All of this depends on the death of Jesus and would not have been possible without it. What happens after that is the subject of the next chapter.

Notes

1. J. Blanchard, *Whatever Happened to Hell?* (Darlington: 1993), p. 46.
2. Quoted by Blanchard, p. 69.
3. *Faber Book of Aphorisms* (London: 1970), p. 80.
4. P. Davies, *God and the New Physics* (London: 1983), p. 10.

8

WHAT HAPPENS WHEN WE DIE?

We come now to look at the Christian teaching on life after death. Christianity is the religion with which most of us in this country naturally identify, even if only to the extent of getting married in church and putting 'C of E' on medical forms. We tend therefore to regard ourselves as being familiar with its teaching. What we often fail to realise, however, is the extent to which we misunderstand that teaching—although this is scarcely surprising when we consider that most of us receive it at umpteenth hand, filtered through centuries of inaccurate representation, adulterated with concepts from other sources, and viewed through a pair of thoroughly twentieth-century spectacles. And our misconceptions are rarely more pronounced than when we consider the Christian teaching on life after death.

Most people know that Jesus taught that there is a heaven and a hell. Our understanding of what he said goes something like this. God, as my three-year-old announced confidently one day, is in the sky. The place where he is is called heaven. One day we might go to heaven. There we will sing, play harps, sit on clouds and try to enjoy ourselves for ever and ever.

The problem with this concept of heaven is that it does not sound very enticing. Prime Minister David Lloyd George spoke for most of us when he wrote:

When I was a boy, the thought of heaven used to frighten me more than the thought of hell. I pictured heaven as a place where there would be perpetual Sundays with perpetual services, from which there would be no escape, as the Almighty, assisted by cohorts of angels, would always be on the lookout for those who did not attend.[1]

So much for heaven. If we don't get to heaven we fear that we will be sent to hell. We envisage hell as a place of fire and worms and darkness and little black devils, the stuff of which nightmares are made. Milton described it like this:

A dungeon horrible, on all sides round
As one great Furnace flam'd, yet from those flames
No light, but rather darkness visible
Serv'd only to discover sights of woe,
Regions of sorrow, doleful shades, where peace
And rest can never dwell, hope never comes
That comes to all; but torture without end
Still urges, and a fiery Deluge, fed
With ever-burning Sulphur unconsum'd
                    (*Paradise Lost* I 61–69)

Our understanding is that which of these places we go to will depend on whether we have been good enough. We all hope that we will have been, not because we like the sound of heaven much (we would far rather stay here), but because we like the sound of hell even less (though we can't really bring ourselves to believe that this is what a God of love can possibly have in mind). In any case, we all have nagging doubts that when it comes down to it we might not have been good enough!

This picture is both naive and oversimplified. Such concepts of heaven and hell do have their basis in the Bible, but they owe more to the popular religion of the Middle Ages than to the teaching of Jesus. Faced with the task of communicating the Christian faith to an almost entirely illiterate population, the medieval church relied a great deal on visual images. It became common practice to decorate the walls of churches with paintings illustrating the life of Christ and scenes from the Bible, including the Last Judgment. Heaven was usually portrayed as rows of saints in flowing robes, sitting on thrones ranged to each side of the throne of Christ. But it was the depiction of hell that gave free rein to the imagination of the medieval artist. Sinners were shown suspended from the genitals, stirred in boiling cauldrons by devils equipped with what look like black fondue forks, force-fed red-hot coins and sucked by snakes.[2]

As we stand now before such pictures we instinctively realise that this must be at best a gross oversimplification of the true teaching, and at worst is to be taken no more seriously as a description of what is to come than are the paintings of the modern surrealists. And so we remark to ourselves that surely nobody expects us to believe *that* kind of nonsense any more.

Written sources—the New Testament

Fortunately, however, we have direct access to a great deal of more accurate information on this subject within the pages of the New Testament.

Much of the teaching of Jesus was concerned with what happens when we die, and it is recorded in the gospels—whose authority and reliability we examined in Chapter 6. Alongside the teaching of Jesus we have the teaching of Paul, who as we have seen claimed to have received it supernaturally from Jesus. Paul's teaching is recorded in the Book of Acts, written by Luke, the author of the fourth gospel, and in the letters written to the early churches by Paul himself. Although original in his approach, Paul's teaching is completely consistent with that of Jesus as later recorded in the gospels, and he personally, as we saw in Chapter 6, had so little to gain and so much to lose from his leadership of the church that we can be confident of his sincerity. He has therefore always been accepted as a genuine authority on spiritual matters.

The third principal source in the New Testament on life after death is John, the author of the Book of Revelation, traditionally identified with John the disciple of Jesus and writer of the fourth gospel, but about whom we have far less information. His prophecy is, however, also consistent with both the teaching of Jesus and Paul and the prophetic writings of the Old Testament. Finally there is Peter, Jesus' most passionate disciple, author of two letters.

These writings have traditionally been regarded as a whole, together reflecting the teaching of Jesus, both because of their inner consistency and because of the evidence subsequent to the resurrection of Jesus that something quite remarkable was happening in and through these early Christians. And taken as a whole, the pages of the New Testament do contain a clear, plausible and comprehensible explanation of what happens when we die. In this chapter I shall therefore not confine myself to the teaching of Jesus alone, but look to the New Testament in its entirety. I will, however, always attribute what is said to the individual sources.

The Second Coming of Jesus

The prophets of the Old Testament had foreseen the coming of a Saviour who would establish a kingdom on earth in which God would be at the centre, and where his people would be restored to their rightful status. Jesus had claimed to be this Saviour, and had been widely accepted as such. His execution had therefore led to very great disappointment and disillusionment. But Jesus had taught that these predictions were to be fulfilled in a way only glimpsed by the later prophets, and far more remarkable than that which had traditionally been expected. He taught that he would come not once but twice, and that it would be his *second* coming which would finally establish the kingdom of God on earth. He urged the disciples to be always prepared for his return, and to work meanwhile to spread the good news of the gospel to all nations. He explained that his second coming would inaugurate a series of cataclysmic events, and that these would lead up to the establishment of a universal reign of righteousness and peace on earth.

His first demonstration that this teaching would be fulfilled was his resurrection. Jesus is not dead; he is waiting. Meanwhile he is alive and active, praying for the church, preparing a place for us in heaven, and pouring out his Spirit on earth.

All this seems rather far-fetched. But Christians believe it for a number of sound reasons. First, because of the resurrection. Jesus said he would rise from the dead, and he did. So when he said he would come again, it seems reasonable to believe him. Secondly, because all the New Testament writers are united on the importance of this teaching; between them they mention the second coming no fewer than 318 times.[3] Thirdly, because every Christian has first-hand experience of the outpouring of the Spirit. And finally, because every Christian has discovered that prayer in the name of Jesus is answered.

And so the second coming of Jesus is the great event to which all Christians look forward. It will be heralded by certain signs, first of which is the end of the age.

The end of the age

We saw in Chapter 5 that the Old Testament prophets foretold a future Day of Judgment and destruction, which they referred to as 'the Day of the Lord'. They insisted that the created universe would come to an end: 'All the stars of the heavens will be dissolved, and the sky rolled up like a scroll' (Isaiah 34:4). On that day evil and sin will be destroyed, and shelter given to those who have sought righteousness and humility (Zephaniah 1:18–2:3). This will happen in the same way that the world was created in the first place—at the instigation of God. A new world will then be created to replace the old, corrupt one.

In the beginning you laid the foundations of the earth,
     and the heavens are the work of your hands.
They will perish, but you remain;
     they will wear out like a garment.
Like clothing you will change them
     and they will be discarded (Psalm 102).

These prophecies were recalled and confirmed by Jesus himself, most clearly on one occasion (recorded in Mark 13, Luke 21 and Matthew 24–25) when the disciples asked him what the signs of the end of the age would be. Jesus replied that first of all there would be a period of wars, earthquakes and famines; that then there would be persecution, and then the darkening of sun, moon and stars foretold by Isaiah. After a time in which many false prophets will roam the earth, he himself would return:

> They will see the Son of Man coming on the clouds of the sky, with power and great glory. And he will send his angels with a loud trumpet call, and they will gather his elect from the four winds, from one end of the heavens to the other (Matthew 24:30).

This is the second coming. It will be followed by the resurrection of the dead and the Day of Judgment.

Apart from describing this sequence of events, Jesus made two further significant points. First, the passing away of heaven and earth is to be regarded not as the end of something but rather as the beginning of something—he likened it to 'the beginning of birth-pains' (Matthew 24:8). This is consonant with our earlier observation that Jesus was concerned primarily with our eventual, eternal destination, and not with what precedes it. Secondly, all this will occur suddenly and with no warning, and so we should be prepared for it at all times. This means that the periodic attempts which have been made to identify the date of the end of the world are a vain exercise.

These warnings of destruction are echoed elsewhere in the

New Testament. Peter points out that destruction will come, but only as a last resort, and as a necessary prelude to reconstruction:

> He is patient with you, not wanting anyone to perish, but everyone to come to repentance. But the day of the Lord will come like a thief. The heavens will disappear with a roar; the elements will be destroyed by fire, and the earth and everything in it will be laid bare. . . . That day will bring about the destruction of the heavens by fire, and the elements will melt in the heat. But in keeping with his promise we are looking forward to a new heaven and a new earth, the home of righteousness (2 Peter 3:7–13).

Paul picks up the image of childbirth in Romans chapter 8, repeating that 'the whole creation has been groaning as in the pains of childbirth right up to the present time', but promising like Peter that it 'will be liberated from its bondage to decay and brought into the glorious freedom of the children of God'. In other words, the world, like us, is flawed and subject to decay; and like us it will need to die and be recreated.

The most detailed description of the destruction of heaven and earth at the end of the age is given in the last book of the Bible, the Book of Revelation. It was written towards the end of the first century, belongs to a genre of literature known as apocalyptic (from the Greek word for 'uncover') and is notoriously difficult to interpret. What is clear, however, is that its central theme is the struggle against evil. This struggle is played out on three different levels.

First, there is the battle of the individual believer to hold fast to his faith in the face of all that would prevent him.

Secondly, there is the historical battle caused by the presence of evil within society. John portrays this in obscure allegorical terms, and may have been predicting particular historical events or just illustrating the principles which lie behind what happens—and which we have seen at work in our own times in, for example, the Second World War, in Iraq, and in Bosnia.

And thirdly, there is the cosmological struggle between good and evil, which is the fundamental one, and which is reflected in the other two. This is the struggle which was won in principle by Christ on the cross, and will be finally won in practice only when the source of evil, the devil or Satan, is bound and destroyed. John describes it in terms of earthquakes, the blackening of the sun, a moon of blood, stars falling to earth, and the destruction of land and sky; a bottomless pit is opened, and fire, smoke and sulphur released over the earth. The 'spirits of demons' gather an army of kings to fight the Battle of Armageddon, the ultimate attempt of evil to take control of the world. But then John sees this:

> I saw heaven standing open and there before me was a white horse, whose rider is called Faithful and True. With justice he judges and makes war. His eyes are like blazing fire, and on his head are many crowns. . . . The armies of heaven were following him, riding on white horses and dressed in fine linen, white and clean. Out of his mouth comes a sharp sword with which to strike down the nations. . . . He treads the winepress of the fury of the wrath of God Almighty. On his robe and on his thigh he has this name written: King of Kings and Lord of Lords. . . . Then I saw the beast and the kings of the earth and their armies gathered together to make war against the rider on the horse and his army. But the beast was captured, and with him the false prophet. . . . The two of them were thrown alive into the fiery lake of burning sulphur. The rest of them were killed with the sword that came out of the mouth of the rider on the horse (Revelation 19:11-22).

Then John sees an angel coming down from heaven, with a key and a chain; he locks 'the dragon, that ancient serpent, who is the devil, or Satan' into an abyss. After 'a thousand years' Satan will be released, and there will be another battle; this time he will be thrown into the lake of burning sulphur with the beast and the false prophet. The battle against evil will have been won, and God's plan can now come into effect:

Then I saw a new heaven and a new earth, for the first heaven and the first earth had passed away (21:1).

John expresses himself in passages such as these in the imaginative language of vision, and the Book of Revelation is best read in these terms; it does not present itself as a literal description of future events but rather as a series of pictures representing a final struggle with evil and its embodiment, Satan. It is striking that despite the poetic presentation, the final victory over evil is the same as that described by Jesus, Paul and Peter in the more ordinary terms cited above.

Resurrection

We know that when we die our bodies will be buried, or cremated, and will exist no more. We believe that our spirits will however remain alive, and continue to exist in paradise or Hades. But will we always exist in this bodiless state? Or will our bodies somehow be restored to us—raised again, or 'resurrected', to use the technical term?

The doctrine of resurrection is hard to understand, because although we are told *what* will happen (that we will receive new bodies), and *when* it will happen (at the end of the age), it is far from clear *how* it will happen. We know that the Jews had not traditionally believed in the survival of the body, but that towards the end of the period which preceded the birth of Jesus the Pharisees had begun to teach it. We also know that both Jesus and Paul taught the doctrine of resurrection—Paul apparently proclaimed it so adamantly that in Athens his hearers thought he was telling them about two new gods, Jesus and Resurrection![4]

During his ministry Jesus often referred to his own future resurrection. Familiar as they must have been with the Jewish doctrine, his disciples still seem to have had difficulty getting their minds round what he meant, doubtless wondering whether

he expected to be taken literally, or whether he was speaking
figuratively in some way:

> Jesus gave them orders not to tell anyone what they had seen until
> the Son of Man had risen from the dead. They kept the matter to
> themselves, discussing what 'rising from the dead' meant (Mark
> 9:9–10).

Some theologians today struggle with the same issue, claiming
that Christ's resurrection could not actually have happened but is
to be interpreted metaphorically; that is, that it must be a fiction
which stands for something else—the survival of the spirit,
perhaps. But as we have seen, the evidence for the bodily
resurrection of Christ is very hard to dismiss. Furthermore, Jesus
demonstrated his power to raise people bodily from the dead by
actually doing it on three earlier occasions, to the astonishment
of everyone concerned. Once he restored the twelve-year-old
daughter of a man named Jairus to life after she had died and
mourning had already begun:

> 'Stop wailing,' Jesus said. 'She is not dead but asleep.' They
> laughed at him, knowing that she was dead. But he took her by the
> hand and said, 'My child, get up!' Her spirit returned, and at once
> she stood up. Then Jesus told them to give her something to eat
> (Luke 8:52–55).

Two details of this story are particularly interesting: first, that
Jesus refers to her (bodily) as 'asleep'; and secondly, that her
spirit 'returned'—her body was sleeping, and her spirit had
remained alive. This is the most natural view to take of those
passages where the dead are referred to as 'asleep'—what is
sleeping is the body, not the spirit.[5]

On another occasion Jesus restored the only son of a woman
who lived in a village called Nain from death to life—this time
from the coffin (Luke 7). But the third instance is perhaps more

striking still. Lazarus, the brother of Jesus' friends Mary and Martha, had died, been wrapped in grave-cloths and buried for four days when Jesus reached Bethany, the village where they lived. Martha knew that her brother would 'rise again in the resurrection at the last day'. But Jesus said,

> I am the resurrection and the life. He who believes in me will live, even though he dies, and whoever lives and believes in me will never die.

Martha replied that she did believe, and knew him to be 'the Christ, the Son of God'. Then Jesus went straight to the tomb, ordered the stone to be removed, and commanded the decaying Lazarus to come out. And so he did. This single event gave Jesus such a large following that the chief priests began to plot how to kill Lazarus and so remove this uncomfortably powerful evidence that Jesus was indeed who he claimed to be (John 11:1–44, 12:9–11).

Here we may remark that the same point applies to these extraordinary passages as to those recording the resurrection of Jesus himself—they may seem hard to believe now, but they were written well within living memory of the events they describe, and would have been no easier to believe then. Indeed, had they not been based on generally recognised fact, they would have made the early church into a laughing stock.

If we believe these accounts, it seems that Jesus raised three people bodily from the dead as a sign of his power over death, and that he then rose from the dead himself in an even more spectacular way, not merely by a revival of his old body but by the acquisition of a new 'spiritual' body and a new spiritual life. In giving a temporary resurrection to Jairus's daughter, the son of the widow of Nain, and Lazarus, Jesus was pointing the way to a permanent resurrection which he demonstrated himself and which one day we shall all experience.

> And this is the will of him who sent me, that I shall lose none of all
> that he has given me, but raise them up at the last day. For my
> Father's will is that everyone who looks to the Son and believes in
> him shall have eternal life, and I will raise him up at the last day
> (John 6:39–40).

Paul also taught clearly that the dead will be raised, and that this
will happen when Christ comes again at the end of the age:

> The Lord himself will come down from heaven, with a loud
> command, with the voice of the archangel and with the trumpet call
> of God, and the dead in Christ will rise first (1 Thessalonians 4:16).

So Christianity teaches that we should look forward to a special
day, the day of the return of Jesus and the resurrection of the
dead. On that day, however, it is not only the dead who will be
changed, but also those who are alive. Paul goes on to explain
that after the dead are raised, 'we who are still alive and left will
be caught up together with them in the clouds to meet the Lord in
the air. And so we will be with the Lord for ever' (1
Thessalonians 4:17). This fits in with what Jesus said about men
being snatched from their work in the fields, and women from
their task of grinding the wheat (Matthew 24:40–41).

It is therefore clear that both Jesus and Paul taught that we will
be raised from the dead. But it may well occur to us to wonder
what this will mean in practice. Does it mean skeletons pulling
themselves out of the ground to be reclothed with flesh, as for
example the Renaissance artist Signorelli painted it in the
cathedral of Orvieto? Does it mean tomb lids creaking open and
people climbing out, as often carved above the doors of Gothic
cathedrals? Does it mean the sea washing up bodies, and wild
animals disgorging missing limbs, as depicted in medieval
manuscript illustrations? This sounds implausible, so perhaps it
means the provision of new bodies to replace the old ones? After
all, apparently the ingredients are easily obtained; all one needs

is some calcium, potassium, sulphur, phosphorus, charcoal and sodium, together with a little iron and a lot of water.[6]

Paul turned his attention to this issue in his letters to the Corinthians, who appear to have continued to believe the traditional Greek view that the soul is immortal but the body perishable. He insists that we will be given new bodies, but that they will not be the same as our present ones. This would fit with what we observed in Chapter 6 about the nature of Jesus' resurrection body—he could, for example, appear in a room of which all the doors were locked, although he was so solid that he could be touched. And so Paul describes these new bodies as spiritual rather than natural, and imperishable rather than perishable, and immortal rather than mortal—although elsewhere he too talked of 'somehow' attaining to the resurrection of the dead:

> I declare to you, brothers, that flesh and blood cannot inherit the kingdom of God, nor does the perishable inherit the imperishable. Listen, I tell you a mystery: we will not all sleep [die], but we will all be changed—in a flash, in the twinkling of an eye, at the last trumpet. For the trumpet will sound, the dead will be raised imperishable, and we will be changed. For the perishable must clothe itself with the imperishable, and the mortal with immortality. When the perishable has been clothed with the imperishable, and the mortal with immortality, then the saying that is written will come true: 'Death has been swallowed up in victory.' . . . Thanks be to God! He gives us the victory through our Lord Jesus Christ (1 Corinthians 15:50–57).

It seems therefore that we are to conclude that our resurrection bodies will be recognisably ours, but that they will be different from our present bodies.

The Last Judgment

The Old Testament prophecies of a 'Day of the Lord' clearly spoke not only of the coming of a Saviour, but also of judgment.

Zephaniah describes it as a day of wrath on which the sinful will be destroyed. Daniel regards it as a day when the Lord's people will be justified, so that they can enter his kingdom: the Son of Man will come 'with the clouds of heaven', the court will sit, and judgment will be 'pronounced in favour of the saints of the Most High'. Evil will be destroyed, and 'the sovereignty, power and greatness of the kingdoms under the whole heaven will be handed over to the saints' (Daniel 7:27). These two passages were both written centuries before the birth of Christ, but already the two major elements of the judgment can be seen: judgment means condemnation, and judgment means justice and security—depending of course on which side one falls.

These prophecies are echoed in the Book of Revelation, where John describes his vision of the future judgment:

> Then I saw a great white throne and him who was seated on it. Earth and sky fled from his presence, and there was no place for them. And I saw the dead, great and small, standing before the throne, and books were opened. Another book was opened, which is the book of life. The dead were judged according to what they had done as recorded in the books. The sea gave up the dead that were in it, and death and Hades gave up the dead that were in them, and each person was judged according to what he had done. Then death and Hades were thrown into the lake of fire. The lake of fire is the second death. If anyone's name was not found written in the book of life, he was thrown into the lake of fire (Revelation 20:11–15).

John the Baptist warned that this judgment would be carried out by the coming Christ. He used two agricultural images to describe it. The first is of a man come to gather in the harvest, threshing the wheat on the floor and separating the grains from the chaff, the one to be stored and the other to be burned. The second image is of a farmer tending his orchard, cutting down the trees which do not bear good fruit and burning them (Matthew 3:10–12).

The concept of a final judgment at the end of time is therefore an integral part of the Christian faith, and it was one of the matters about which Jesus spoke the most often and the most clearly. It will involve the division of humanity into two groups, the saved and the lost, the righteous and the wicked, the alive and the dead. Jesus described it in various ways, but perhaps this is the most famous:

> When the Son of Man comes in his glory, and all the angels with him, he will sit on his throne in heavenly glory. All the nations will be gathered before him and he will separate the people one from another as a shepherd separates the sheep from the goats. He will put the sheep on his right and the goats on his left. Then the King will say to those on his right, 'Come, you who are blessed by my Father; take your inheritance, the kingdom prepared for you since the creation of the world.' . . . Then he will say to those on his left, 'Depart from me, you who are cursed, into the eternal fire prepared for the devil and his angels.' . . . Then they will go away to eternal punishment, but the righteous to eternal life (Matthew 25:31–46).

On another occasion he compared the judgment to the separation of the weeds from the wheat at harvest, explaining that the wheat stands for the 'sons of the kingdom', and was sown by the Son of Man, and that the weeds stand for the 'sons of the evil one', and were sown by the devil. He also likened the kingdom of heaven to a net let down into a lake, which caught both good and bad fish, causing the fishermen to have to separate them and throw away the bad ones (Matthew 13).

It is important to understand that we need have absolutely nothing to fear from the prospect of facing this judgment. Without the death of Christ on the cross, and the victory over evil which it represents, we would, as we saw earlier, all be lost, for we have all sinned and fall short of the glory of God, to use the words of the prophet Isaiah. But the cross gives us a choice, and the Last Judgment is a ratification of the choice we have made. It is not about whether I have been good enough, whether I have met this criterion or that criterion; it is about whether I am spiritually alive or spiritually dead, whether I have already been restored to a relationship with God through the death of Christ and the intervention of the Holy Spirit, or whether I am still caught up in sin:

> To those who by persistence in doing good seek glory, honour and immortality, he will give eternal life. But for those who are self-seeking and who reject the truth and follow evil, there will be wrath and anger (Romans 2:6–8).

If I have accepted the life that Jesus offers I can be absolutely certain that I will enter into heaven. It does of course matter that I try to live according to the standards of the love which I have received, and this should be clearly visible. It may be reflected in all sorts of ways, but Jesus summarised them under two headings: in my love for God, and in my love for other people. Paul put it, in the passage quoted above, in terms of seeking glory, honour and immortality. I am enabled to do this by the power of the cross and its victory over evil, by my new reliance on the help of the Holy Spirit, and by seeking God's forgiveness when I fail—which of course at times I will, as all Christians do. The crucial thing is that I must persist—Christianity is not a licence for pleasing myself. If on the other hand I choose not to do this, but to live my life without God, separate from God, then I must expect to continue to be separate from God after I die. God will respect the choice I have made.

That is the personal way of looking at the Last Judgment. But we may still wonder why it is necessary at all. A number of concepts are important here.

First, judgment brings justice. We may not like the idea of facing judgment, but we are all in favour of the dispensation of justice. The victim receives neither vindication nor protection if the aggressor is not punished. We are used to a society which takes judgment and justice out of the hands of the individual by the appointment of impartial judges and juries; it should reassure us that ultimately such justice will be dispensed not by an imperfect legal system but by an all-knowing God.

Secondly, without justice there can be no love. How can God love a rape victim if he merely tells her he forgives her aggressor? How can there be a heaven for that woman if the rapist has neither turned from his own evil (which, as we saw when we discussed the cross, is God's preferred solution), nor been removed from the scene altogether? The pages of the Bible resound with promises that God will protect and vindicate his people, because he loves them. He won't just sit there.

Thirdly, love and hate, good and evil, cannot mix. The existence of evil is intolerable to a loving and perfect God. In light there can be no darkness; evil has to go. God is awesome, holy, perfect, and his standards for us in eternity are the same. He sent his Son to enable us to choose between good and evil, light and darkness; if we choose light, we shall live in the light; if darkness, then in the darkness. What judgment does is separate those who have made one choice from those who have made the other. In effect in the light of our response to the cross of Christ, we judge ourselves.

Finally, judgment brings reward. Paul looked forward to receiving 'the crown of righteousness' (2 Timothy 4:8), and states with confidence that 'each will receive his praise from God' (1 Corinthians 4:5). John was told that

the time has come for judging the dead, and for rewarding your servants the prophets and your saints and those who reverence your name, both small and great—and for destroying those who destroy the earth (Revelation 11:18).

This is what Jesus came for; this is what he offers.

Between death and the Last Judgment

Jesus taught that he would return on an appointed day at the end of time, that the dead would be raised and judgment then take place. He said that some would be alive on the day of his return, but that others would have died. This prompts an interesting and difficult question. For those who have died, what happens between the day of their death and the Day of Judgment?

This is a question which has perplexed many Christians from the first century to the present. Early theologians believed that we would wait in a pleasant neutral place. By the twelfth century, perhaps building on this concept, the Western church had developed the notion of purgatory, which received its first formal definition in 1274, and which remains an official doctrine of the Roman Catholic Church.[7] According to this teaching we will spend a period of time undergoing purgation for our sins before being admitted to heaven. Others believe that the period between death and the end of time will be spent asleep; this has perhaps been the most popular view. And others believe that we will be admitted to heaven or hell straight away, without having to wait for the Day of Judgment.

It is possible to discern answers to this question from the Bible. But it may be that we are asking the wrong question altogether. First, it was never a major concern of Jesus to give a detailed description of the afterlife, or to explain exactly what our progress through the other world would be. There was only one issue which he regarded as of real importance throughout the time of his ministry on earth: whether a person was lost or saved, floundering in darkness or living in light, believing lies or knowing the truth, spiritually dead or spiritually alive. In the long run that is all that matters. If your daughter is in a coma, your major concern is whether she will come out of it, not how much she will sleep or where she will live afterwards.

Secondly, even had he wanted to, Jesus probably could not have given an answer that we could understand. This is because of the nature of time itself, and its relationship to eternity. We usually think of time as an absolute, something which passes in an ordered, regular way, like moving along a piece of string.

Every event occupies a fixed place on the piece of string, and comes either before or after all the other events. Thinking about our own lives in these terms, birth is marked at the beginning of the string; school, job, perhaps marriage, at points along it; and death at the end. Then we think of the string as continuing to stretch into eternity, except that we can't see it from here, and wonder what events will be marked as we travel along it. Eternity just means the string never ends.

This is the way we experience time. We exist within time and space and cannot move outside the parameters they set for us— or even think outside them. But God is not bound by time and space in the same way; he is outside them in some sense. He sees the whole of the piece of string at once. His understanding cannot therefore be the same as ours, and our questions about eternity may well be meaningless, because they presuppose that eternity is just an extension of time. It may not be.

Modern physics gives us a glimpse of God's perspective on space and time. We now know that they cannot be measured on a constant scale; they stretch and shrink. We are therefore not altogether wrong when, as we saw in the last chapter, we subjectively perceive time to pass quickly or slowly. Time is related to gravity—gravity makes it go slower. Furthermore, time and space are not two separate things, but part of the same thing. Physicists refer to them in one breath as spacetime.

The principle that spacetime is affected by gravity is described in Einstein's general theory of relativity, and it is very hard to understand, locked as we are into the familiar concepts of time as something which ticks constantly and regularly onwards, and of space as, well, space! But all we really need to grasp is that for the physicist, time is not a sequence of events which happen, but rather something which is simply there; and space is not a finite place or even an infinite place, but something related to time. So it may not be possible to explain eternity in terms of time, or heaven in terms of space. If at the death of our bodies we were to leave the world of space and time, all questions about when and where simply could not be asked—which is perhaps why Jesus gave no cut-and-dried answers to them.

The 'intermediate state'

The general theory of relativity, challenging though it is, is nonetheless not a reason for refusing to think about life after death altogether. It gives us grounds for caution, and explains why the particular issue of what theologians call the 'intermediate state'—what happens between death and the Day of Judgment—is a tricky one. This is in fact the only aspect of the nature of life after death about which Jesus offered no clear teaching, and it is the aspect on which the church has found it hardest to come to a common view. Remembering therefore why we are unlikely to find a clear doctrine of measurable progress through the other world, we shall attempt to proceed from within the perspective of space and time.

Although the New Testament offers no single explanation of what will happen to us immediately on death, there are a number of passages which address the issue and from which we may build up a picture of what things may be like.

The first thing that is clear is that although our bodies die, our spirits remain alive and conscious. As Jesus hung on the cross, one of the other two men crucified alongside him asked, 'Jesus, remember me when you come into your kingdom.' Jesus immediately gave him a promise: 'Today you will be with me in paradise' (Luke 23:42–43). This would seem to rule out, at least for this man, a period of sleep or purgation. Paul was so confident that on death he would go to be with Jesus that he stated that in many ways he would prefer to die straight away, for 'every moment we spend in these earthly bodies is time spent away from our eternal home in heaven with Jesus' (2 Corinthians 5:6). On another occasion he wrote, 'I really don't know which is better, to live or die. Sometimes I want to live and at other times I don't, for I long to go and be with Christ. How much happier for me than being here!' (Philippians 1:22–23). And in chapter 7 of the Book of Revelation John describes his vision of a great crowd 'from every nation, tribe, people and language' standing before the throne of God, with the clear implication that they have been there since death and will stay there until the Last Judgment. It is interesting to observe that these passages are consistent with what subjects of near-death experiences report, both in that we retain our conscious identity and in that we are transported to some other place after leaving our bodies.

It seems therefore that for some at least there is an agreeable destination of some kind immediately after death. This may not however always be the case, since other passages suggest that judgment, or division into two groups, does not wait until the Day of Judgment itself. Peter wrote that 'the Lord knows how to rescue godly men from trials and to hold the unrighteous for the day of judgment, while continuing their punishment' (2 Peter 2:9), which suggests that there is an intermediate destination of an unpleasant kind as well as the one Paul longed for. Jesus himself described these two destinations, or states, in terms of the story of a rich man and a beggar. It is recorded in chapter 16 of Luke's gospel:

> There was a rich man, who was clothed in purple and fine linen and who feasted sumptuously every day. And at his gate lay a poor man named Lazarus, full of sores, who desired to be fed with what fell from the rich man's table; moreover the dogs came and licked his sores. The poor man died and was carried by the angels to Abraham's bosom. The rich man also died and was buried; and in Hades, being in torment, he lifted up his eyes, and saw Abraham far off and Lazarus in his bosom. And he called out, 'Father Abraham, have mercy upon me, and send Lazarus to dip the end of his finger in water and cool my tongue; for I am in anguish in this flame.'

Abraham declines, on the grounds that people may not cross from one place to the other. And so the rich man asks:

Then I beg you, father, to send him to my father's house, for I have
five brothers, so that he may warn them, lest they also come into this
place of torment.

Abraham again declines, explaining that they have received their
warning already in the scriptures.

The purpose of this story is to give a warning against
complacency, and not to paint a detailed picture of life after
death. But nonetheless it seems clear that there are two
immediate post-mortem states, and that one of them, referred to
as Abraham's bosom, is pleasant, and the other, referred to as
Hades (see below), is not. Abraham is the ancestor of the Jewish
nation, and the representative of their security as God's chosen
people. The name Lazarus means 'God-help-me', and
summarises the attitude Jesus is urging upon us. The passage as
a whole reflects Jesus' teaching that humanity falls into two
categories—those who have eternal life and those who do not.
These are the categories into which we will ultimately be
divided; they are the categories into which we by our own choice
divide ourselves now; and it is not surprising that they should be
the two categories into which we will divide on death. In this life
we are able to pass from one to the other, but it seems that
thereafter we are not.

Paradise

In the story of Lazarus, the intermediate dwelling place of the
spiritually alive is referred to as Abraham's bosom. In another
three passages in the New Testament it is called by the more
familiar name of paradise. One of these passages we have
already discussed. Jesus assures the thief crucified beside him
that he will go straight to paradise. This is the only reference
Jesus makes to paradise.

The second reference occurs in Paul's second letter to the
Corinthians, in chapter 12 of which Paul describes his own

experience of being 'caught up to paradise', which he says is in the 'third heaven'. He is unsure exactly how this took place; it may have been what we now refer to as a near-death or out-of-the-body experience: 'Whether it was in the body or out of the body I do not know—God knows.' He gives no details of what he saw, except that it was inexpressible and he is not permitted to reveal it.

The third reference comes in the Book of Revelation, in which God promises that 'to him who overcomes, I will give the right to eat from the tree of life, which is in the paradise of God' (Revelation 2:7). This is a clear reference back to the Garden of Eden, where we remember that 'in the middle of the garden were the tree of life and the tree of the knowledge of good and evil' (Genesis 2:9). It is a promise that God will restore to us the freedom from evil and the spiritual life which we have lost, and which are symbolised in these two trees.

We have become used to regarding the word 'paradise' as meaning the same as the word 'heaven', and as referring to the place we hope to go to at the end of time. In fact it is quite clear that this was not its original meaning. 'Paradise' comes from the Persian word for a pleasure garden, and this is why we traditionally use it of the Garden of Eden. A lush garden represents all that is most attractive to a people living in an arid landscape; the hanging gardens of Babylon, with their sophisticated systems of irrigation, were commonly regarded as one of the seven wonders of the world. People reporting positive near-death experiences often describe the place they glimpsed as being like a beautiful garden. So it seems that we should think of the 'intermediate state' of the spiritually alive in terms of a garden-like place called paradise.

Hades

We come now to the question of an 'intermediate state' for the spiritually dead—that is, for those who have not received the life that Christ came to bestow on them. We saw in Chapter 2 that the Old Testament refers to the abode of the dead as Sheol, and describes it as a shadowy realm where there is no hope. The Greek translation of Sheol is 'Hades', and this is the name used in the New Testament to refer to the post-mortem state of those who remain cut off from the source of life. It is more clearly described as a state than as a place.

The word 'Hades' is not translated consistently in the various English versions of the Bible, which makes interpretation difficult. Jesus referred to it three times: once in the story of Lazarus and the rich man, once as a warning to those cities which ignored his message that Hades is where they would go, and once as a promise to Peter that the 'gates of Hades' would not overcome the church (Luke 16:23; Matthew 11:23–24, 16:18). Peter referred to Hades when announcing to the people of Jerusalem that Jesus had risen from the dead, reminding them of David's prophecy that the Christ would not be 'abandoned to Hades' (Acts 2:27, 31).

The other references to Hades come in the Book of Revelation. John reports a vision of the 'Son of Man'—the title Jesus most commonly used to refer to himself—who said to him: 'I am the living One; I was dead, and behold I am alive for ever and ever. And I hold the keys of death and Hades' (Revelation 1:18). Later John sees a horse whose 'rider was named Death, and Hades was following close behind him' (6:8). Perhaps the clearest indication that Hades is a temporary condition is given in the description of the Last Judgment in Revelation chapter 20, where we read that 'death and Hades gave up the dead that were in them, and each person was judged according to what he had done. Then death and Hades were thrown into the lake of fire' (20:13–14). Such a lake of fire has been seen by at least one person during a near-death experience; others have reported terrifying experiences of isolation, darkness, tunnels and despair. Many have returned from such experiences firmly convinced of the truth of the Christian faith.[8]

It seems therefore that viewed from our limited perspective, we all continue to exist after the death of our bodies, either in a place or state of life called paradise, or in a place or state of death called Hades. This is the conclusion which best fits the little information that the scriptures give us, and it is the one adopted by most modern commentators.[9]

Hell

Whatever may be said about the intermediate state, the teaching of the Bible on what happens after the Day of Judgment is clear and unambiguous: we go to one of two destinations, heaven or hell. We will look first at what is taught about hell, and then at what is said about heaven.

Hell is not a popular concept; belief in its existence is declining fast even among committed Christians, and within the general population it has been almost completely discarded. A poll taken in the United States in 1978 suggested that over seventy per cent of people believed in hell; by 1988 the figure in Australia was found to be thirty-nine per cent, and by 1989 in Britain it was twenty-four per cent. Another series of polls conducted between 1977 and 1991 revealed that even those who do believe in hell do not expect to go there themselves: no more than four to six per cent of Americans anticipate this destiny. Hell, it seems, is for other people.[10]

I think this is due to a number of factors. First, the New Testament gives us very few details of hell; Jesus spoke of it often, but always only as a warning—his emphasis was on the life he came to offer, not on the death that was the alternative. Secondly, we tend to think of hell in terms of the popular concepts of the Middle Ages, and not in terms of what the New Testament tells us. And thirdly, we bring to bear on it a set of late twentieth-century secular assumptions which are not always helpful. The most powerful of these is the post-Freudian assumption that we are not responsible for our actions; we are

victims of the things that happen to us. This in turn is based on
the post-Enlightenment (eighteenth-century) assumption that
man is basically good, and just needs encouragement for
everything to go well. Christianity teaches the opposite: that the
human race was created good ('and God saw that it was good' is
the constant refrain of the creation story in Genesis), but was
infected by the principle of sin soon after the beginning. G.K.
Chesterton once remarked how surprising it is that we have
rejected the Christian doctrine of original sin, as this principle is
known, because it is the only doctrine which can be empirically
verified—we have only to open the pages of any daily
newspaper to find incontrovertible evidence that all is not well
with humanity.[11]

Let us therefore begin by looking at what Jesus said about
hell. First, the word. Our word 'hell' is completely unrelated to
any word used in the New Testament. It comes from the Old
English 'hel', which in turn derives from a Germanic root
meaning 'cover' or 'conceal'. The Latin word for hell,
'infernus', from which we derive the words 'inferno' and
'infernal', simply means 'lower', and relates to the Roman
concept of an underworld. Jesus did not use either of these
words, or anything like them. The word most often used by Jesus
to designate the destiny of the lost was 'Gehenna'. This word
carried with it a very clear set of associations, and we will begin
by looking at these associations.

'Gehenna' is a transliteration of a Hebrew phrase, 'valley of
Ben Hinnom'. This valley is a ravine on the south side of
Jerusalem, and it has a very particular history. In the eighth
century BC it was used as a site for the burning of children as
human sacrifices to the Ammonite god Moloch.[12] Later it became
the city rubbish dump, which meant that a fire was kept
constantly alight to incinerate the garbage thrown there. This
was the place which Jesus chose as a metaphor for the
destination of those who are cut off from God, warning his
disciples not to be afraid of anything that men could do to

them, but rather to 'fear him who, after the killing of the body, has power to throw you into hell [Gehenna]' (Luke 12:5), and telling the Pharisees, the religious leaders whom he constantly accused of hypocrisy, that they would not escape being condemned to hell (Matthew 23:33).

This is the essence of Jesus' teaching on hell. And while we may usefully look at other passages from the Bible which develop the associations of Gehenna, this remains the core of the Christian teaching. Most of the rest of what we believe to be the Christian hell comes not from Jesus himself but from the exercise of our own fertile imaginations, and we do well to heed the warning of theologian Reinhold Neibuhr:

> It is unwise for Christians to claim any knowledge of either the furniture of heaven or the temperature of hell.[13]

In so far as Jesus spoke of hell, then, he spoke of it as a place; a specific place; and a specific place which carried a specific set of associations to contemporary hearers. It is a rubbish dump. Those who go there are those who have put themselves outside God's plan and become redundant; it carries associations of rejection, of waste, of superfluity, of having come to the end of useful life, of being thrown out. It is a place characterised by the presence of fire, and Jesus often referred to fire as the means by which God's judgment would be effected, using the imagery of the burning of dead wood, chaff and weeds. He warned against sin, urging us to do everything we can to avoid being 'thrown into eternal fire', the 'fire of hell' (Matthew 18:7–9)—saying that it would be better to have a millstone hung round your neck and thrown into the sea than to experience this fire. One commentator has calculated that there are twenty-one biblical references to fire as an eternal punishment, drawing from both the Old and the New Testaments.[14] Some of these occur in the Book of Revelation, the main source for Milton's description of hell, where the destination of the unrepentantly sinful is described as a 'fiery lake of burning sulphur' (Revelation 19:20). It is important to realise that this lake was never intended for man, but was 'prepared for the devil and his angels' (Matthew 25:41).

A first-century rubbish dump would have been characterised not only by fire but also by the presence of worms, and so we find Jesus referring to hell as the place where 'their worm does not die, and the fire is not quenched'—a quotation from Isaiah's description of what will happen to the bodies of those who rebel against God (Isaiah 66:24).

It is scarcely likely that Jesus intended to say that those who do not enter heaven will remain in this particular valley on earth, particularly since we know that heaven and earth are to be destroyed and replaced by new ones. Most modern commentators agree that it is similarly unlikely that the dwelling of the lost will be a place of fire and worms, preferring instead to see these as part of the Gehenna imagery. Jesus' central message was that man is in a wrong relationship with God, and needs to enter into a right relationship. Gehenna with its fire and worms is a description of what it will feel like to be in that wrong relationship for eternity; the torment will be the torment of separation, of exclusion, of unfulfilled thirst for God, of the gnawing of remorse and regret.[15] The same must apply to Jesus' comment that in the 'fiery furnace' there will be 'weeping and gnashing of teeth' (Matthew 13:50); those in hell will suffer from the despair and fury of knowing they didn't have to be there—of making the discovery made by the rich man in the story of Lazarus, but too late.

However, Jesus did not always refer to the destiny of the lost in terms of Gehenna. On other occasions he compared it to being thrown into prison. God will treat us just as a king might treat those who owe him money, and Jesus tells the tale of a king who had a servant who owed him 10,000 talents—a vast sum. Having legitimately ordered him to be thrown into prison, he listened to his plea for mercy and freed him with his debt cancelled—only to find the man demanding payment from someone who owed him a far smaller sum. He threw him back into prison. Jesus warns that this is how God will treat us. We all owe him a debt; he will freely cancel that debt, but only on condition that we treat others in the same way (Matthew 18).

The concept of hell as a prison again seems entirely appropriate when we consider that this is precisely how the Bible describes our current state of separation from God, and is precisely the situation from which Jesus said he came to rescue us—'he has sent me to proclaim freedom for the prisoners' (Luke 4:18). Hell is the continuation of what we already have, not some new set of unimaginable horrors. Jesus was sent, as Isaiah prophesied, to set the captives free and release the prisoners. Those who choose to remain in captivity will remain there for ever, and this is what hell is.

One of the predominant characteristics of first-century prisons would have been darkness, and we find that this also is given as a description of the conditions of the lost. Jesus warns that many who expect to find themselves in heaven will in fact 'be thrown outside, into the darkness' (Matthew 8:12), and refers to a similar fate in two of the parables which he tells to illustrate the nature of life after death (Matthew 22 and 25). Peter states that 'blackest darkness' is reserved for those who lead others astray (2 Peter 2:17), and another New Testament writer, Jude, says that 'blackest darkness has been reserved for ever' for godless men who deny Christ (Jude 13). It is not spelt out exactly what this darkness means, but again it makes perfect sense if we look at it in terms of the teaching given by Jesus and his disciples concerning this life. Darkness is the opposite of light; to be in darkness is to be lost, frightened, in despair, dead. Light, on the other hand, is used throughout the New Testament as a metaphor for life, truth and salvation. John wrote of Jesus: 'In him was life, and that life was the light of men. The light shines in the darkness, but the darkness has not understood it' (John 1:4–5). Jesus himself said, 'I am the light of the world; he who follows me will not walk in darkness, but will have the light of life' (John 8:12). Paul reported that Jesus appeared to him in a vision and said:

> I send you to open their eyes, that they may turn from darkness to light and from the power of Satan to God, that they may receive forgiveness of sins and a place among those who are sanctified by faith in me (Acts 26:18).

Spiritually speaking, to be in the darkness is to be dead, and to be in the light is to have eternal life. Hell is therefore another way of describing what it is like to be in the darkness, eternally.

Hell, like prison, is also a place of punishment. Paul wrote this to the Thessalonian church:

> God is just: He will pay back trouble to those who trouble you and give relief to you who are troubled, and to us as well . . . He will punish those who do not know God and do not obey the gospel of our Lord Jesus. They will be punished with everlasting destruction and shut out from the presence of the Lord and from the majesty of his power on the day he comes to be glorified in his holy people (2 Thessalonians 1:8–10).

The punishment consists, we note, not of physical torment at the hands of little black devils (little black devils are not mentioned in the Bible), but of everlasting destruction—the opposite of everlasting life—and of exclusion from the presence of Christ. This is precisely the aspect Jesus stressed when he described heaven as a wedding feast to which many of those who are invited fail to turn up, and to which others come in scruffy clothes, with the result that they have to be thrown out (Matthew 22). This sense of unexpected exclusion recurs throughout Jesus' accounts of the other world. On another occasion he expressed it in terms of knocking at the door of someone's house, only to be told from within, 'I don't know you or where you come from' (Luke 13:22–30). Another time he put it as baldly as this:

Not everyone who says to me, 'Lord, Lord,' will enter the kingdom of heaven, but only he who does the will of my Father who is in heaven. Many will say to me on that day, 'Lord, Lord, did we not prophesy in your name, and in your name drive out demons and perform many miracles?' Then I will tell them plainly, 'I never knew you. Away from me, you evildoers!' (Matthew 7:22–23).

Again it seems that the criterion is relationship—the saved will be those who really know Jesus, and who actively live their lives in the light of that relationship, and not those who just know of him. The rest must continue in their separation. As one commentator puts it, 'At the judgment the unbeliever's separation from God is consummated.'[16] Hell is a second death, the final and irreversible separation of the person concerned from God. If heaven is described as eternal life, then hell is eternal death. If eternal life is the fulfilment of the life the Christian has on earth, then eternal death must be the fulfilment of the death the non-Christian has on earth. Death is separation from God; and if that is what we are experiencing now, we can be sure, if we believe the teaching of the Bible, that we will experience it far more fully—and far more painfully—later.

Heaven

No eye has seen, no ear has heard, no mind has conceived what God has prepared for those who love him—but God has revealed it to us by his Spirit (1 Corinthians 2:9–10).

This is how Paul wrote of the glory of heaven. In a sense we know very little about heaven and what it will be like. And yet in a sense we know a great deal. The essence of heaven, as described by both Jesus and Paul, is relationship with God—the restoration of what was lost in the Garden of Eden. We are certainly given pictures of what it will be like, and plenty of them; but it is not in essence a place of material delights, as it is for example for the Muslim. And we are certainly told that we shall find release from the troubles and desires of this world; and yet we do not lose our own individual identity, as anticipated by the Hindu and the Buddhist when they contemplate nirvana. Heaven is the place where by entering fully into a relationship with God we will find fulfilment of all our needs, and where we will fully become the people we were created to be. In the quotation above, Paul states that God has revealed this to us by his Spirit because through the Holy Spirit we are already able to experience that relationship, albeit in an incomplete way. Heaven for the Christian is more of the same, but better; in Paul's words again:

> Now we see but a poor reflection as in a mirror; then we shall see face to face. Now I know in part; then I shall know fully, even as I am fully known (1 Corinthians 13:12).

When Jesus spoke about heaven he usually used the phrase 'the kingdom of heaven', or 'the kingdom of God', and it is clear that he too regarded this kingdom as having what has been described as 'an already and a not-yet aspect'—that is, in one sense it starts now, and in another it belongs in the future.[17] When Jesus talked about the kingdom of God as a present phenomenon, he usually pointed to healings and miracles as evidence of the presence of God, and these still happen today.

When Paul talked about it, he usually focused on internal evidence, such as joy or peace, and these too are experienced by the believer today. The opportunity to move in this way from being spiritually dead to being spiritually alive is one which nobody who has experienced it would forgo. But both Jesus and Paul taught that there is a sense in which the kingdom of heaven lies in the future, and it is at this that we will look now.

Heaven as a place

Heaven, the heaven which follows the Day of Judgment for all believers, is described in the Bible as a definite place. It is more than just a relationship, although it is that; it is a home, a destination where God is to be enjoyed for ever and ever, a kingdom which will be established on earth, but not on this one. We have already seen that the old order will be destroyed, and a new heaven and new earth be created, in such a way that they are no longer, as at present, separate, but rather fused. The two realms will become one, a place where God and man may live together. So this realm will have a real geographical existence— it is not a misty realm in a land of sunspecked clouds, but rather a continuation, or a recreation, of what we have already, not just in terms of our renewed relationship with God but also in terms of place.

The most important characteristic of the new heaven and earth is that there will be no distance between them. We will return to the state we were in at the creation, enjoying the companionship of God as did Adam and Eve in the Garden of Eden. This is often pictured as living together with God in a perfect city, a heavenly version of the city with which the first recipients of Jesus' message were familiar—Jerusalem. This is how John describes it:

> Then I saw a new heaven and a new earth, for the first heaven and the first earth had passed away, and there was no longer any sea. I saw the Holy City, the new Jerusalem, coming down out of heaven from God, prepared as a bride beautifully dressed for her husband. And I heard a loud voice from the throne saying, 'Now the dwelling of God is with men, and he will live with them. They will be his people, and God himself will be with them and be their God' (Revelation 21:1–3).

This city is situated on a mountain, point of union between heaven and earth; it is surrounded by high walls with gates guarded by angels, symbols of perfect security and protection. It is built from the most precious and beautiful materials known to man:

It shone with the glory of God, and its brilliance was like that of a very precious jewel, like a jasper, clear as crystal. . . . The wall was made of jasper, and the city of pure gold, as pure as glass. The foundations of the city walls were decorated with every kind of precious stone. The first foundation was jasper, the second sapphire, the third chalcedony, the fourth emerald, the fifth sardonyx, the sixth carnelian, the seventh chrysolite, the eighth beryl, the ninth topaz, the tenth chrysoprase, the eleventh jacinth, and the twelfth amethyst. The twelve gates were twelve pearls, each gate made of a single pearl. The great street of the city was of pure gold, like transparent glass (Revelation 21:10–11, 18–21).

The choice of which precious stones will be used is extremely interesting, as David Pawson has pointed out, in that those selected share three important characteristics. First, they are all extremely hard. Secondly, they all have an approximately oblong crystal structure. Both these characteristics make them more suitable for building than other precious stones not mentioned. But it is the third characteristic which is the most remarkable. The chosen stones are all anisotropic in pure light (and John states that the city will be illuminated not by sun or moon but by the light of God); that is, 'when viewed in light refracted through a cross-polarised filter, they produce all the colours of the rainbow in an infinite variety of patterns, whatever their original colour'. Other precious stones are isotropic, and lose their colour altogether in pure light; diamonds and rubies, which would have seemed ideal choices for the heavenly city, are of this kind. John could not possibly have known of this property, since pure light is available only in laboratory conditions. Pawson cites this as evidence that John's vision was indeed inspired by God.[18]

The heavenly Jerusalem is not however seen as a purely urban environment. A river, described as the river of the water of life, flows down the main street of the city, and the tree of life grows on both sides, yielding a different crop of fruit every month.

Although this is the most famous representation in the Bible of heaven, and although it occurs not just in Revelation but also in, for example, Isaiah and the Epistle to the Hebrews, Jesus himself never chose to describe heaven in terms of a city. He almost spoke of it in parables, stories intended to illustrate one particular aspect of what they describe. Some of these parables stress the enormous value of heaven—it is like a treasure hidden in a field, worth selling all you have to purchase the field and dig it up; or like a beautiful pearl, worth selling all you have to buy it (Matthew 13). Other parables stress the extent of its growth from insignificant beginnings—it is like the large shrub which grows from the tiny mustard seed (six feet of shrub from one millimetre of seed, apparently), or like the risen dough which comes from the addition of a minute amount of yeast to flour (Matthew 13; Luke 13).[19]

On another occasion, recorded in both Matthew 22 and Luke 14, Jesus compared the kingdom of heaven to a wedding reception. A king prepared a wedding feast for his son, and invited many guests. When the day arrived, however, the guests failed to turn up, excusing themselves on the grounds of more pressing business. The king was furious; he sent out his servants to invite anyone they could find, and soon the great hall was full of those who wanted to be there—including the poor, the crippled, the blind and the lame. This, Jesus explains, is a picture of what will happen in heaven. Two points stand out here; first, that heaven is a celebration, a party. And secondly, that heaven will be full of ordinary people, and not those who regard themselves as important.

The picture of heaven as a wedding feast also occurs in Revelation. John sees God seated on his throne, and hears what sounds like a multitude of people shouting:

'Hallelujah! For our Lord God Almighty reigns.
Let us rejoice and be glad and give him glory!
For the wedding of the Lamb has come, and his bride has made herself ready.

Fine linen, bright and clean, was given her to wear.'
(Fine linen stands for the righteous acts of the saints.)
Then the angel said to me, 'Write: "Blessed are those who are
invited to the wedding supper of the Lamb!"' (Revelation 19:6–9)

God gives the invitations; the wedding is between Christ,
represented according to Jewish sacrificial tradition as the Lamb,
and the community of the church. The relationship between
Christ and the church is also described in terms of a wedding by
Paul in his letter to the Ephesians.

Who will be in heaven?

Heaven, therefore, is a restored relationship, a beautiful city, a
wedding feast. In all these aspects it is defined by the presence of
God and of Christ. But there will be many people there as well,
and the New Testament gives us a clear idea of who they will be.

Jesus said that 'no-one can enter the kingdom of God unless
he is born of water and the Spirit' (John 3:5). This is the basic
criterion for entry into heaven: one must first experience spiritual
rebirth here on earth, which is why Jesus often said that we must
become like little children in order to enter heaven. We cannot
earn a place there; it is a gift, just as life itself is a gift. And so we
don't have to be models of tireless service like Mother Teresa;
we don't have to be spiritual giants like Paul; we don't have to be
disciplined ascetics like St Francis of Assisi; we don't have to be
great theological thinkers like Thomas Aquinas or founders of
revivals like John Wesley—although of course we expect to find
all these people in heaven. We just have to be children of God in
our daily lives.

I first saw Christ in an old lady, bed-ridden with multiple
sclerosis; then in a fellow student at university. One of the
Christians from whom I have learned the most is a nurse in the
Corby Diagnostic Centre. Another runs a nursery school in
Leicester. These are just ordinary people; but chosen by God and
living their lives in obedience to him. These, as Jesus put it, are

the members of my eternal family: 'Whoever does the will of my Father in heaven is my brother and sister and mother' (Matthew 12:50).

We are told little beyond this about relationships in heaven. Jesus did say quite clearly that there will be no marriage (Luke 20:27–38); we know that there will be no death. We must assume that there will be people there of all ages, and people who have discovered the secret of eternal life on their deathbeds as well as those who have been living as Christians for years. And we must trust that God is perfectly fair, and will judge each of us according to the light we have received. It is not possible for us while on earth to say that this or that person will or will not be in heaven.

What is clear, however, is that those who do go to heaven will receive a reward there. The greatest reward is of course heaven itself; but Jesus seems to imply that there will be more even than that. The poor, the hungry, the tearful, the persecuted will all receive a great reward in heaven, according to Luke's version of Jesus' Sermon on the Mount (Luke 6). Matthew quotes at greater length, commending peacemakers, the merciful, the meek, the pure in heart and those who hunger and thirst for God. On the same occasion Jesus urged his hearers to love even those who hate them, to do good even to those who do evil to them, to lend even to those who will not repay the loan, for this is how God has treated us, and he will reward us for treating others in the same way (Matthew 5–7). We are also encouraged to give to others in secret, to pray unseen, and to fast without mentioning it, so that we will be rewarded not by men but by God; Jesus calls this storing up treasure for ourselves in heaven.

And yet we will all, irrespective of our success in these areas, receive the same fundamental reward, heaven itself. This is illustrated in Jesus' parable of the workers in the vineyard, where those hired in the morning, those hired at lunchtime and those hired at teatime all received the same pay from the owner, the point being that each received the sum offered and for which he had agreed to work (Matthew 20).

The appropriate response to receiving the reward of heaven is thanks and worship, and the clearest statement that this is, in part, what we shall want to do in heaven is found in the Book of Revelation. Its pages are punctuated with descriptions of praise, singing and thanksgiving before the throne of God.

So heaven is a place of rewards and of celebration. It is also—and this may come as a surprise—a place of work. It is abundantly clear from the Bible that we will not just worship and celebrate, but that we will be given other tasks to do, each according to what seems appropriate. Jesus told his disciples that they would sit on thrones with him, judging the twelve tribes of Israel (Matthew 19:28), and that they would then rule over a kingdom (Luke 22:29). Paul demands of the squabbling Corinthians, 'Do you not know that the saints will judge the world? . . . Do you not know that we will judge angels?' (1 Corinthians 6:2–3). In the Book of Revelation John quotes Jesus' promise to anyone who does his will that he will be given authority over nations and will rule over the whole earth (Revelation 2:26–27, referring to Psalm 2). Later he writes, 'You have made them to be a kingdom and priests to serve our God, and they will reign on the earth' (5:10).

Two other New Testament passages suggest that we will have different roles or at least statuses in the kingdom of heaven. One of these is chapter 5 of the Gospel of Matthew, where Jesus is recorded instructing his hearers to continue to obey the law, warning them that 'anyone who breaks one of the least of these commandments and teaches others to do the same will be called least in the kingdom of heaven, but whoever practises and teaches these commands will be called great in the kingdom of heaven'. Secondly, Jesus implies in one of his parables that we will be given responsibility in heaven. He tells the story of a manager who was called to account by his master, recommends shrewd management of wealth in order to receive a welcome into heaven, and comments that whoever can be trusted with very little can also be trusted with much, and whoever is dishonest with very little will also be dishonest with much. So if you have not been trustworthy in handling worldly wealth, who will trust you with true riches? And if you have not been trustworthy with someone else's property, who will give you property of your own? (Luke 16:10–12).

Finally, what will it feel like to live in this new heaven and new earth? We know that we will have new bodies. We know that we will live in a community. Our best guide to the nature of life in this community is the description of the heavenly Jerusalem with which we began. John writes that in this city there will be no tears, no death, nor mourning, crying or pain; there will be no sin, since the cowardly, the unbelieving, the vile, the murderers, the sexually immoral, those who practise magic arts, idolators and liars will not be there. There will be no darkness, nothing impure, nothing shameful or deceitful. There will be rejoicing, singing, music, eating and drinking.

The last two chapters of the Book of Isaiah paint a similar picture of life in the heavenly Jerusalem, although written centuries earlier; here too we are told that it will be a place of rejoicing, where there is no more weeping or distress, where children do not die in infancy or men in old age. In this Jerusalem we will build houses and plant vines, enjoying our work and not labouring in vain. There will be animals there, but wolves and lambs will feed together, lions will become vegetarian and snakes eat dust instead of biting man. It will be a place of material prosperity and emotional comfort. In short, it sounds rather like exactly what it says it is—a new heaven, and a new earth, in which 'the creation itself will be liberated from its bondage to decay and brought into the glorious freedom of the children of God' (Romans 8:21).

The world has seen many theories proposed concerning life after death, and we have looked at the major ones in this book. Which is the true picture? The only one which seems to stand up to rigorous examination and to make sense of all the evidence is the Christian one, and this is the one which I have come to believe in. Since I decided, twelve years ago, to believe it, I have found its teaching to coincide perfectly with my experience of the new spiritual life which Jesus promised would be mine. I know that one day I will die. And I know that I am not afraid of death, any more than my friend Ruth was. Indeed, I expect to find in it the fulfilment of my life here on earth. Meanwhile that life continues, full of the purpose and meaning which in my experience only belief in Christ can bring.

Notes

1. David Lloyd George, *Lord Riddell's Intimate Diary of the Peace Conference and After* (London: 1933), pp. 122–23.
2. For a list of the major medieval paintings of the Last Judgment see Alison Morgan, *Dante and the Medieval Other World* (Cambridge: 1990), pp. 199–200. For illustrations see R. Cavendish, *Visions of Heaven and Hell* (London: 1977).
3. The most detailed single account of this teaching is given in Matthew 24–25.
4. See Acts 23:6–8.
5. This view is taken by D. Hunt, *Whatever Happened to Heaven?* (Eugene, Oregon: 1988), pp. 34–35.
6. I. Barclay, *Death and the Life to Come* (London:1988), p. 36.
7. For discussion of this see P. Ariès, *The Hour of Our Death* (Harmondsworth: 1983), chs 3–4; and J. Le Goff, *La Naissance du Purgatoire* (Paris: 1981).
8. Accounts of such experiences are given by M. Rawlings, *Beyond Death's Door* (London: 1979), ch. 7.
9. See for example J. Blanchard, *Whatever Happened to Hell?* (Darlington: 1993), ch. 3, 6; D. Pawson, *The Road to Hell* (London: 1992), ch. 3, pp. 32–34.
10. See Blanchard, 1993, pp. 13, 250–51.

11. Cited by A. Fernando, *Crucial Questions About Hell* (Eastbourne: 1991), p. 96.

12. See for example 2 Chronicles 28:3; 33:6; Jeremiah 32:35. For the history see Blanchard, 1993, pp. 41–42; Fernando, 1991, p. 26.

13. Quoted by Blanchard, 1993, p. 126.

14. Blanchard, 1993, pp. 136–40.

15. See for example Blanchard, 1993, pp. 140–41; Hunt, 1988, pp. 29–30.

16. Fernando, 1991, p. 29.

17. B. Witherington, *Jesus, Paul and the End of the World* (Exeter: 1992), p. 74.

18. D. Pawson, *The Road to Hell* (London: 1992), p. 70.

19. M. Zohary, *Plants of the Bible* (Cambridge: 1982), p. 93.

FURTHER READING

Zaleski, C., *Otherworld Journeys: Accounts of Near-Death Experience in Medieval and Modern Times*, Oxford University Press, 1987.

Sullivan, L.E. (ed.), *Death, Afterlife and the Soul*, Macmillan Publishing, 1987.

Cavendish, R., *Visions of Heaven and Hell*, Orbis, 1977.

Rawlings, M., *Before Death Comes*, SPCK, 1980.
Beyond Death's Door, Sheldon Press, 1979.

Kastenbaum, R., *Is There Life After Death?*, London, 1984.

Wilson, Ian, *Reincarnation? The Claims Investigated*, Penguin, 1982.

Bruce, F.F., *The New Testament Documents: Are They Reliable?*, IVP, 1943.

Anderson, N., *Jesus Christ: The Witness of History*, IVP, 1985.

Barclay, I., *Death and the Life to Come*, Hodder and Stoughton, 1988.

Pawson, D., *The Road to Hell*, Hodder and Stoughton, 1992.

Fernando, A., *Crucial Questions About Hell*, Kingsway, 1991.

Graham, J., *Dying to Live: The Christian Teaching on Life After Death*, Marshall Pickering, 1984.

Tiede, D., *Jesus and the Future*, Cambridge University Press, 1990.

MacArthur, J., *Heaven: Selected Scriptures*, Moody Press, 1988.

Toynbee, A., et al, *Life After Death*, Weidenfeld and Nicolson, 1976.

Wilson, C., *Afterlife: an Investigation of the Evidence for Life After Death*, Harrap, 1985.

Badham, P. and L., *Immortality or Extinction?*, Macmillan, 1982.